LEISU   J   ᴇ

1

2

Leisure and Culture

Chris Rojek
Professor of Sociology and Culture
Theory, Culture and Society Centre
Nottingham Trent University

Published by PALGRAVE
Houndmills, Basingstoke, Hampshire RG21 6XS and
175 Fifth Avenue, New York, N. Y. 10010
Companies and representatives throughout the world

PALGRAVE is the new global academic imprint of
St. Martin's Press LLC Scholarly and Reference Division and
Palgrave Publishers Ltd (formerly Macmillan Press Ltd).

Outside North America
ISBN 0–333–68000–6 hardcover

In North America
ISBN 0–312–22591–1 hardcover

Worldwide
ISBN 0–333–68001–4 paperback

This book is printed on paper suitable for recycling and
made from fully managed and sustained forest sources.

A catalogue record for this book is available from the British Library.

Library of Congress Cataloging-in-Publication Data
Rojek, Chris.
Leisure and culture / Chris Rojek.
p. cm.
Includes bibliographical references and index.
ISBN 0–312–22591–1
1. Leisure—Sociological aspects. 2. Recreation—Sociological
aspects. I. Title
GV14.45.R657   1999
306.4'812—dc21
99—15308
CIP

Transferred to digital printing 2002

Printed and bound in Great Britain by

Antony Rowe Ltd, Chippenham and Eastbourne

For Robert Rojek

Contents

Acknowledgements

This is the first book I have written in the congenial circumstances of the Theory, Culture and Society Centre, Nottingham Trent University. I would like to thank my immediate colleagues and students for stimulation and support. In particular, Mike Feather-stone, Roger Bromley, John Tomlinson and Sandra Harris have been boon companions.

I would also like to thank Ellis Cashmore, Barry Smart, Bryan Turner, George Ritzer, Maggie O'Neill, John O'Neill, Lauren Langman, Doug Kellner, David Frisby, Paul Willis and Penny Dole for their diverse ministrations and modes of assistance. Extracts from the book were tried out at conferences in Massey University, New Zealand; Massey University, Auckland; University of Ottawa, Canada; and Sydney University of Technology, Australia; the World Congress of Sociology meeting in Montreal (1998) and the American Sociological Association annual meeting in San Francisco (1998). Many thanks to everyone who invited me to these events and responded to the arguments made in the presentations.

There is in nature and there subsists in man a movement which always exceeds the bounds, that can never be anything but partially reduced to order.

Georges Bataille, *Eroticism*

1 From Ritual Culture to Performative Culture

Every society must devise principles for organizing time and space. Without this, the production activity that is necessary for economic and social survival cannot be accomplished. However, no society can exist on production alone. In addition, society requires principles for raising children, protecting territory, managing property, maintaining the elderly and burying and remembering the dead and, of course, relaxing and playing. A surplus of energy and unused resources always remains. The problem of leisure is how to use this surplus.

In traditional societies the question of surplus energy is coordinated by binding occult and religious institutions and practices. Culture is characterized by highly repetitive, ritualized processes of behaviour. To refer to a well-known example, Evans-Pritchard (1976) demonstrates the importance of magic in the social and political organization of the Azande. His discussion shows that everyday life for members of the tribe is dominated by the observance of witch-doctors and oracles. These are the instruments which reveal the mystical forces which are believed to hang over an individual and determine the individual and general life-course. The Azande notion of time holds that the present and future overlap. Thus, the well-being of an individual depends on future conditions which are already in existence and can be revealed by magic. By revealing these conditions, magic gives the individual the foresight to alter the disposition of mystical forces, so that a future which is revealed to demonstrate a negative outcome can, through actions in the here and now, be transformed to achieve a positive result. Eliade's (1957) discussion of shamanism and Sahlins's (1985) account of belief systems in Polynesian societies describe a similar world order. Time does not have the linear, discrete character of Western concepts; space is not segmented according to rational-legal criteria. As Sahlins (1985: 57) puts it in respect of the Maori attitude to time:

(The) past is a vast scheme of life-possibilities, ranging from ancient myth to recent memory through a series of epochs parallel in

1

structure and analogous in event, while successively changing in content from the abstract and universal to the concrete and individual, from the divine to the human and on to the ancestral group, from the separation of Heaven and Earth to the delimitation of clan territories.

Many traditional cultures believe that the division between the body and soul that followed the first death was accompanied by a rupture in the entire cosmos. The sky was hoisted above the land and communication between earth and heaven was severed. The gods now resided in the highest heavens. Access to them became more difficult. Only through the ecstasies of the shaman or medicine man could earth and heaven be joined again and the word of the gods made known to man. Shamanism is therefore intimately connected with the notion of the epic journey and a break from the mundane world. By momentarily separating the soul from the body through achieving the state of ecstasy, the shaman is able to travel in the superhuman world of the gods and bring back knowledge of the future.

This idea of a journey or an escape from everyday life is of course preserved in the contemporary attitude to leisure and travel. Both are commonly associated with 'escape experience' in which the elements of character which are suppressed in the arenas of work, family and community life are released through the act of 'going away'. Of course, the religious origins of this yearning for escape are now exchanged in a secular form. Yet the notion that some forms of leisure and tourism have a semi-religious connotation will be readily understood by most readers. For example, we commonly think of a football cup final as having an 'other worldly' significance and we speak of 'pilgrimages' to selected tourist sights.

The argument that leisure and tourism connote 'other worldly', 'escape' experience is central to the general discussion in this book. Both will be interpreted as one of the primary means through which contemporary secular life is made and remade. In traditional society the question of how to handle surplus energy is bracketed as a metaphysical matter. It is up to the Gods to decide how the surplus will be absorbed. The highly ritualized character of group life can be interpreted as a method of diverting the surplus to solidify the group. In secularized, individualized society a different set of problems is posed. Surplus energy is diverted and absorbed in ways which befit the fragmented, differentiated character of life.

This does not mean that modern life has lost its ritual character.

Rather, this character is displayed through a different repertoire of social performances. The performative qualities of everyday life have been extensively commented upon (Goffman 1967, 1971, 1974). In this study performance will be understood as the social cement which binds life with others. Human life is full of passion and terrors, highs and lows. But these qualities are never expressed *au naturel*. They are always mediated by performance scripts. It is not enough to feel passion or terror, others must witness it too. The human animal is so bound to the wheel of ceaseless performance that he or she is often prey to feelings of inauthenticity. It is not just that our performances seem unreal, we are aware of the artificial character of performing and the faulty pastimes and enthusiasms that are often affixed to it. For much of this book leisure will be treated as a performance activity. Far from fulfilling the function conventionally ascribed to it of 'getting in touch with ourselves', leisure makes status statements about ourselves to others. It is status-positioning activity. Of course, this is not to say that bodily pleasure and leisure never go together or that all forms of leisure are at bottom, inauthentic. Rather it is to insist on the performance-related aspects of 'getting away from it all' or 'getting in touch with our real selves' which are usually glossed over in the literature. Moreover, and crucially, it raises the proposition that some forms of performance of activity have no ulterior value beyond placing us culturally in relation to others. Leisure behaviour is part of the complex system of representation and signification which organizes life with others. It is perhaps not the most important part. As activity which belongs to the surplus it remains secondary to the productive activity which creates the surplus in the first place. On the other hand, much of this study will be concerned to establish the proposition that economic and technological forces have rendered the work ethic, as it is conventionally understood, obsolete. We are moving into post-work societies but the ethical framework devised to regulate life with others in industrial society has not caught up with this transition. An important sign of the move to post-work is the growing importance of leisure in cultural life. The main challenge facing students of leisure is to devise ethical principles of private well-being and public responsibility which are compatible with post-work society.

Evans-Pritchard (1976) and Eliade (1957) both emphasize that in traditional societies the collective rituals designed to produce a journey away from 'normality' are repetitive. The timing of the

ceremonies are predetermined by the will of the gods. When birth
or death occur, or when the tribe is threatened by external hazard
such as drought or war, the shaman acts not through choice but by
obeying immemorial superhuman laws. Eliade (1957) stresses the
sacred and reconfirming character of tribal festivals:

> Every religious festival . . . represents the reactualization of a sacred
> event that took place in a mythical past, 'in the beginning'. Re-
> ligious participation in a festival implies emerging from ordinary
> temporal duration and reintegration of the mythical time
> reactualized by the festival itself. Hence sacred time is indefi-
> nitely recoverable, indefinitely repeatable.

Festivals are optimistic events in the tribal calendar because they
enable men to live closer to their gods. They do not simply com-
memorate a mythical event, they reactualize it. The repetition of
cosmology through festivals and celebrations has the effect of
regenerating time. In a sense, traditional culture is bound up in a
closed cosmology in which time is circular. Collective leisure is often
about revisiting earlier times to honour their significance or intensity. Temporality is not confined by the human life cycle. Rather
there are gradients of temporality, and collective ritual or ecstatic
ceremonies are ways of tunnelling into them. But the tunnelling
process requires collective assent. If only some members of the
group devote themselves to escape experience, the surplus energy
in the collectivity is not evenly distributed. The lack of even distribution may be a source of unrest which ultimately threatens the
viability of the group as a collective entity. Everyday life in traditional societies is therefore regular and paced. Even the ecstasy of
the shaman is designed to renew an essentially unchanging order.
To depart from it risks offending the gods and inviting calamity
upon the tribe. As Evans-Pritchard (1976: 201) notes, magic and
oracles constitute an intellectually coherent system. Since both transcend ordinary life they cannot be easily contradicted by ordinary
experience. For a Zande, innovation, deviation and diversity are to
be discouraged and even repressed because they run contrary to
the law of the gods. Time is not a matter of choice but destiny.
The question of how we are to spend the day does not arise, because
the order of the day is appointed. Hence, to repeat a point made
earlier, the question of how to deal with surplus energy is always a
metaphysical question. It is not a matter for tribal members to decide,
instead it is in the lap of the Gods. The Zande understand as well

as anyone else that no individual can be programmed to act with 24-hour metronomic precision. Even so, everyday life in tribes like the Azande is highly regulated. The line of events from dawn to dusk and season to season follows a primordial pattern and there are strong prohibitions which prevent individuals from challenging or breaking the pattern.

However, while ritual may celebrate surplus energy it does not expend all of the energy in the group. The surplus available to each individual depends upon their physiological and mental characteristics. This is not a matter for tribal leaders to decree. They may seek to lay down the law about human behaviour in the group. But as with all human gatherings an unaccounted surplus is bound to remain. This unaccounted surplus can be the source of dialectic movements which challenge ascribed authority structures.

In the case of the Azande, opposition is organized at the institutional level through the organization of *Mani*. The *Aboro Mani* or 'People of Mani' are distinguished from lay members of the tribe by various practices and secret formulae. They act as conduits for new types of medicine and magic imported from foreign people. These have value for many lay members of the tribe because they break the monotony of Zande ritual and may introduce forms of knowledge which are more effective in producing results. Interestingly, Evans-Pritchard (1976: 214–15) notes that a feature of *Mani* practice is that women join in more or less equal numbers with men. This is contrary to Zande lay practice where sexual segregation is strictly enforced. The *Aboro Mani* are tolerated, but they often act in ways which directly contradict the authority of Zande hierarchy. In addition *Mani* challenges the status order of the Azande. Lay tribal leaders are accorded high status throughout Zande life. But in *Mani* practice they do not usually attend or participate in ceremonies. Even when a tribal leader does enter a *Mani* lodge he is not assured leadership over lay folk unless he owns the medicines which the lodge uses. Even then, he is obliged to respect lay people and defer to them. Not surprisingly *Mani* practice is not popular with tribal leaders. For it lies outside ordinary social life where the authority of the leaders reigns supreme. *Mani* sorcery may even contradict tribal laws and therefore undermine the authority base upon which the power of the tribal hierarchy rests.

Yet *Mani* are tolerated. In explaining why, Evans-Pritchard (1976: 218) speculates that they are a symptom of the social disintegration of the Azande. The closed cosmology of the lay members has been unable to resist the forces of expansion. The more the Zande lay hierarchy struggle to resist endogenous expansionary tendencies and to police foreign influence, the greater the risk that they will appear out of touch and reactionary. Yet in making concessions to expansionism they invite the forces which sow dissent and conflict. For the Zande leaders it is a no-win situation. Either they suppress endogenous and foreign tendencies for diversity and run the risk of counter-revolution, or they allow these tendencies to proliferate and experience a drip-by-drip diminution of their authority. Thus, there is no escape from cultural formations which challenge the ruling order of things either by inverting that order or counterposing it with alternative values.

Evans-Pritchard conducted his fieldwork in the late 1920s. As Gillies (1976) shows, by the 1970s the authority of the Zande elite had indeed diminished. Even in Evans-Pritchard's day, power was clearly shifting to the colonial powers of Britain, Belgium and France who each claimed portions of the tribal homeland. After the war these colonial forces in turn gave way to the post-colonial nation-states of Sudan, Zaire and the République Centrafricaine. The *Aboro Mani* may not have overturned the power of the traditional Zande elite, but they paved the way towards the consolidation of the Zande into broader geopolitical units. In this sense *Mani* certainly signalled the disintegration of traditional Zande ways of life.

What do these accounts tell us? The following points must be made:

1. Relations in traditional society are overtly bound by rituals of conduct. Forms of activity are closely patterned by primordial, hierarchical lines of authority. Ritual is the method for diverting and absorbing surplus energy.
2. Repetition and regularity follow from the need to manifest performance. They are mechanisms for expressing qualities of performance which involve the social totality.
3. Social energy, like physical energy, cannot be absolutely contained. Traditional society has no concept of individual choice. Even the decisions of the Head of the tribe and the shaman follow the dictates of the gods. Persons are, as Durkheim (1902; 1915) said, cells which stand in relation to the tribe just as cells stand in relation to the host organism of a living presence. Yet persons do not behave mechanically. They have the capacity to act in ways which are contrary to the rules and habits of the collective.

4. Cultural existence imposes shape upon human behaviour. Traditional societies radiate immediate and obvious recognition of approval or censure in respect of human behaviour. Yet because human capacities are dynamic, the actions of humans are never contained by the categories of human culture. The pattern of daily order, one might say, possesses immanent tendencies to challenge the limitations of cultural custom, habit and decree. In all cultures, antistructures of behaviour are the corollary of the structural rules of everyday life. Because leisure belongs to the surplus it stands a close relation to the gestation and expression of antistructures of behaviour.

5. Our conventional understanding of leisure as personal freedom, choice and self-determination has no place in traditional society. The ecstatic states evoked by the shaman through ritual may carry over into self-expression. Thus in the journey to meet the gods, individuals may experience bodily pleasure and emotional catharsis which transports the psyche and viscera beyond the ordinary experience of the collectivity. However, the thrust of the culture is to compel the individual to conform. The ecstasy of the shaman is a momentary break from the monotony of daily existence. Yet its purpose is conservative in that it always functions to return excited senses to the normality of tribal order. Play and work are woven into the seamless religious fabric of the tribal order.

6. The collective remaking of the group is accomplished through conspicuous ritual. These frequently adopt the means of play forms such as dances, chants, masks and intoxicants. But play is rarely an end in itself. It is part of the closed magical and religious cosmology which meshes the tribe together. Play forms take the tribal members away from the cares of everyday life, but they also insist on returning the individual to everyday normality. One might say that the classic cosmology of traditional society is an hermetic system in which time, circumstance and action are explained by the mechanics of supernatural forces. Ritual provides a way of tunnelling into hidden gradients of time. But the overall system is essentially circular and closed. This supports a lifeworld dominated by homologies rather than difference. The cosmology, customs and habits of the tribe evoke a universal order. However, universality is challenged by exogenous forces, notably colonialism and post-colonialism. Traditional society persists in a modern world order in which science, technology and the nation-state predominate.

7. Finally, bodies in traditional society are often 'busy' – for example,
   in the pursuit of hunting and gathering, the defence of the tribe
   and the reaffirmation of tribal culture through ritual form. But
   above 'business', bodies are always 'occupied', always performing. That is, the various activities of the individual body are marked
   by the obligation to be congruent with the interests of the tribe.
   The *Mani* are tolerated so long as they refrain from taking things
   too far. Serious transgression invites punishment. Durkheim (1902,
   1915) characterized the moral ethos of tribal life as 'repressive'.
   He contrasted this with the 'organic', elastic, differentiated activities cultivated in modern industrial culture. Durkheim was
   only partly right. The trait of modern industrial culture which
   he never wrote about in detail was vacancy: vacant bodies, killing time, avoiding commitments, filling the space between
   gemeinschaft and *gesellschaft*. If there is one reason why Durkheim
   missed this, it is his failure to recognize the extent to which
   relations in urban-industrial cultures are performative. That is,
   the extent to which modern ways of dealing with surplus energy
   are simply about status positioning activity as opposed to productive labour or a search for authenticity.

PERFORMATIVE PLURALISTIC CULTURE

Eliade (1957: 205) notes some features of mythical systems that
have carried over into modern society. For example, popular culture embodied in the cinema, comics and literature employs several
motifs that would be familiar in tribal society: the conflict between
good and evil; the fight between the hero and the monster, initia-
tory combats and ordeals. The tribal ideology of the journey often
involves battles between these positive and negative forces and similar
motifs can still be found in today's travel literature, with its references
to 'no-go' areas, 'dangers' and so on. There are also paradigmatic
figures that remain: the maiden, the hero, the paradisical landscape
and hell. Similarly, the attachment to fixed festivals in today's calendar is reminiscent of conditions in tribal society. Social development
is always a mix between continuities and discontinuities. This much
is clear from Eliade's account.

However, in terms of the temporal character of everyday life one
key discontinuity divides modern experience from its traditional
counterpart. In Eliade's (1957: 107) words:

Repetition emptied of its religious content necessarily leads to a pessimistic vision of existence. When it is no longer a vehicle for reintegrating a primordial situation, and hence for recovering the mysterious presence of the gods, that is, when it is desacrilized, a cyclic time becomes terrifying; it is seen as a circle for ever turning on itself, repeating itself to infinity.

Ever since Tonnies (1887), one can read social theory as a response to the decline of ritual culture with its fetishes of religion and cyclic time. A social form based upon collective ritualized performance is replaced with a social form based upon patterns of performance which are more varied, differentiated and de-differentiated. The sociological works of Marx and Durkheim describe the Modernist project of replacing religion with secular humanism and the notion of cyclical time with that of an expanding, controllable future. Weber's work is more sceptical about the potential of secular, rational humanism. His (1968, 1976) discussion of the work ethic and the imprisoning effect of calculability, precision and standardization implies that modern men and women have gained rational control of the social universe at the expense of losing traditional features of closeness, flexibility and spontaneity which make life worth living. Veblen (1899) and Simmel (1971, 1978) develop the theme of the irrationalities of the rational world order. Simmel (1971) even attributes morbidity to Modernity in his accounts of the symptoms of neurasthenia and the blasé attitude which, he insists, are generated by modern life.

The culture which these classical social theorists are writing about is already recognizably, performative pluralistic culture. That is, a culture in which there are strong social pressures to make individuals behave in predictable, standardized ways; in which the quality of the performance is the main criterion for establishing validity in the power and authority relations between actors; and where the patterns of performance are becoming more varied, differentiated and de-differentiated; and crucially, where some people perform merely for the sake of performance. Performative culture literally requires people to be performers. They consciously submerge aspects of their own character in order to present a face to society that will enable them to be accepted for educational training, to participate in paid employment, to have authority over others, to engage in play activity with others, to symbolize acceptance and continuity.

Although the term 'performative culture' is associated most readily today with Lyotard's (1984) work, Goffman's (1959, 1967, 1971) writing on 'facework' remains the best guide to the characteristics and dynamics of performative pluralistic culture. Goffman presents social order as a continuous and interlinked process of staged performances. Credible performances do not simply stem from the individual, they rely on a series of supporting buttresses. Goffman (1959: 245) identifies three buttresses as indispensable:

1. *Back regions.* That is, the concealed elements in a performance which make the performance believable. They are contrasted with the 'front region' which is the locus of the performance. Back regions remind us that performers require training and support in order to deliver credible performances. For example, in delivering a company plan to shareholders, the managing director relies on knowledge and protocols of behaviour learnt from the family, the education process, the coaching culture of the company and the expectations of the audience. Every successful performance relies on back regions of knowledge, expertise and activity.

2. *Props.* That is, the visible accompanying details that make a performance credible. To continue with the example of the company director, to gain the immediate respect of colleagues, he or she must be well groomed, well dressed, convey authority, manage and formulate strategies. Props are essential to every performance. A performance which takes place without the right props will typically flounder.

3. *Teams.* That is, the network of social actors who act in conjunction with the performer to sustain the performance. With respect to the company director, one thinks of secretaries, personal assistants, financial advisors, personnel staff and so forth. The team adds to the credibility of the performance, bringing out certain features through their sustaining activity and glossing over others.

Goffman (1959: 245) draws a contrast between the character as performer and the individual as performer. Successful performances require the performer to stay in character, at least for the duration of the performance. Out of character the performer returns to being an individual. Interestingly, when Goffman speculates on characteristics of the individual out of character, issues of worry and anxiety dominate his list. Thus, he (1959: 245–6) writes:

He has a capacity to learn, this being exercised in the task of training for a part. He is given to having fantasies and dreams, some that pleasurably unfold a triumphant performance, others full of anxiety and dread that nervously deal with vital discreditings in a public front region. He often manifests a gregarious desire for team-mates and audiences, a tactful considerateness for their concerns; and he has a capacity for deeply felt shame, leading him to minimize the chances he takes of exposure.

Goffman presents these characteristics as general features of the individual. Several points follow from his discussion. In the first place, his distinction between the performer as character and individual suggests that contemporary life is saturated with artifice. Thus, in performing any social role, the individual is, at some level, simultaneously conscious of being in and out of character. The degree to which a successful performance is accomplished depends upon fixing this consciousness to the performance so that the hidden, reflexive part of the individual does not intrude.

Secondly, out-of-character activity is a source of anxiety. When individuals are not performing, they have an unpleasant sense of being cast adrift. Performing is necessary not only for social cohesion but personal health. But if the general impulse is towards continuous performance, it follows that some performances are not as necessary as others. If individuals are continuously performing they logically require powers of discretion to determine the suitability of performance styles in different social situations. Yet, as Weber (1968) argues, the character of modern life is bureaucratic and rational. Individuals are under strong pressures to be 'busy' even in circumstances where the value of what they produce is irrelevant or unimportant. The façade of the busybody was nicely revealed by Merton (1968) in his famous discussion of the bureaucratic personality. Merton argues that some bureaucrats develop patterns of ritualistic overconformity to the means of behaviour so that the ends of behaviour are lost. Bureaucrats adhere so closely to the rules of what they are doing that the goals of their behaviour become relegated to matters of secondary importance. So, for example, it is more important to arrive at work on time, in the right suit and to establish role distance between oneself and one's colleagues than to solve the problems that the bureaucracy has been assigned to solve. Central to the present study is the notion that some forms of leisure can only be explained by positing a disjuncture between the means and ends of leisure. In plain language, many people in their leisure are busy doing nothing. The performance of appearing to be busy conveys status and a sense of personal security. Yet it cannot neutralize a deeper inner sense of voluntarily choosing activity which has no value. Hence, the emptiness and meaninglessness which is often a feature of contemporary leisure experience.

Thirdly, Goffman's distinction suggests that social life is composed of privatized, interior regions in which individuals can 'be themselves'. The space for sustained self-reflexivity and relaxation is particularly important because Goffman's discussion clearly presents front region activity as having strong tendencies to be stressful. He speaks of 'anxiety', 'nervousness', 'shame' and 'vital discreditings' as normal parts of daily encounters. In order to perform we need to have parts of our life to which we can retreat and establish what Giddens (1992), following Laing (1960) terms 'the ontological security' necessary for active life. This is because performing in public often requires us to behave in standardized ways, not only to other 'faces' but also to abstract or invisible audiences. We need time and space in which our sense of 'real' self as an individual is reinforced and developed. This is not necessarily a privatized confirmation of self-worth. Establishing our own ontological security involves relating to 'significant others' closely. But it is activity that necessarily takes place away from the hurly-burly of the public sphere. Yet – and this is critical – modern social life provides less and less time and space in which individuals can rebuild a sense of ontological security. Instead it proliferates criteria and monitoring systems to measure the degree of business in individuals and society. Surplus is automatically associated with either waste or unused capacity. The time that we need to construct a sustainable sense of an inner life is eaten into by the drive to perform. We are actors who frequently have no conviction in the scripts that we are required to speak.

Fourthly, Goffman's discussion implies that front region activity is occupied activity. A performer is, precisely, somebody with something to do. In a sense his sociology assumes that only infants have nothing to do and require constant supervision from adults in order to participate in ordinary social life. Certainly his (1961) account of the inmate world and the mechanics of total institutions insists that even mentally ill adult patients routinely play roles and perform. That is, patients who are labelled as people who must be withdrawn from ordinary everyday life still perform. The observation is consistent with Goffman's general sociology.

Fifthly, Goffman suggests that although individuals require space to be themselves, few of us want to be alone for very long. We may relish solitary moments and we may value our own company, but we shun fully privatized existence. The individual, he (op. cit.) states manifests a 'gregarious desire' for team-mates and a 'tactful considerateness' for their concerns. *Contra*, Sennett (1974), who characterizes the rise of modern society as involving 'the fall of public man', Goffman identifies the public sphere as an indispensable component of modern existence. At the same time he goes to some lengths to insist that successful public performances require extensive private preparation and support work.

Goffman is generally understood to have produced a sociology which exposes how ritual behaviour is conducted in modern industrial society. However, his comprehension of what ritual means is very different from say, Evans-Pritchard's account of ritual in the life of the Azande or Eliade's account of repetition in pre-modern cultures. First of all, Goffman suggests that modern life is less interwoven with collective principles. In pre-modern society, the sense of the individual as an independent person is blotted out by tribal consciousness. As Durkheim (1915) argued, pre-modern formations possess a highly developed *conscience collective*. People are bound together by mechanical ties of solidarity and they are controlled by a repressive system of discipline which punishes infractious, transgressive behaviour. Modern society may rely upon interdependent conduct between social actors. But private time and private space is built into the fabric of daily existence. The sense of the individual as a reflexive, independent entity is far more highly developed. The boundaries of acceptable behaviour are more loosely defined. Transgression is a negotiable characteristic of ordinary human relations. The absolutist systems of pre-modern formations, which distinguish between absolute right and absolute wrong, are seen as too mechanical because they ignore the ambivalence which is integral to social life. The space and time for private play forms and types of leisure which avoid the monitoring eye of the public are greater. Leisure and travel become means both of renewing the existing order and engaging in deviant or profane forms of behaviour which challenge established rules and practices. They are ways of diverting and absorbing surplus energy which conflict with the assigned values which are meant to govern everyday life.

Secondly, the presence of ambivalence in ordinary relations reflects a collapse of hierarchical authority structures. In traditional society, power is invested in the tribal head with clear, indisputable ranks of authority below him. Thus, the children of the chief, his wife or wives and witch-doctors each possess a level of power which is automatically evident to the rest of the tribe. Modern societies have produced a knowledge and information glut in which positions of authority develop counterveiling ideologies and positions. There are more antistructures of behaviour which are either opposed to, or contrast with, the structural rules of everyday life. In such circumstances it is harder to determine the best course of action or to know what to believe. For example, the conservative proposition that the market is the best mechanism for allocating resources and achieving distributive justice is routinely opposed by socialists and social democrats. They argue that the market distribution is iniquitous and they call for higher levels of state regulation in order to achieve justice. The opposition is a very familiar one in Western democracies. The conduct of managing economy and society is always a matter of dispute. One important consequence of it is that political authority is always a contingent, tension-ridden construction. Persons in power are always conscious of contrary forms of knowledge which openly circulate in society to undermine their position. This consciousness is shared by the electorate. For example, in November of 1996 the electorate of the most powerful nation in the world contrived to vote President Clinton into office for a second term with just 48 per cent of the eligible voters. Clinton had fared better in 1992 when he achieved 55 per cent of the turnout. But this in itself broke the trend of voting in American elections since the Kennedy administration of 1960. Victory on a minority turnout raises obvious questions about legitimacy and mandate. Clinton's victory demonstrates Goffman's point that in a performative pluralistic culture appearances matter more than substance. In a democracy, power can be won and sustained by making the right gestures to standardized external criteria of legitimacy, as opposed to genuinely achieving legitimacy through garnering popular support.

Goffman's discussion implies that performativity is a precondition for action in modern societies. The impression that a performance gives is a requirement for placing trust in the performer. Order depends upon trust being reproduced. This applies to the micro-level of everyday life as well as the macro-level of Presidential elections, stock exchange trading, economic management and social administration. Social life would be unthinkable without a high level of trust routinely built into everyday connections and practices. We relate to strangers as faces occupying positions. However, Beck (1992) and other writers have drawn attention to the increased consciousness of risk in contemporary everyday life which undermines trust relations. In some part, this heightened consciousness derives from a realization that there are some regional and global risks which are now so large that they cannot be insured against. But it has also been fuelled by the glut of information in contemporary culture and the enriched knowledge that we have of repertoires of facework and the partial legitimacy of authority positions. Beck's work on risk problematizes the Modernist twinning of leisure with escape. For it suggests that risk consciousness dwells in leisure activity. For it is precisely when we have nothing to do that we become engulfed by worries and fears about all that can go wrong. If this is correct, risk consciousness will form a larger component in the ideologies of some forms of leisure. This is already evident in contemporary life in the health scares associated with smoking, drinking, eating certain types of food. It is also evident in tourism in the fears articulated by eco-tourists that some forms of tourism have been environmentally damaging. Beck's work can be criticized for over-exaggerating the omnipresence of risk consciousness in everyday life. Most of us continue to perform our mundane, day-to-day activities, with a low expectation that very much will go wrong. In contrast, Beck's work suggests that risk consciousness is a brooding presence in our typical relations with each other.

Despite being vulnerable to the charge of over-statement, risk is an important concept. Another leisure response to risk is to translate risk into a play form. Bunjy jumping, sky diving, undisciplined drug and alcohol use to test limits, can all be interpreted as ways of playing out global risk through voluntarily chosen, ultimately containable, leisure pursuits. Together with the argument that leisure experience possesses an other-worldly significance in our culture, the uses of leisure to cope with risk consciousness will be a major theme in the book.

LYOTARD AND PERFORMATIVITY

In recent years the concept of performativity has received its most significant application in the work of Jean-François Lyotard (1984).

He argues that performative cultures typically establish criteria of relevance to establish legitimate performances. Action and legitimacy become matters of achieving these criteria. Inevitably, as Merton (1968) noted, there is the possibility of a disjunction between means and ends. Social performers become so wrapped up in the task of achieving the standard criteria of the means involving a given performance that they lose sight of the ends. Part of Lyotard's criticism is founded in the proposition that this disjunction exists in chronic form in contemporary society. Social performers are absorbed in the detail of their performances. Their servitude to the *minutiae* of performance activity means that they cannot register the full range of effects that their performances have on themselves and on others. Lyotard uses the example of the modern university to illustrate the point. The move from elite to mass higher education requires the construction of performance criteria to assess efficiency. Thus, the value of a discipline or module may be judged by the number of students it attracts. Modules or disciplines which attract few students invite the possibility of being valued as inefficient resource investments. As such, in fully developed performative pluralistic culture the lecturers who run them will be subject to pressures to change curriculum content and pedagogic methods, or risk termination. Hence, in the UK in the 1980s, many philosophy and sociology departments were threatened with closure by a right-wing government bent on extracting quantifiable monetary value from the investment in higher education. Lyotard's objection to performative culture is that it makes standardization the primary operational value of social interaction. 'When it comes to speaking the truth or prescribing justice,' he (1984: 52) comments, 'numbers are meaningless.'

Basic to Lyotard's critique is the assumption that performativity is not universal. Performative and counter-performative cultures abound. In any system that claims to have total control, there is always a surplus. His critique points to a powerful tendency in contemporary culture rather than a crystallized state of affairs. We should speak of the omnipresence, rather than the universality of performative culture. However, because we find it so easy to identify with the notion of performativity and the criticisms which follow from it, we should give due importance to the significance of the concept in the organization of identity, association and practice. To be noticed in modern industrial-urban culture we must be adept performers. If we cease to have the capacity to perform through physical or mental illness we cease to be figures of value in the culture. Our rights and responsibilities are taken away from us. We enter the composed, unvarying world of the total institution described so well by Goffman (1961). But in dedicating our work and leisure time to performing we may gain the approval of our peers, but lose our lives.

THE ANTINOMIES OF PERFORMATIVE CULTURE

Performativity is then, a key feature of modern organizations. To make people work together in modern organizations, performance standards and indicators must be laid out and instilled through regular contract. From school to death, we are enmeshed in a ceaseless process of monitoring and evaluation. At school we undergo IQ tests, we study to pass exams, we try to fulfil the academic criteria that will gain us a university place; aiming for work we present our performance capacities to employers in the form of job applications; in work we are set targets; we set ourselves goals; in our familiy lives we attempt to show our love to our spouses and children in measurable ways, but evaluate their behaviour according to our innate standards of what is expected and what is required; and when we are dying our bodies will be evaluated according to medical criteria which determine our medication and when to switch our life-support machines off. Leisure is often presented as the antithesis of performative culture. It is not.

Stebbins's (1992) important work on 'serious leisure' illustrates the importance of performativity in common leisure practice. Serious leisure consists of voluntary leisure activity in which the individual develops a sense of a career, self-worth and progress. It is usually associated with an intensification of relationships with others because the leisure activity involves coordinated, co-operative activity. Stebbins (1992) uses the example of barber-shop quartets to illustrate how leisure contributes to both the individual's sense of self-esteem and self-actualization and to the integration of the community.

An auxiliary concept used by Stebbins is casual leisure. This consists of desultory, opportunistic, circumstantial leisure activity which is motivated by a desire for automatic stimulation and immediate gratification. Examples of casual leisure include channel hopping, hanging around shopping malls, random drinking and smoking. Although Stebbins claims to use these terms in non-evaluative ways it is self-evident that the term 'serious' carries with it strong moralistic connotations. In a later work Stebbins (1997) recognizes this, and argues that casual leisure is not insignificant. He acknowledges that casual leisure forms may be more popular than serious forms in contemporary society. Even so, he (1997) retains the proposition that serious leisure forms are more important to the wellbeing of the individual and society. There are two reasons for this. First, serious leisure permits the development of a sense of career in the individual and hence a basis for self-monitoring and progress. Secondly, it enhances the integration of the community and this contributes to the stability and harmony of society. In sum, serious leisure is a vehicle for the cultural and moral reaffirmation of communities as places in which the individual recognizes relations of belonging.

The concept of serious leisure has met with wide approval in the study of leisure (Jackson and McQuarrie 1996). It is an interesting attempt to clarify the conceptual minefield of leisure studies by introducing a new categoric distinction between forms of leisure activity. For this it should certainly be welcomed. But it is unsatisfactory in a number of respects. In particular, three points must be made.

First, it lacks a tenable moral dimension. Stebbins (1992: 3–4) defines serious leisure as 'the systematic pursuit of amateur, hobbyist, or volunteer activity sufficiently substantial for the participant to find a career there in the acquisition and expression of a combination of its special skills, knowledge and experience'. He clearly intends this definition to apply to leisure activities which further the goal of social integration. But the definition could apply just as well to the construction of deviant leisure identities and deviant leisure careers. Drug-abusers, pornographers and trespassers all use special skills and experience in the pursuit of their activities. They develop techniques for disguising their behaviour from public view and while their activities may be reprehensible to many of us, they are serious and essential to them. These techniques and skills are very considerable. They are the basis for developing a personal sense of career development and although the values that they mobilize and celebrate may offend others, they also produce the basis for developing self-esteem and self-actualization. Stebbins provides no tenable moral basis for distinguishing between leisure practices. But as Bailey (1987), Cunningham (1980), Corrigan and Sayer (1985) and Wagner (1997) point out, the history of leisure is surrounded by issues of moral regulation. Leisure is not simply about 'free time' activity, it is about free time activity that is evaluated as morally good or evil by others. My position is that a moral element must be included in any satisfactory theory or conceptual framework that refers to leisure. Further, it is not satisfactory to discount law-breaking activity as 'deviant' and hence of no interest to students of leisure. I propose that in most cases, law-breaking activity does not lead to trial, penalty or imprisonment. Law-breaking is a *popular* activity. By engaging in it we demonstrate performative capacities that transcend the mundane categories of everyday life. We gain fun, excitement and pleasure (Katz 1988). Any approach to leisure which fails to take central account of the fun, excitement and pleasure to be gained from deviant behaviour is, I think, unrealistic.

Secondly, by conjoining the concept of serious leisure to the concept of career, Stebbins reproduces a paradigm which paints leisure as driven by rational-purposive activity. True, he contrasts serious leisure with casual leisure. However, despite a brief amendment he (1997) does not develop the concept of casual leisure very much and the tone of his discussion is dismissive. Casual leisure is, as it were, the 'white noise' of leisure conduct. For Stebbins, it may be popular but essentially it is desultory and inconsequential in explaining personal or cultural patterns of leisure conduct. But is society moving in the direction of more organized, community-based leisure pursuits? Are we going to have more barbershop quartets, closer social integration and less drug addiction, alcoholism, dependency-based leisure consumption and social isolation? A considerable body of literature in the study of culture suggests that social conditions are becoming more episodic and anonymous (Castells 1996, 1997, 1998; Wagner 1997; Katz 1988). What Kracauer (1995) called the 'distraction industries' of mass capitalism – television, cinema, popular music – provide a wealth of stimulation for individuals who wish to escape moral commitment. Individuals may be pressed back onto leisure as a sphere to develop a sense of career and personal worth by the vagaries of the employment market. But at the very least, one might propose that there will be problems in developing self-actualization through leisure in conditions in which rejection or a lack of certain employment develops in the labour market.

Thirdly, Stebbins provides no basis for regarding leisure as a lever for social change. Instead, his discussion of serious leisure tends to emphasize the integrative effect of leisure in reinforcing social order. Casual leisure may disrupt order, but precisely because it is disorganized and desultory it provides no basis for transforming society, Of course, much leisure activity can be explained in terms of Durkheim's (1915) concept of 'the remaking of social life'. But to ascribe a reproductive function to leisure is too narrow. The position that I will develop here, especially in Chapter 4 of the book, is that leisure is partly a catalyst for social change. Turner (1969, 1982, 1992) has devised the category of 'liminal leisure' which refers to a time and space in the flow of collective life in which individuals can legitimately stand outside the axioms, mores and conventions of society. I propose that the culture of leisure includes a strong transgressive element. Leisure enables us to objectify the rules and mores of everyday life and subject them to critical appraisal. It is no accident that organizations like trade unions and political parties have part of their origins in pub meetings and coffee-house gatherings (Habermas (1962). In these settings individuals could let their hair down and, in relatively private settings, pose wider questions relating to inequality and injustice. I propose that there is a close historical and current relation between some forms of leisure activity and transformation of the public sphere. Leisure events like concerts, recreational education, discussion groups and the like, have generated political strategies and movements which have transformed society. If some forms of casual leisure are read as contributions to liminal activity their role in transforming relations must be acknowledged. The history of popular culture in the post-war period provides countless examples. The development of popular music challenged the staid family values of the pre-war years and contributed to the informalization of everyday life. The growth of sport and exercise in leisure promoted a new popular consciousness of health. Body piercing challenged the notion of 'the normal body' and suggested that traditional patterns of social inclusion were too narrow.

In sum, Stebbins's work has produced an important counter to the commonsense view that leisure is subordinate to work in everyday life. He shows convincingly that serious leisure pursuits are often more central in the development of notions of self-worth and self-actualization than work experience; and further, that serious leisure has a significant role in contributing to social integration. The latter is a useful antidote to policy-makers who define social questions solely in terms of a twin strategy on employment and welfare. Creating satisfactory conditions of leisure for all of the population also has a part to play in social engineering. However, having given

Stebbins his due, I also want to insist that there is good reason to hold that the paradigm that he applies is too inflexible and uniform. To put it candidly, Stebbins's conclusion of the leisure groups that he investigated may be right, but his analysis of the society in which they are situated is wrong.

Recently, in the sociology of culture and cultural geography writers have claimed a paradigm shift around the concept of flow (Castells 1998; O'Connor 1997). An ancestor of the concept has cropped up before in leisure studies, notably in the work of Csikszentmihalyi (1975). He identifies flow with autotelic activity. He argues that flow occurs when the task matches the individual's ability and competence. In this condition the individual becomes fully absorbed and experiences a sense of self-actualization and pleasure. For the purposes of understanding how contemporary thinkers apply the concept of flow, Csikszentmihaly's concept is too psychologistic. In these concerns flow is contrasted with what might be called the reified categories of experience that prefigure in the work of Stebbins. What then, is being claimed for the concept of flow? And what are its consequences for Stebbins's categoric distinction between serious and casual leisure?

Shields (1997) provides a useful summary of the concept of flow and its paradigm implications. He acknowledges that the concept has its origins in the philosophical work of Deleuze and Guattari (1988). It is also prefigured in the work of Elias (1978a, 1978b, 1982) whose attack on what he called 'static (or reified) thinking' culminated in a methodological injunction to consider all social entities as 'in-process'. As far as the application of the concept of flow in the social sciences is concerned, Shields (1997: 3) claims the following characteristics for the concept of flow:

> (It recognizes that activities) have a tempo and rhythm as well as direction. The significance of the material quality of flows is that they have content, beyond merely being processes. They have the advantage of recasting the idealist notion of processual change into the changing material itself. Process generally indicates the transformative 'gap' between states or dispositions. Process is thus strongly defined on the basis of origin and terminus as a definite line or path between two points, waystations in a further process. Process is conventionally defined by its objectives ... (b)y contrast, flows signal pure movement, fluidity and direction. They are relational, but not in a positional, instructural sense.

Shields goes on to note that Lefebvre (1991: 206) was one of the first social scientists to deploy the concept of flow. Lefebvre's application allowed for changes in the intensity of flow activity. He acknowledged peaks and troughs in the pattern of movement.

Seizing on the idea of peaks and troughs, Virilio (1986) argues that the speed of technological, social and cultural change in contemporary society is accelerating. A significant feature of our culture is that life is speeding up. I think this is something that is widely felt on an intuitive level. Of course, some sociologists of leisure argue that nothing fundamental has changed. For example, Roberts (1998) maintains that the central questions of leisure relating to the distribution of time and space and the inequality of power in industrial society remain intact. Yet the mere fact of increased acceleration in flow alters the quantity and intensity of our relationships with others and, through this, the character of leisure is also altered.

Analytically, it may be useful to distinguish between fast and slow leisure. Fast leisure refers to mobile, fragmentary, varied leisure relations. Slow leisure refers to stable, sustained and regular leisure relationships. I think that these terms are more useful than the serious/casual dichotomy, because they are descriptive rather than evaluative. They also highlight something that is missing in Stebbins, which is a sensitivity to the role of movement and change in leisure orientations. Stebbins's dichotomy implies that it is possible to plot individuals along a continuum between serious and casual orientations. In addition, the emphasis on career and integration suggests a solidification of personalities and community forms around serious and casual types. In contrast, the distinction between fast and slow leisure suggests a fluidity of movement and encapsulation of variety and contradiction which, I think, is absent in Stebbins. Fast and slow orientations to leisure can be posited or examined in the same personality or community. Let me go into the question in more detail.

As Figure 1.1 shows, it is necessary to distinguish between two levels of velocity: individual and capitalism. I'm assuming here that the focus of interest in this study is contemporary Western society and that this society retains the essential characteristics of the capitalist form. At the level of the individual, fast leisure simply refers to an acceleration in the velocity and density of leisure relations with other leisure actors. For example, to take a simple example of supply-led acceleration, the phenomenal growth of computer

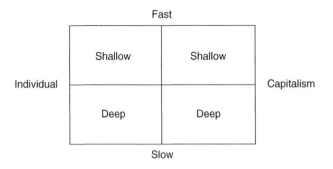

Figure 1.1   Fast and Slow Leisure

games, gameboys and playstations over the last decade is built on the hunger for constant novelty. It is an industry requirement for games to be replaced rapidly so that the market continuously expands. Computerized games typically involve attention spans to be concentrated in short bursts rather than continuously developed. They encourage the development of fragmentary consciousness since they permit the individual to concentrate on one part of the game instead of the unfolding whole. Speeding up and slowing down the game is practised so that boring bits or slow bits can be left out. In addition, the use of TV and computer monitors enables the game player to treat the game as part of a multi-media system of provision. The individual can drop out of the game, channel hop, browse the internet and engage in a variety of multi-media activities while nominally engaged in playing the computer game.

This form of leisure is fast because it requires fragmentary, superficial levels of consciousness and offers high levels of mobility to the individual enabling him or her to switch activities rapidly. It contrasts with a slow form of leisure, like reading a novel. Enjoying fiction requires the discipline of allowing narrative and character to develop in the imagination. Although the imaginative possibilities are limitless, the medium is inflexible and narrow. The only major technical innovation of note since the invention of the printing press has been the introduction of the talking book. This development is perhaps indicative of the fast leisure orientations in lifestyle, since it increases the flexibility of the medium by allowing the individual to read the book by listening to it on a Walkman while doing something else at the same time.

Societies, not just individuals, can be analyzed in terms of fast or slow orientations to leisure. In the twentieth century the 1920s, 1960s and arguably the 1990s are all periods of 'fast' leisure. That is, they are associated with an acceleration in the velocity and density of leisure relationships. The catalyst in each case is often technological. Thus, the invention and mass production of the phonogram in the 1920s was a crucial factor in precipitating the jazz age; the development of the pill, the extension of mass communication systems, especially television, the improvement to private transport systems, all contributed to the permissive leisure lifestyles of the 1960s; while the 1990s have witnessed the development of the Internet which has the potential to revolutionize ordinary orientations of leisure by dramatically increasing our sense of interdependence and our accessibility to information and entertainment.

But it would be a mistake to fall into a determinist mind-set. Technologies always exist as techno-cultures. The emergence and success of all technologies is dependent upon a range of cultural, social and economic factors. For example, the vitality of the jazz age owed much to a general sense of liberation from the horrors of the First World War, full employment and a spurt of rising real incomes which only ended with the 1928 Crash and the onset of the Great Depression. The ferment of the 1960s also rested on a bed of full employment and rising real income. Added to it, was the growth of higher education which contributed to the general criticism of central social institutions and values which occurred at that time. Students, one should remember, were part of the spearhead of social unrest. The May events in Paris in 1968, which were heralded by many commentators as signifying the downfall of capitalism in the West, involved the student body as one of the leading protaganists. The 1990s communication revolution has occurred in the context of the expansion in the number of cultural intermediaries in society. The growth of numbers working in the service and knowledge-based sectors of the economy has been propitious for the rapid expansion of computerized leisure pastimes in non-work time. The expansion of higher education has reinforced this tendency by increasing computer literacy in the leisure and employment markets.

Pace Roberts (1997) states that the fast leisure forms emerging in the 1990s represent new ways of absorbing and diverting surplus energy in the social system. They are often explicitly oriented to global networks of leisure. Indeed, the rise of network society raises serious questions about the viability of the nation-state as the prime units of analysis in making sense of the lifeworld. Life with others today is increasingly lived with an awareness of cultural and economic interdependence. The expansion of mass communication, and the growth of tourism, has made the barriers of the nation-state more and more porous. Several commentators are now openly asking if culture and civil society have moved into a post-nation-state condition (Giddens 1990, Robertson 1992, Vattimo 1992, Turner 1993).

I propose that the evidence suggests that flow is a crucial concept in explaining how people actually behave in their leisure time. Stebbins's (1992) concepts of serious and casual leisure have idealist connotations since they evoke states of being rather than the process itself. For example, serious leisure does not always involve engrossing, self-actualizing experience, just as casual leisure is not always meaningless and desultory. The concept of flow conveys more faithfully the anti-climactic gap between aspiration and achievement that is a common feature of leisure experience. It is also better able to handle variations in the intensity and tempo of experience that occur in leisure.

In wider social theory it is now commonplace to argue that the acceleration of everyday life has transformed the character of performativity. It has contributed to the sense of fragmentation and de-differentiation which are often cited as hallmarks of postmodernism (Vattimo 1992; Lash and Urry 1994). Our received ideas of performance and performing selves are no longer commensurate with the technical conditions of everyday life. This is especially evident in intimate life, where lifelong marriage is no longer the standard adult experience and in the area of work, where the traditional notion of a job for life has disappeared.

In the field of leisure, two of the most significant recent attacks on performative culture have come from Judith Schor (1992) and Aronowitz and Di Fazio (1994). Significantly, each advocates a reformed view of leisure on the basis of a critical estimate of the work ethic. This is significant because, as Weber (1976) showed, in contemporary urban-industrial-market culture the work ethic is the principle of performativity *nonpareil.*

OVERWORK AND THE LEISURE DEFICIT

Schor (1992) contends that, in contrast to Europe, American workers in the postwar period have found themselves trapped on a treadmill of increasing work hours and declining leisure time. Schor estimates that over the last 20 years working hours have risen by the equivalent of one month per year. While there are variations between strata, the trend applies to all levels in American society. Parallel research by Martin (1994) suggests that leisure time in the USA declined by 37 per cent between 1973 and 1994. Confronted with the choice of more work or more leisure, the overwhelming majority of American workers have chosen more work. The implications and consequences of the choice are striking. Technological innovation and improvements in systems of management have delivered a huge productivity dividend to the US economy. GNP has doubled over 1948 levels. Schor (1992: 2) attests that the theoretical savings in the organization of worktime delivered by this dividend are dramatic. Since American workers now take only half the year to deliver 1948 levels of production, it is theoretically possible for every US worker to take every other year off on full pay. Yet consistently, US workers have chosen to work longer hours. In other words they have chosen to perform according to the performance-script laid down by the work ethic. Surplus time has not been devoted to leisure but to more work.

It is important to put this in historical context. As Hunnicutt (1988) demonstrates, the struggle for shorter hours and more free time was a prominent traditional goal in the American labour movement. For most of the nineteenth century, it was regarded as equivalent to securing the best terms and conditions of work. The results are not in doubt. Between 1900 and 1920 working hours fell sharply from just under 60 to just under 50 hours per week. During the Great Depression the average working week fell to below 35 hours. However, this was partly due to the effects of short-time working and unemployment. After 1945, the 40-hour week became the norm. Schor (1992: 21) calculates that today 30 per cent of American males in employment work above 50 hours per week. She puts the hours of work for American women (including unpaid 'housework') at 70–80 hours per week.

What has caused the postwar return to work? According to Schor the root of the answer lies in the conditioning processes which have evolved in consumer culture. Consumer culture has exerted a performative effect upon how individuals choose to spend not only their free time but their work time. She argues that the main standard of success and failure in consumer culture is defined by one's ability to buy commodities in the market. Personal worth is represented by the commodities that one possesses. In order to accumulate commodities, and to comply with the tendency of capitalist industry to constantly update and transform commodity culture, one must have disposable income. The pressure is so acute that dangerously high levels of debt accumulation are now a normal part of the American way of life (see also Ritzer 1995). Living on credit is now the norm. This holds good for the rest of the industrialized world. Hence, the pressure in consumer culture is to get work which delivers the highest possible income. If one job cannot provide this, workers take two or three jobs in order to build up a portfolio of jobs. The effect on leisure and quality of life is obvious. More work means less leisure.

Schor's (1992: 11) list of the negative effects of this choice provides a depressing litany of the ills of modern America: broken homes, divorce, under-socialized and anti-social children, lack of sleep, a huge increase in stress-related illnesses such as heart disease, hypertension, gastric problems, depression, exhaustion and a general sense of dissatisfaction and purposelessness. By choosing work over leisure, people contribute to the devaluation in the quality of their lives. This is done without direct external coercion. Rather individuals are caught up in the pressure to work which derives from the continued ascendancy of the work ethic and the pressure to consume which stems from the seductions of consumer culture.

Hochschild's (1997) study of 'the time bind' provides supportive evidence. She argues that women follow the magnetic logic of men in regarding the workplace as a haven. Women's liberation has taken women out of the home and into the office and factory in ever greater numbers. She describes the rise of 'the parent-free household' and the 'participant-free civic society' and relates it to crime, unrest and *anomie*. We do not need to work so long or so hard, Hochschild concludes, and the quality of life in society would be better if we reduced our commitment to pecuniary labour.

At this point a note of caution should be injected into the discussion. By laying all of the main ills of contemporary industrial culture at the door of work, Schor and Hochschild are overstating their case. The ills to which they allude are the result of a complex set of circumstances involving overpopulation, lack of education, inadequate health and welfare services. Overwork plays a highly significant part here, but it is not necessarily the lead factor.

Nevertheless, Schor's study is a valuable antidote to the post-industrial society theorists of the 1960s and early 1970s who identified the mechanization of work and the expansion of computer technologies with the coming of the leisure society. Certainly, there was much in this thinking which now seems over-optimistic and naive (Webster 1995). Notably, the belief that the requirement to engage in paid labour would gradually shrink; that civic society would be dominated by altruistic voluntarism which would counterbalance the state; and that mass society would be replaced by a new bohemianism which would emphasize cultural creativity. At the same time, there are several important continuities between Schor's analysis and the post-industrial society perspective. For example, Riesman's (1950, 1964) famous work on 'the lonely crowd' of mass consumers anticipated Schor's stress on the alienated, isolated conditions of modern urban-industrial existence. Moreover, just as Schor stresses the contradictions between work and leisure, Bell (1973), in what is today an unfairly neglected book, discussed 'the cultural contradictions' of mass consumer culture. The brief comparisons between Schor's work and these writers is not made to take anything away from Schor's analysis. Her arguments are timely, relevant and persuasive. The post-industrial society authors generally believed that the move toward 'the leisure society' was assured by the so-called 'logic of industrialization' (Kerr *et al.* 1973). Their work also denoted a palpable faith in modernization as an essentially progressive force in human affairs. In the worst cases, post-industrial society authors seemed to propose that technology would automatically solve the problems of economic scarcity and create 'the good society'.[1] Schor writes in a situation in which the limits of modernization are stressed. New worries about risk society, the over-exploitation of Nature, pollution, the destruction of human groups and the proliferation of illnesses associated with industrial society are in the air. They prevent Schor from adopting the meliorist stance of the post-industrial society school.

Even so, it is worth making the comparison in order to underline the deep-seated nature of the trends in work and leisure upon which Schor comments. At several points in her discussion Schor (1992: 2, 81) implies that conditions in Western Europe are demonstrably better than in North America. Western Europeans, she argues, have retained a commitment to shorter hours and leisure and quality of life issues. She (1992: 82) points to the large German union IG Metall which has gained a 35-hour week for its members. However, the European feminist literature on part-time and casualized women's labour and the work on the 'informal' or 'black' economy suggests a less sanguine picture.[2] For example, the tendency to put in more hours for more pay is only too familiar in the British context. Several observers submit that sectarian wage bargaining between the British trade unions contributed to producing high levels of unemployment in the 1980s and 90s; and others argue that the hours of work put in by British women have increased dramatically since the Thatcher years (Hindess 1986; Walby 1997). Schor's picture of increasing work hours, moonlighting and declining quality of life will ring true with the experience of most of her European readers. Another reason for remembering writers from the 1950s and 60s in the context of Schor's analysis of work and leisure, is that her solutions to the problem of the leisure deficit have a rather familiar ring to them. Thus, she (1992: 142–65) makes five policy proposals:

Incentives for Employers to Cut Hours

The practice of 'adding time on' to contracted labour by working over contract time to finish a job should be discontinued. Schor calls for the establishment of a binding worktime schedule for all jobs. Going over the allotted time, must be paid for by higher wages. Similarly, workers who voluntarily work over the allotted time should receive units of time rather than money which they deposit with the company 'time-bank' to enable them to take time off when it suits them.

Similar ideas are present in the work of Galbraith (1974), Kerr *et al.* (1973), Gorz (1989) and Hochschild (1997). Gorz's discussion of 'the politics of time' is especially important and mirrors the ideas of Schor in several particulars. However, its significance merits separate treatment and I will postpone that until the final chapter of the book. The main problem with the proposal is that it implies that there is a reserve of qualified, available labour to fill the gap when one worker chooses to take time off. One can envisage that it might be relatively easy to replace unskilled or semi-skilled manual workers who cash in surplus time. But it is precisely these jobs that are disappearing in greatest numbers through the automation and digitalization of production (Lash and Urry 1987). The reason why many skilled workers are working longer hours in many branches of industry and business is that their jobs cannot easily be done by anyone else. There may be some truth in the cliché that 'no one is irreplaceable'. But the complexity of modern industrial and organizational processes means that businesses will suffer an immediate decline in performance when key staff leave. That is one reason why top managers and technical staff command high salaries. Businesses are judged by standards of technical performance. Variation in these standards by bringing in new fixed-term contract workers creates obvious apprehension among clients. Most employers would dismiss it as a dangerous business practice and point to the decline in competitive advantage that it invites.

Moreover, the idea of bringing in workers to fill the gap is very familiar to what already exists for many part-time workers in European and North American universities. A large and fluctuating casualized labour force of part-time postgraduates has been used to plug variable teaching demands for a number of years. When a full-time lecturer is ill or on sabbatical the casualized labour force benefits by being offered more hours. But these hours disappear once the lecturer returns. While there are undeniable benefits in developing experience and confidence for the part-time lecturer, there is also unsatisfactory job security and a sense of being permanently exploited. There is little in Schor's proposal to prevent one from predicting that the same feelings of dissatisfaction and exploitation would be evident if the move to a time bank system led to the creation of a general pool of casualized labourers.

Another problem is that the rigid quantification of the labour process carries the high probability of destroying goodwill between employers and employees. Many employees who surpass targets are already rewarded with performance-related pay bonuses. In a free labour market, with current levels of unemployment, employers are likely to replace workers who refuse to work overtime with others who would be only too eager to be given the work opportunity.[3]

Beyond all of this, there is the problem that Schor's idea of time banks merely turns time into a form of currency. Workers will compete with each other to store up larger reserves of time and this will be the basis for new forms of inequality based around committed and uncommitted time. Schor's argument attacks consumer culture and condemns it for the toil and trouble associated with paid employment. But consumer culture is a symptom rather than a cause. The real motivating influence behind consumer culture and the work ethic is the competitive character of society. Possessive individualism will not stop when reward is apportioned in time as well as money. It will simply find a new way of expressing itself through the unequal distribution of time.

Giving up Future Income for Time-Off

Companies would have the obligation to offer annual reward increases either in terms of more money or more time-off. This is vulnerable to most of the objections raised in relation to Schor's suggestion to cut hours by creating 'time banks'. In the highly interdependent business and production systems that operate today, teamwork is highly valued. The disruption to productivity that would be caused by some members of a work-team opting to have their reward in time-off rather than money is obvious. Although Schor mentions some counter-evidence from work experience in the USA and the UK, she (1992: 148) admits that it is marginal.

Improve Wages for the Lowest Paid

One reason why many workers have a great deal of work and little leisure is that they are low paid and need to put in hours to gain the standard of living which they desire. Schor makes the populist proposal that wages for the low paid should be increased. Again, one finds this in much post-industrial society thinking of the 1960s and 70s (Touraine 1971; Galbraith 1974; Kerr *et al.* 1973). Schor proposes that mandatory non-work time for low-paid workers should also be increased. In principle, few would disagree with either aim. However, in practice many will stop short of supporting Schor in her belief that the state should reduce large wage differentials between the high and low paid by paying more to the low earners and less to the high earners. Others will balk at the suggestion of higher general taxation in order to support the raising of the minimum wage, or the establishment of a minimum wage. There is little evidence to suggest that these policies stand any chance of being accepted. Punitive levels of taxation in the UK in the 1960s and 70s acted as a disincentive for workers to work harder. Many reacted by contributing to the black or informal economy. Other top-wage earners emigrated to competing countries where the taxation policy was more generous. Moreover, while the national mood in America, Britain and many other countries in the West may have turned away somewhat from the tax-cutting Reagan and Thatcher years, there is little evidence that people will vote for serious increases in their personal levels of taxation. Tax increases are only electorally possible if they are confined to the margins of pay structures. Any assault on the heart of pay inequality is likely to be unpopular and untenable.

Market society does not spontaneously engender high trust relations. People are suspicious of 'new deals' and 'fresh social contracts' and with good reason. The postwar welfare state was presented as a permanent settlement. Yet by the mid-seventies successive administrations throughout the West were retreating from commitment to universal health, education and pension provision. Improving wages for the low paid logically implies state intervention and a state-controlled system of funding. Why should we believe that this system would be any more permanent than the postwar commitment to free education, universal health care and inflation-proof pensions?

Overcoming Consumption

Workers are trapped in a work and spend circle because they are conditioned to covet the commodities of consumer culture. Schor advocates that we must try to break our addiction to consumption. Materialism, she argues, is ultimately a hollow value. It doesn't matter how many possessions you have or how much money you have in the bank, if your struggle to consume involves depression, social disintegration and health risk. Again, this is familiar from the writings of post-industrial society theorists (Galbraith 1972; Kerr *et al.* 1973; Bell 1976) and also critical theorists (Adorno and Horkheimer 1944; Marcuse 1964). The dream of opting out of the rat-race is as old as market society. The trouble with it is that most people are never remotely in a position to turn the dream into reality. The liberal democracies of the West have built up the general expectation in the labour-force that work is the normal feature of adult life after higher education until retirement. The years after retirement are presented as 'the leisure years'. This is why in adult working life we follow such strong incentives to save and contribute so assiduously to pension schemes. Of course, there will always be some people who decide that enough is enough and opt to scale down their income in order to have more leisure. However, as Schor (1992: 158) herself admits, they have always been statistically insignificant. There is little in her analysis of trends to suggest that the position will be reversed.

Moreover, her criticism of consumer culture is too indiscriminate. It presents all commodities as vessels of enslavement. Schor ignores consumer recodings of commodities. As Kellner (1994) and

Willis (1990) point out, the presentation of consumer culture as an ideological or hegemonic rat-trap seriously underestimates the reflexive and critical powers of consumers to make meaningful cultures out of this situation.

Rediscovering Leisure

Capitalism has always treated leisure as secondary to work. Schor (1992: 5–6; 43–8) goes to some lengths to demonstrate that this is a departure in Western history. Citing the work of Webster (1926) and Glotz (1927), she notes that the Ancient Greeks enjoyed 50 to 60 holidays a year. In the old Roman calendar, 109 days were designated as 'work-free'. By the mid-fourth century the figure climbed to 175 days. *Prima facie* the leisure dividend in Ancient society is an appealing model for industrial society to follow. But what Schor does not say is that the societies of Ancient Greece and Ancient Rome eventually collapsed. In both cases the collapse is partially attributed to the decadence, idleness and lack of innovation in Ancient culture.

Schor (1992: ibid), also tells again the old story of the relaxed work relations which prevailed in the Middle Ages. The calendar of feast days is certainly hugely generous by today's standards. For example, France allowed for 52 Sundays, 90 rest days and 38 holidays; medieval peasants in England had approximately one-third of the year off; and in Spain, travellers reported that holidays accounted for five months per year (Rodgers 1940; Cheney 1961; de Grazia 1962; Gurevich 1985). The figures are open to dispute. Still, there is no doubting the general point that medieval culture was more generous in the leisure time that it provided. However, what is not sufficiently stressed by Schor is the poverty and uncertainty that prevailed in the Middle Ages. This was a social formation locked in a low-growth trap, which was regularly unable to feed or care for its population. There are huge dangers in exaggerating the bucolic charm of the pre-industrial world.

Leaving the one-sidedness of Schor's account of history aside, there are other problems with her discussion. More free time for all is an attractive sentiment. It draws on the utopian argument that unfettered human creativity is bound to express itself in positive and ennobling ways (Arendt 1958). In the era of post-industrial society, Kerr *et al.* (1973) identified the growth of more pluralism, leisure and the 'new bohemianism' as being corollaries of 'the logic

34   *Leisure and Culture*

of industrialism'. But like Schor, they neglected the problems relating to overpopulation, overcrowding, human aggression and the
velocity of life that haunt industrial and post-industrial societies.
There is a dark side to leisure. It is evident in the presence of
alcoholism, drug-addiction, violence, distraction activity and vandalism in metropolitan cultures. The rediscovery of leisure is unlikely
to amount to very much if we think of it solely in terms of an
expansion of 'serious leisure' (Stebbins 1993). There is an ethical
dimension to face as well. The question of the proper use of leisure
time raises desperately thorny questions about who 'we' are and
what 'we' value in society and culture. Schor may be right to argue
that the productivity dividend in Western economies already offers
the possibility of substantial reductions in work time. Yet it would
be irresponsible to look at the matter in the same way that an
accountant looks at a balance sheet. Leisure unlocks doors. But a
binding ethical code for the care of ourselves, let alone care for
others, is not yet in place. More free time does not necessarily
increase the public good.

There are then deep problems with Schor's policy analysis. Yet at
least she is thinking about these issues and attempting to offer
solutions. Her work draws on much of the postwar conventional
wisdom in the study of leisure. Thus, she reiterates the findings of
Linder (1970) and Harriman (1982) regarding the emergence of
'the harried leisure' class. But her economic analysis is more sophisticated and provides a more convincing picture. The existence of
overwork and the leisure deficit corrects the optimistic view of some
functionalist writers that there is an in-built tendency in the process of industrialization which automatically increases leisure for
all. Schor also confirms the links made by many historians between
leisure and consumer culture (Ewen 1976, 1988; Cross 1988). In
particular, she argues persuasively that leisure in Fordist society is
focused on consumption activity. Shopping and accumulation become the focus of non-work time. Workers become entangled in a
cycle of work and spend. So that traditional notions of leisure as
involving the 'freedom to be' (Kelly 1987) become ever more irrelevant in the 'quest to have'.

However, the strengths of Schor's analysis of leisure should not
blind readers to the evident weaknesses in her suggested solutions

to overwork and the leisure deficit. Her policies to regulate leisure time presuppose levels of public taxation and state control that would almost certainly be unacceptable to the electorate in most of the Western democracies. In addition, she underestimates the rigidities in the labour market which prevent the sort of flexible arrangement that 'time banking' would require. Employers would oppose the move to break up successful work teams by allowing employees to take time off in lieu of greater earnings; and customers would be apprehensive about service delivery. Finally, Schor's study uses a compressed view of history which is skewed to emphasize the positive features of leisure in pre-industrial society. The process of industrialization has changed our attitude to time from a task orientation to time orientation (Thompson 1967). It does not follow that more leisure time will lead to enriching activity. Leisure in industrial and post-industrial settings contains strong tendencies towards social distraction and social criticism. Channel-hopping, fashion, *flânerie*, computer games are all examples of fast leisure forms in which the short attention span and addiction to novelty dominate. Without a strong affirmation of a new leisure ethic which neutralizes the work ethic by producing socially and economically acceptable criteria of time regulation, the switch to leisure will cause more problems than it solves. But we do not have a leisure ethic; we are still harnessed to the work ethic. In the final analysis, Schor provides little tangible reason or evidence to suggest that the situation will change.

LEISURE AND TECHNOCULTURE

Aronowitz and DiFazio (1994) provide an important contrasting view of the contemporary culture of work and leisure. They follow Schor's analysis in a number of significant respects. Thus, they argue that overwork is a common feature of contemporary society; many traditional job sectors have contracted, while a significant percentage of others have disappeared; and leisure revolves around commodity consumption, thus reproducing cultures of dependence and inertia. However, their discussion of the motivation for overworking and the reproduction of dependency and inertia is more sophisticated.

The backdrop to their analysis is the Frankfurt School critique of instrumental reason. The Frankfurt School derived the concept from Weber's sociology of rationalization (Adorno and Horkheimer 1944; Marcuse 1964). They understood instrumental reason to refer to that form of consciousness which judges performance by economic and bureaucratic effectiveness alone. From the nineteenth century onwards they identified an inexorable tendency to structure science, industry, business, public administration and entertainment around these criteria. Thus, the value of actions was determined in terms of the effect they had in achieving rationally calculated goals. Instrumental reason under capitalism, relates wholly to narrow problem-solving issues. It carries no undertaking to achieve an organic understanding of the relationship between the problem-solving activity and the wider human whole. Adorno and Horkheimer (1944) argued that the application of instrumental reason was a central factor in the prodigious increase in wealth achieved under industrial capitalism. At the same time, they insisted, it reinforced commodification, dehumanization and false consciousness making workers and consumers the slaves of capital. Furthermore, following Weber, they contended that the unintentional consequence of the general pursuit of instrumental reason is the spread of irrationality. Pursuing problems instrumentally cuts off individuals from everything except their discrete area of self-interest. They pay no heed to the impact of their actions upon nature or the wider web of human relationships beyond their immediate sphere of interest. Thus, they may grow prosperous through economic activity, while others around them become increasingly poor, emiserated and desperate; the scientific knowledge they apply may solve their narrowly defined set of problems but destroy the physical and natural environment about them; they may maintain their positions of power but lose any sense of authority over the people that they command. More generally, they apply reason to solve problems but bankrupt their emotional lives.

The Frankfurt School critics did not have to search very far for compelling metaphors of irrationality. The holocaust had driven them from Europe to the United States. Similarly, the defeat of the Nazis ushered in a headlong and deadly race for nuclear supremacy between the USA and the USSR. Atomic destructive power seemed to threaten the very survival of the human species. Moreover, while the developed world poured resources into its nuclear arsenal, third world poverty became more entrenched and immovable.

By the 1960s, Marcuse (1964) had formed the view that instrumental reason could not be uprooted. The capacity of the system to deliver a cornucopia of ever-changing commodities and illusory security had fatally seduced the masses and removed any hope of radical change. The society of organized oppression where the workers 'voluntarily' chose enslavement by feeding their addiction to the world of goods, had reached a stage of development in which it is, as Marcuse (1964) put it, 'without opposition'.

Aronowitz and DiFazio take over many features of this analysis. Most obviously, they contend that instrumental reason dominates science, business, education, public administration and the amusement industry. The success of technology in delivering the goods and conjuring the illusion of a world of universal affluence has elevated it into the transcendent cultural value. It has squeezed out loyalty, care for others and moral considerations to the periphery of everyday social concerns. Quality delivery of service and measurable output for input are now worshipped as the preconditions of effective action. This applies not only to the production of goods and services, but to the intimate relations one has with one's parents, partner, children, co-workers, neighbours, students and remaining 'significant others'. Aronowitz and DiFazio suggests that we now automatically judge all of these relations in our lives by a set of technical performance criteria. Leisure does not escape this regime.

Leisure is frequently conceptualized as non-work. But actually, as Baudrillard (1998) working in rather a different tradition of social analysis also recognized, it is non-work *activity*. Instrumental reason may allow that leisure time and space is not bound by the conditions of the employment contract, above all by the requirement to achieve pecuniary gain. Nonetheless, it ensures that leisure time and space must be devoted to generalized goal attainment activity. For example, from the era of the rational recreationists to the 'commonsense' of the silent majority today, the primary purpose of rest and relaxation in leisure is to renew or increase the market value of individuals by replenishing their energies for more work or extending their capacity for more demanding labour tasks.

Yet leisure activity is also oriented to conferring distinction upon individuals. Following Veblen (1899), and anticipating Bourdieu (1984), Baudrillard argues that leisure is indissoluble from performance criteria. Our participation in leisure activity is a way of demonstrating to others who we are and what we believe in. It is *status-placing* activity. According to Baudrillard (1998: 155–7), there is no such thing as 'free' time, because non-work time requires the individual to honour the work ethic by 'doing something'. 'Leisure,' writes Baudrillard (1998: 158), 'is not the availability of time, it is its *display*' (emphasis in original). The performance requirement to display leisure to others in various ways means that leisure is not autonomous activity, but bound activity. What it is bound to is the work ethic and the rule of instrumental reason.

Aronowitz and Di Fazio use the term *technoculture* to denote the general situation in which work and leisure relations are currently located. They see the move towards the computerization of work, learning, administrative and leisure functions as symptomatic of the triumph of all that Baudrillard and the Frankfurt School feared:

> Having permeated everyday life, technology has become a culture; hence the conflation *technoculture*. It is no longer critical. It accepts, even celebrates, computer mediation as liberating. In the postcritical perspective, we are informed of the wonders of cyberspace, where innovations such as virtual reality offer overworked professionals play therapy to counteract stress (Aronowitz and Di Fazio 1994: 79).

So far their analysis retells the story told by the Frankfurt School between the 1940s and 60s. The growth of technoculture catches the individual in ever more sophisticated interludes of fast leisure which fragment consciousness, provide an exaggerated view of human freedom, distract critical consciousness and prevent transformative action. In pointing to the iron grip of technoculture, Aronowitz and DiFazio inadvertently succeed in recalling the conclusion that Adorno (1991) drew towards the end of his life. Namely, that the current technological, social and cultural conditions do not objectively suggest the prospect of social transformation. Accordingly, Adorno concluded that the objective conditions of life demand the social response that he called 'resignation'. This was widely misunderstood as a weary acceptance that social revolution is impossible. Actually, Adorno was not forsaking the hope of revolutionary transformation. He was merely observing that this hope is incompatible with the objective conditions of this 'moment' – the 1950s and 60s – in advanced capitalism.

Aronowitz and Di Fazio stop well short of proposing that Western societies are teetering on the brink of revolution. However, much of the force of their argument springs from the passionate conviction that the principles of performativity advanced by instrumental reason have reached a dead end. While the inadvertent effect of their analysis is to suggest resignation, their outward intent is to increase activism and engagement to transform the technoculture in ways which contribute to human emancipation. In a multi-layered and rich analysis, which continuously moves between recorded personal experience and an analysis of abstract necessity, they expose the terminal contradictions of instrumental reason in late twentieth-century capitalism. Four trends are singled-out for special mention:

The Progressive Disappearance of Jobs

The mechanization of work in the manual labour section is now matched by the cybernation of work in the service, knowledge, information and professional sectors. Increasing numbers of workers in both manual and non-manual sectors are being made not simply redundant but irrelevant. Their jobs are not disappearing temporarily through a blip in the trade cycle, they are disappearing for ever. We are witnessing a major structural transformation in the labour market. The replacement of labour with machinery offers competitive advantage by increasing productivity. It is therefore unlikely to be cut back or postponed.

The Proletarianization of Labour

Income levels are being driven down by the surplus of workers relative to demand. Professionals and graduates are encountering resistance in the traditional markets for their skills and expertise. Scientifically based technologies are displacing and reconfiguring professional skills. The elimination of work is no longer a problem for the uneducated and unskilled or semi-skilled labourer. The scientific-technological revolution means that everyone is potentially surplus to requirements. Doctors, university lecturers, lawyers and engineers are becoming like assembly-line workers. The hallowed guarantee of a well-paid professional job for life is now shot through with holes. The result is greater uncertainty in the professional sector as everyone realizes that they may slip down the hierarchy and into the unemployment statistics.

The Collapse of Self-help Philosophy

A characteristic prop of capitalist legitimacy has been the philosophy that self-help can triumph over adversity. Energy plus imagination, plus a little bit of luck, will enable individuals to dig themselves out of the morass of poverty or low income and participate in the good life. In conditions of an absolutely shrinking labour market, the philosophy of self-help is nullified. The traditional escape route of social mobility which offered the underprivileged a way out of their circumstances is now blocked. Fewer and fewer experience upward mobility. The lower chances of progress leave people with a sense that their work effort is worthless.

Technoculture Negates Democratic Process

In the words of Aronowitz and DiFazio (1994: 67): '"Modern technology creates its own politics" – not one of the commonweal, in which its applications are subject to public debate, but one of managerial domination of nearly all public institutions: the economy, the state and local communities.' The technoculture supports the illusion of free and open participation in decision-making. In practice, it disenfranchises the masses by rationing the data which enters the public domain and creating professional strata who monopolize relevant knowledge.

In addition, Aronowitz and Di Fazio note that the twin imperatives to work and consume which instrumental reason demands, ravages environmental stability, destroys complete relationships between husbands, wives and children and shatters the spirit of community. Like Marx, they conclude that the existing relations of production act as a fetter on the forces of production. However, whereas Marx saw this contradiction as ending in proletarian revolution, Aronowitz and Di Fazio see it as producing the general reconstruction of national time budgets and the rehabilitation of the notion of self-governing time. They (1994: 331–4) reject the Marxist notion that work is a 'species need' in human beings. They refer to Di Fazio's (1985) study of unemployment among US East coast longshore fishermen which found that, given certain preconditions, active nonwork is an attractive time option for workers. In the words of Aronowitz and Di Fazio (1994: 336):

> Contrary to the ideologically conditioned theory shared by sociologists, psychologists and policy analysts that 'nonwork' produces,

and is produced by, social disorganization and is symbolic of irresponsibility and personal dysfunctionality, recipients of guaranteed annual income who are relieved of most obligations to engage in labour do not fall apart. The incidence of alcoholism, divorce and other social ills associated with conditions of dysfunctionality does not increase among men who are not working. Nor do they experience higher rates of mortality than those of comparable age who are engaged in full-time work. Given the opportunity to engage in active nonwork, they choose this option virtually every time.

Aronowitz and Di Fazio are therefore in favour of a substantial reduction in working hours and an equivalent increase in leisure time. They (1994: 37) call for an immediate reduction of the working week from 40 hours to 30 hours for all levels of society; a maximum working day of 6 hours for all; and the progressive reduction of working hours as technological transformation erodes the amount of necessary human labour in the production process. These demands raise the question of policies to achieve their ends. Aronowitz and Di Fazio (1994) recommend four policies:

(1) The Establishment of an Adequate Guaranteed Income for All
A 25 per cent reduction in the working week for all presupposes a guaranteed minimum wage. Determining a fair level of guaranteed income is a notoriously difficult task. Aronowitz and Di Fazio (1994: 353) are somewhat vague about the appropriate level of guaranteed income. They (ibid) state that it should be 'equal to the historical level of material culture'. In practical terms, this means setting a level which meets basic nutritional, housing and recreational requirements. But they do not show why an equal level for all will not breed new forms of symbolic competition, or why those who feel that their work is better than others will cease to agitate for a higher rate of return. A Rousseauian view of man underlies their outlook. It is by no means clear that cladding Rousseau in modern dress does anything to make his view of human nature more plausible.

(2) Enlarging the Scope of Public Responsibility
The reduction of the working week implies the transfer of resources and responsibilities from designated public bodies to the end-users. Aronowitz and Di Fazio (1994: 353) envisage the revival of altruistic voluntarism. The main mechanisms for this are the labour movement

and communities. Altruistic voluntarism implies the construction of a culture in which providing and maintaining common goods and services will be the responsibility of all citizens. This presupposes a major reorientation in the attitude to work. It ceases to be a matter of personal gain and becomes a voluntarily chosen responsibility which is discharged for the mutual benefit of all.

(3) Regulating Capital
The proposal to reduce the working week obviously implies the potential for gaining competitive advantage in economies which elect to be non-signatories to the agreement. Aronowitz and Di Fazio (1994: 349–50) call for international co-ordination in regulating capital to ensure a level playing field. In addition, they demand restrictions on the unhindered progress of capital's exploitation of nature. Alternating current electricity should be replaced with direct current, solar and wind energy. New regulations on automobile use should be introduced and new laws placed upon air and water pollution. For Aronowitz and Di Fazio this is more than a matter of ecological survival. It bears upon the survival of the human species. 'There is little doubt,' they (1994: 356) contend, 'that the two main killers – cancer and heart disease – and another key cause of premature death – automobile accidents – can be reduced only if we decide to reverse the blind, compulsive march of industrial culture.'

(4) Popularizing the Concept of 'Self-managed Time'
The industrial era has been dominated by the injunction that work must be the central life interest. This has created a false and unnatural division between work and leisure. This division has prevented citizens from playing a full part in civil society because it presupposes that the majority of their conscious time is organized at the behest of employers, while the remainder is left over for rest, relaxation, family life and leisure. Aronowitz and Di Fazio (1994: 357–8) aim to rediscover the Ancient Athenian ideal of a self-managing community in which the individual participates as an informed, cultured citizen rather than a harried, mutilated member of industrial class society. They envisage the reconstitution of civil society. Popular governance would be executed through popular assemblies with ample time for discussion and decision-making.

It is perhaps unnecessary to emphasize the far-reaching nature of these proposals. They amount to a fundamental reconstruction of the economy, civil society and the polity. One of their logical consequences is that leisure, as we know it, will disappear. For in a society in which the self-management of time and enlargement of personal participation in community life are recognized as general principles, leisure will quickly be dismissed as a hang-up of an outmoded industrial structure which prioritized work as the key to personal livelihood and social well-being. By replacing the working self with the self-managing self through the cybernation of the labour process, the paraphernalia of the work/leisure distinction collapses. The era of 'the whole individual' will begin. This, in turn, raises the question of how self-managed time will be used.

Aronowitz and Di Fazio's (1994) description of what the self-governing individual will do in cybernated society pays homage to Marx's (1965) picture of the individual under fully developed communism which situated 'free and full development' in the foreground. The notion of popular governance sketched out by Aronowitz and Di Fazio (1994) presupposes a high level of personal control over time allocation but this is in the context of a generalized intensification of collective bonding. Individuals will 'freely and fully' develop their own capacities, but because they no longer relate to the economy, polity and civil society in an alienated state, they will also spontaneously expand their participation in the management of community affairs. An important caveat to this proposition, is the argument that education must be expanded to develop the self-governing skills that individuals will require to play a full part in the new civic order. Aronowitz and Di Fazio support the principle of 'education throughout the lifecycle'. Teaching in Universities is currently organized on the basis of providing a hothouse of education and training which lasts for spans of three to four years at undergraduate level and one to five years at graduate level. However, the enhanced significance of 'knowledge work' in cybernated society will require the universities to transform their structures. Aronowitz and Di Fazio (1994: 350–51) envisage growth in the traditional University function of research. But teaching will increasingly adapt to a 'colloquia' pattern in which conventional undergraduate training is complemented by open seminars and discussion workshops at the postgraduate level.

Aronowitz and Di Fazio look forward to a grass-roots transformation in the body politic. The labour movement will be a catalyst for improving society rather than pursuing the narrow sectarian goals of wage bargaining. Yet in the postwar period the economistic goals of the labour movement have dominated over altruistic concerns. Faced with the option of higher wages or social reconstruction, workers have chosen higher wages. Aronowitz and Di Fazio are left with the argument that altruistic voluntarism will revive through the collapse of the system. This is actually very similar to Marx's argument that capitalism will collapse when the relations of production become fetters on the forces of production. But capitalism grinds on. The postwar evidence hardly supports the view that impending collapse is round the corner. On the contrary, with the disintegration of 'presently existing socialism' in Eastern Europe, capitalism gives every appearance of having triumphed. 'There is no alternative', as Mrs Thatcher was fond of saying – repeatedly.

Also Aronowitz and Di Fazio's (1994) hopes for education are civilized, desirable but sociologically naive. As with Schor's (1992) programme to achieve a reduction in work time, their discussion of the enlargement of knowledge work and the role of the universities in generating vital civic culture is oddly reminiscent of the post-industrial society theorists of the 1960s and 70s. Recall that Bell's (1973) vision of 'post industrial society' predicted a decline in industrial labour; the emergence of 'robotic factories'; the continuing and sustained increase in production because of the dividend of rationalization; the higher significance of knowledge in production and the conduct of everyday life; and an enhanced role for universities in the management of civic culture. Aronowitz and Di Fazio (1994: 43) dismiss Bell's thesis for over-exaggerating the harmony produced by technological change. There is no 'end of ideology' in the offing, argue Aronowitz and Di Fazio, no prospect of the reduction of social and moral questions to technocractic logic. Yet their own analysis assumes a harmonistic movement to the 'end of work' society. There is a disturbing tension in their analysis. They marshal a very cogent case that instrumental reason is omnipresent in the conduct of personal and collective life. It is presented as leading to wasteful competition, short-termism in the exploitation of the environment and a variety of physical and social ills. At the same time, they insist that we are on the brink of making a momentous rational settlement to reduce the working week, revitalize civic culture and regulate capital. The evidence used to support this proposition is very thin. Like Schor (1992) they refer to the case of the German Metalworkers Union (IG Metall) which represents auto, steel and metal fabricating workers. In 1985 the Union struck to achieve a 35-hour week to be implemented over five years. Aronowitz and Di Fazio (1994) interpret this as a vote for leisure and imply that it is the start of a move to put leisure above wages on the collective bargaining agenda. But it is surely fanciful to use the experience of one semi-monopolistic union as a guide to the entire labour market of Germany, to say nothing of the rest of Europe and the USA. And it is even more fanciful to suggest that the experience of IG Metall can act as a template for low wage economies in South East Asia, Latin America and China where restrictions of labour time and union strength tend to be weaker. Even allowing for the theoretical desirability of Aronowitz and Di Fazio's argument, the evidence for this is very uneven. It is misleading to imply that IG Metall started a trend in Western Europe. On the contrary, in the context of high unemployment, the deindustrialization of economies and competitive bargaining between unions, the emphasis in collective bargaining has been on increasing wages and defending the right to work (Sayers 1987).

But leaving aside the paucity of supporting evidence, Aronowitz and Di Fazio (1994) may be criticized for misunderstanding the ingrained character of the work ethic and consumer culture in the organization of personality and the conduct of economic and civil relations. To put it succinctly it remains the axis of system integration. Reduce its salience and the cultures of family life, industry, welfare, leisure, the arts and government are undermined. For over two and a half centuries we have been taught that work is the centre of healthy existence; we have been urged to praise industry and shun idleness; we have been schooled to forgo immediate gratification in order to achieve deferred goal attainment. The life cyle has been organized to support effective working lives, with childhood acting as a preparation for working life and old age as the reward. The foundation of the system is the work ethic and it is this which Aronowitz and Di Fazio (1994) propose should be replaced by a twin ethic of responsible self-government and altruistic voluntarism. The enormity of the proposition must not be mistaken. The move to post-work is presented as achievable without a significant reduction in living standards and with the continuation of consumer culture. But it does not follow automatically that the international regulation of capital will deliver guaranteed living standards to the economically advanced countries. The required capital transfer to the underdeveloped world is of such magnitude that it will depress living standards in the advanced core. Aronowitz and Di Fazio (1994: 307, 343) answer this by claiming that reducing the wealth of the rich and progressive taxation policy will minimize unrest. But to return to British experience in the 1960s and 70s again, when the tax rate for the highest paid reached 98 per cent in the pound this proposition did not hold true. On the contrary, less tax was collected because the high tax rate produced a twin disincentive. People chose to work less and to mask the real level of their income through a variety of 'creative accounting' practices. Moreover, framing the subject in terms of a transfer of wealth from the rich to the poor is over-simplistic. It fails to allow for the differentiated character of the labour market. *Contra* Aronowitz and Di Fazio (1994) the cybernation of work has not produced the universal deskilling of the workforce. The cybernated workforce still requires computer mechanics, management strategists, marketing personnel and service delivery staff. For many of these workers cybernation and rationalization have produced *reskilling* tendencies in work experience. For example, in Britain the move towards modularization in higher education has created a demand from employers for increased research activity. University staff have become involved in master-minding and applying competitive strategies to attract students, especially full fee-paying postgraduate students. They have also developed new methods of teaching to make courses more attractive and informative to students. Similarly, in publishing the development of computerized book-pricing schedules and stock control systems has not eliminated editorial, sub-editorial and warehouse jobs. Rather, it has created the scope for workers to become strategically involved in list management, company service policy and efficiency improvement. For these workers, reskilling and job enlargement has increased the commitment of individuals to work and enhanced job satisfaction. The question of reskilling is not raised to deny the existence of deskilling. Rather it is mentioned to counter the one-sided view that emerges from Aronowitz and Di Fazio's analysis. It is important to recognize that reskilling raises questions about who decides on the nature of new and enhanced skills; and further that these questions are often monopolized by management rather than workers. Even so, it is important to note the presence of reskilling tendencies in economy and culture.

Turning now to the question of the persistence of consumer culture, Aronowitz and Di Fazio (1994: 189–91) adopt a disapproving tone to advertising and commodity culture. They follow Marcuse (1964) in emphasizing the superficiality of consumer desires and wants. Consumer culture is presented as a rat-trap of false satisfactions. Kellner (1983) points out that this kind of criticism is too undiscriminating. Consumer culture is not an undifferentiated category. Many of its products may offer empty promises, but others give consumers genuine satisfaction and expand their consciousness and life experience in positive ways. Fiske (1989) develops the point by contending that consumers also have the capacity to play with the codes of consumption and subvert them. He (1989: 37) sees youth cultures as 'shopping mall guerillas' who disrupt the controlling codes of mass consumption by redefining the meaning of commodities and the chains of denotation attached to them. Fiske's work assigns *positive* values to consumer culture. In actuality, consumer culture is obviously a mixture of good and bad, positive and negative. But the superficial and meretricious qualities that can be found there are unlikely to disappear with the coming of cybernated society. Aronowitz and Di Fazio misread the character of consumer culture because they fail to give sufficient importance to the density of contemporary life and the velocity and flexibility of relations of communication and interpersonal relationships.

Modern societies are heavy with people. There are more of us than ever before. We are linked to each other by complex economic and social division of labour and manifold emotional chains of interdependency (Gershuny 1993; Du Gay 1996). It may be necessary to allude to the character of work and organization under capitalism in order to explain the impersonality and anonymity of contemporary life. But it is not a sufficient explanation. The sheer density of populations perpetuates a sense of emotional distance from one another. Scientific, urban-industrial societies require high levels of structural differentiation in order to function (Offe 1984). Population density calls upon some members of the community to specialize. We cannot all become doctors of medicine, computer engineers, fashion designers, political organizers, university lecturers, social workers or atomic physicists. The presupposition of Aronowitz and Di Fazio's (1994) argument is that these capacities are bottled up in the labour force and will pour out as soon as the working week is subtantially reduced. There is little reason to suppose that a reduction in the working week will precipitate convergence between the spheres of family life, education, work, government, science, technology, the arts and so on. In self-governing communities people will follow their own interests and there is no guarantee that these interests will be prosecuted in order to enhance the common good. One might wish that these interests are multi-dimensional and enhance one's personal sense of involvement with others, but one cannot impose this wish upon genuinely self-governing individuals. It is the right of the self-governing individual to pursue a narrow set of self-interests and to hunker down in a privatized existence if that is what they choose to do. It is also a right of the self-governing individual to forgo deep relations with others and the refinement of creative capacities for the avid pursuit of monetary gain in order to consume pleasures which he or she acknowledges are momentary. Faced with the option of a reduction in the working week, we cannot assume that people will opt for more leisure. Schor's (1992) analysis of US consumption patterns in the postwar period indicates that they have voluntarily chosen to gain more work *instead* of leisure.

CONCLUSION: THE PERSISTENCE OF INGRAINED PERFORMATIVITY

It is perhaps necessary to state again the *ingrained* character of performativity in the organization of personality, economy and civil society. For two and a half centuries we have been encouraged to perform well in our work; to look the part to land a job; to be a useful member of the community who adds value to the common good; and to participate in the goods and services bonanza. These work-performance disciplines carry over into our non-work emotional relations and leisure activity. We want to do well with our partners and our children; we want to use our leisure time and space to the best advantage. The competitive urge has been modified by collectivist and communitarian initiatives (Etzioni 1993). Neighbourhood associations have combined together to improve the quality of life in the neighbourhood; settlements in regions have affiliated to use their regional status to bargain for resources from federal government, and so on. But, as Etzioni's (1993) paean to the 'reaffirmation' of community values makes clear, these developments have tended to exemplify and reinforce the competitive spirit of self-help rather than meaningfully challenge it. Typically the purpose of combination and affiliation has been to raise the level of resources and life chances available for all within the category of 'community', leaving those outside to make their own way.

Davis's (1990) analysis of the Los Angeles 'city of quartz' with its images of walled rich communities, policed by security staff while the rest of society is left to fend for itself, is very much to the point here. Civic culture contains strong tendencies towards social isolation which are not going to be countered by a general plea to 'be more altruistic'. Indeed, when progressive taxation policies have been applied to redistribute wealth more evenly in the general population they have been fiercely resisted by individuals and collectivities who see 'their' resources at risk. Aronowitz and Di Fazio's arguments depend upon the masses abandoning competition and performativity in favour of sharing and helping. To be sure, the weight of evidence in the Western democracies suggests that motives of sharing and helping are alive and well. We give to charities, we are conscious of those who are worse off than ourselves, we worry about and sometimes fear the 'excluded'. But there are limits to people's willingness to abandon their own interests and the interests of their families and neighbours in favour of abstractions such as 'the common good', 'the poor' and 'the needy'. There is no compelling reason to suppose that we have reached a stage in which the majority regard the benefits of abandoning self-interest in favour of improving the collective good outweigh the perceived costs. Indeed, the current philosophical fashion is to repudiate 'grand narratives' and castigate universalizing, totalizing concepts in favour of reaffirming the importance of difference (Lyotard 1984; Bhabba 1994).

As with the arguments of the post-industrial society theorists of the 1960s, the propositions of Schor and Aronowitz and Di Fazio that we must prepare to move to 'the leisure society' have to be treated with scepticism. To repeat Baudrillard's (1998) proposition, contemporary leisure is not about the consumption of free time, but about the use of time for the purpose of social display. It is *status placing* activity. We perform in our leisure, just as we do in our work. The opportunities for escape, dropping out or time off are nugatory even if the mythology supportung these goals is rich and abounding (Rojek 1993).

However, this is not to say that the character of performativity remains unaltered. Equally, it is not to suggest that the technological and cultural tendencies identified by Schor and Aronowitz and Di Fazio are mistaken. Leisure and work cultures are undergoing changes. But these changes are not primarily turning on the question of having more leisure or less leisure, more work or less work.

They are turning on the twin issues of the velocity of everyday life and the need to develop flexible life strategies. In a remarkable work on the meaning of leisure, Veblen (1899) touched upon some of these issues a century ago. He outlined a theory of leisure which identified leisure as a discipline, a profoundly *motivated*, performative activity, designed to signify meaning to others. He disrupted the commonsense notion that leisure is activity pursued for its own sake through the exercise of choice. Instead, he showed how instrumental reason structures leisure and our concepts of 'time off', 'self-fulfilment' and 'life satisfaction' before the concept of 'instrumental reason' had been invented. Veblen's (1899) theory is an appropiate jumping-off point to explore the questions of velocity, flexibility and inequality that dominate contemporary leisure experience.

2 'The Leisure Class' Today

The central issue addressed by Veblen (1899) in *The Theory of the Leisure Class* is the honorific value of leisure in mass culture. He shows little interest in the intrinsic character of leisure activities. Indeed, his argument questions if leisure can be understood as activity 'for its own sake' or as a 'natural' expression of human capacities. Rather his focus is upon what leisure practice signifies symbolically in mass culture and, of course, the connection between symbolic and economic power. This anticipates many of the most salient themes in contemporary discussions about performative culture. In fine, Veblen is claiming that we possess a strong tendency to emulate the standards set by the most economically powerful strata in society. This implies that cultural capital derives from economic capital and further that the stratification hierarchy in industrial society is relatively unambiguous.

Veblen's confidence in these propositions can be ultimately traced back to his belief that all known societies have been stratified. He recognizes stratification on sexual lines but identifies the decisive principle of stratification as manual labour. The slaves and plebeians in Ancient Rome were distinguished from the patrician class by many features. Education, dress, speech styles, cultural capital were all relevant. But the key difference is that slaves and plebeians were obliged to engage in manual labour to gain a livelihood; the patrician class recognized no equivalent discipline for themselves.

Feudal society, Ancient Greek, Islamic, Hindu, Buddhist, North American tribal and Aztec civilizations and industrial capitalism, all operate with the same dichotomy. They all acknowledge a division between a minority class, which is free from the necessity to engage in manual labour, and the majority who must submit to manual labour so as to gain a livelihood. In addition, they all recognize that the essential behavioural standards in society derive from the minority class. Their practice of 'good' or 'civilized' behaviour sets the context for general behaviour. The historical principle underlying Veblen's theory is that manual labour is always associated with the inferior class. The men of the upper class are exempt and, in many cases, debarred from work. Just as the Ancient Romans and Aztecs acknowledged that an elite range of activities was suitable for the

sons of the Chief and the warrior class, the industrial citizen of
the nineteenth and early twentieth centuries – Veblen's own time
– recognized that the sons of the capitalist class must follow an
elaborately coded set of 'gentlemanly' pastimes and interests.
Familiarity with these activities established a person's rank in relation
to other members of society.

To the eyes of contemporary readers who have followed the colonial and postcolonial debate,[1] Veblen's remarks about 'savage'
cultures may appear rather offensive. *Prima facie*, Veblen is apt to
appear as an untroubled evoutionist who takes it for granted that
'barbarian' culture is primitive, and modern industrial culture is
superior. Yet this is a superficial reading of his argument. Veblen's
anthropology is certainly questionable. But the questions do not
hinge on his alleged belief in the superiority of the West. On the
contrary, he was criticized in his own day for attributing 'barbaric'
values to industrial capitalism (Riesman 1964: 385). This was not
without reason. For Veblen argued that industrial capitalism *is*
barbaric in its veneration for competitiveness, conspicuous consumption and institutionalized sexism. His anthropology is most faulty
in respect of his idyllic view of 'savage' society as peaceful, harmonious and industrious. He contrasted this with the aggression, brutality
and parasitism of industrial civilization.

The dichotomy is false and is the cause of fundamental errors in
Veblen's analysis of industrial civilization. Veblen (1899: 33–40)
noted that 'savage' culture pins its authority structure upon the
monopolization of the means of violence and the ownership of women
by the Chief and his retinue of warriors. Possession of property
gradually develops into a requisite of male esteem and self-respect
and extends to the male offspring. Industrial capitalism inherits and
elaborates the same principle. Thus, the state monopolizes the legitimate use of aggression and typically acts to protect the interests of
the ruling class; and men still relate to women as objects to own,
display and produce healthy and legitimate offspring. Veblen may have
believed in the technical and economic superiority of industrial society,
but as his (1899: 107, 230–33) discussion of male power evidences, he
was no apologist for the moral values and codes of conduct sanctioned by industrial civilization. Indeed, one reason why his analysis
has remained topical for nearly a century is precisely that it offers
a compelling critique of the immorality of industrial civilization.

A corollary of Veblen's twinning of leisure with power is that it
is not enough for leisure activity to be practised, it must be *seen* to

be practised. His (1899: 41–79) account of conspicuous leisure and conspicuous consumption clearly acknowledges the importance of visual culture in power relations. *Contra* Sennett, (1977) who, many years after Veblen's death, argued that the privatization of life is a consequence of industrialization, Veblen's theory of leisure emphasizes the continuing significance of public ritual and display. Sennett's argument logically points to the attentuation of the public sphere. Veblen's argument is that the public sphere remains a meaningful concept and that leisure is one of the chief ways of participating in it.

Veblen's sensitivity to public culture is no accident. It relates to his observation of technological changes in mass communications. The 1890s witnessed the climax of a number of technological and cultural developments which combined to increase consciousness of the significance of mass representational codes, and the general increasing velocity of life. Improvements in printing technology, the creation of international news agencies and the spread of literacy supported the development of mass circulation daily newspapers. Their *forte* was sensational and amusing items which grabbed public attention. The first photographic motion pictures became available to the general public from 1895. They consisted of short silent comedies, dramas and documentaries. They were usually shown in fairgrounds and sideshows. Advertising had been a feature of mid-seventeenth-century broadsheets in London. But it was not until the last quarter of the nineteenth century that the industy became effective in reaching a mass audience through the growth of popular newspapers (Hartley 1996).

Turning to mass transport, Daimler introduced the first motorcycle in 1895. This was the origin of the automobile. Automobiles developed their own codes of etiquette and influence upon visual culture. The first motor cars were considered to be so dangerous that the law required a man carrying a red flag to walk in front of them. The rule was abolished in 1896. A few months later, Bridget Driscoll, a Croydon housewife, became the world's first fatal car accident victim when she was run over by a car on a demonstration ride for the Anglo-French Motor Car Company.

In short, Veblen's book was written and published in a moment of intense ferment in technologies and lifestyles – the cross current of twin revolutions in communications and transport which spread the idea of a global popular culture. Of course, these revolutions were built on groundwork laid down from at least the mid-eighteenth century. For example, Hartley's (1996) study of the rise of popular journalism shows how the press and advertising in the eighteenth and early nineteenth centuries dovetailed to construct national popular cultures. Moreover, the state participated in the construction of national popular cultures through health and education reforms, licensing laws, military recruitment and training programmes (Corrigan and Sayer 1985). Relgion was also an important part of the process. The antecedents of all of these processes can be traced back much earlier. Elsewhere, Rojek (1993: 23–49) I argued that the role of the state and religion in creating national popular cultures reaches back to at least the Middle Ages, and that mercantile capitalism was addressing popular cultures of consumption from at least the fifteenth century. However, it was not until the 1870s that the state and business corporations can be said to work with the concept of a 'people's capitalism'. McLintock (1995: 208–31) shows brilliantly how companies like Pears, Huntley and Palmers and MacFarlane Lang, invented advertising campaigns that mixed commodity domination with colonial triumphalism. The 'free' market of imperial goods and services girdled the globe with a moral system and a commodity culture which automatically associated the West with progress.

Veblen could hardly have remained indifferent to the capacity of capitalism to remake the world in its own image. Just as Marx lived in a period when the replacement of use value with exchange value had become a popular realization, Veblen witnessed the first throes of the replacement of exchange value with denotational value. The value of commodities and services were no longer described simply by the ratio at which a commodity or service exchanges against others, but also by the ratio of social aplomb or kudos which the commodity or service denotes. This denotation process was not located primarily in discursive culture but in visual culture. In Marx's day participation in commodity culture was organized around exchange relationships involving the consumption of goods and services. Advertising was starting to open a gap between the representation of commodities and the exchange relationship leading to consumption. By Veblen's day, the gap had widened into a chasm. Consumers with marginal capacity to consume could nevertheless participate in the fantasy worlds of commodity culture through advertising, shop window displays and images circulating in the popular press (Williams 1982). The communications and transport revolutions that occurred at the turn of the century, when Veblen researched and published his book, added significantly to the separation of representational codes from reciprocal exchange relations. They all pushed leisure into the direction of becoming increasingly fast. The velocity of leisure experience was a function of the velocity of technological and cultural innovation. Everything solid was melting into air in Marx's day, but by Veblen's time culture appeared to acquire pure transparency. This was why he was able to take the slow leisure practices of the aristocracy as an object of social criticism. They were no longer rooted in 'immemorial time'. The dislocation of social conditions caused by economic change and technological innovation rendered them as conditional and corruptible as everything else in society and culture.

It is the continued power of the wealthy leisure class to set the standards of consumption throughout the whole of society which Veblen denounces. He does so because he believes that the standards of conspicuous waste cultivated by the leisure class exert a pernicious effect upon the behaviour of the lower orders. For Veblen, the tragedy of American capitalism is that it has created a leisure class which defines its *raison d'être* as freedom from economically productive labour. It is a tragedy because the American revolution was waged in the name of breaking European codes of status and honour which derive from pecuniary wealth, and replacing them with a system of esteem based on rational, humanist and democratic values of self-worth. Love of liberty and a chance for everyone to prosper, was the American way. The astounding and unexpected profligacy of American capitalism destroyed this principle. Veblen believed that the American leisure class became too rich too quickly. As a result they had forgotten the lessons of thrift learned by their revolutionary forefathers, and taken to squandering their wealth in displays of wasteful finery, pointless etiquette, useless learning and conspicuous consumption. Veblen reacts to these phenomena viscerally, as a veritable circus of profane vanities. In fairness, the parties, dinners, balls and receptions that dominated the social calendars of the wealthy did have an important set of practical purposes. They forged introductions, reinforced a sense of elite solidarity and solidified elites through marital arrangements (Davidoff 1973). But Veblen chose to concentrate upon their wasteful role in engendering conspicuous consumption. His work points to a spiral of waste which was out of control. Grand parties had to become ever grander; sumptuous dinners had to become more sumptuous; and last year's grand reception was the standard by which the grand reception in the following year would be judged.

In this respect, Veblen anticipates some aspects of Mauss's (1925) famous study of the gift relationship and the importance of the potlatch in social integration. Yet arguably, the conclusions that he drew were more radical. Mauss analyzed the gift relationship as strengthening the power of some tribes and weakening the power of others. The gift-receiving tribe that was forced to surpass the beneficence of the gift-donating tribe would find its assets concentrated in the resources of the latter. In contrast, Veblen implies that the emulatory codes attached to gift-giving in industrial civilization threaten to bankrupt the wealth and vitality of the entire civilization. The abhorrence of paid labour breeds an elite culture devoted to the refinement of non-pecuniary pastimes. As examples, Veblen mentions the cultivation of archaic languages, hunting, equipage, elite sports, occult sciences and developing the canons of taste and dress. The leisure class is not necessarily lazy. Rather it devotes itself to activities which are non-pecuniary and non-wealth creating. The purpose of this devotion in leisure activity is precisely to demonstrate the remote distance that the leisure class enjoys from the necessity to labour of the toiling masses.

Veblen identifies this social distance as a condition of class society from Ancient times. He does not disapprove of the principle of conspicuous consumption because he believes that it has integrated all known class societies. What agitates him is the evident success of the mass communication and transport revolutions in diminishing the gap between the elite class and the masses. In particular, the practice of the masses in emulating the wasteful consumption of the leisure class, and the readiness of corporate capitalism to cater to this appetite, in Veblen's mind, converge to signal the putrefaction of industrial civilization. The democratization of leisure neutralizes the work ethic and deprives industrial civilization of the primary incentive behind growth and wealth creation. It opens the abyss of the leisure society, in which leisure becomes the central life interest.

Veblen's work involves a coherent theory of the body. It identifies the body as occupied with the insignia of the leisure class. Conspicuous consumption among the rich translates into ersatz conspicuous consumption among the humble. In Veblen's analysis the body is never vacant. It is forever posturing, preening and signifying. Of course, Veblen is aware of resistance to the codes of the leisure class. Yet the logic of his discussion is that resistance will be co-opted by the leisure class. For Veblen, a vacant body is a meaningless body, a body that does not fit with the social norm

and is therefore rendered transparent or invisible. There is no discussion in Veblen's work of tramps, drop-outs or bandits. The
question of transgression is implicitly posed by his discussion but
not answered. His is a functionalist theory of power which assumes
that control is exercised from the top. It is therefore vulnerable to
the conventional sociological criticism that it is unable to explain
change. Veblen's theory anticipated the collapse of American society through the addiction to conspicuous consumption and generalized
fecklessness. It did not come to pass.

CRITIQUE OF VEBLEN

Veblen can be criticized on three main counts. In the first place,
he overestimated the homogeneity of the leisure class. Mills (1956)
pointed to decisive cleavages within the economically dominant
formation in society. He eschewed the concept of class domination
in favour of elite influence. Society, he argued, is dominated by
three elites, with two lesser elites flanking them. The three dominant elites are the business elite, the celebrity elite and the military
elite. The lesser, conjoining elites are the political elite and the
traditional aristocracy. Post-Watergate it is hard to agree with Mills's
view that the political elite tends to act neutrally. But despite the
endless public fascination with the Royal family today, there is little
doubt that his assessment that the emulatory power of the traditional aristocracy is declining, is a sound proposition. I shall return
to take up this point in more detail later.

Mills (1956) argued that the power elite is capable of concerted,
interlocking action. However, he was careful to avoid the mistake
that Veblen made in his discussion of the leisure class. Mills refused to present the power elite as an homogenized unity. As he
(1956: 287) puts it:

> Despite their social similarity and psychological affinities, the
> members of the power elite do not constitute a club having a
> permanent membership with fixed and formal boundaries. It is
> of the nature of the power elite that within it there is a good
> deal of shifting about, and that it does not consist of one small
> set of the same men in the same hierarchies.

Mills presents the power elite as more porous and divided than
Veblen's concept of the leisure class. This is quite consistent with

his wider belief that industrial society was producing huge new
opportunities for rapid, long-distance upward mobility. In the 1950s,
the power of the self-made capitalist, or the immense wealth of
popular entertainers who had risen from rags to riches overnight,
became benchmarks of personal progress in popular culture. The
idea of Veblen's leisure class setting the standards of emulatory
behaviour for the rest of society was hard to sustain in a consumer
culture that was trying to come to terms with the new postwar icons
of Elvis Presley, Marilyn Monroe, Marlon Brando and Jimmy Dean.

The second criticism of Veblen is that he overestimates the pas-
sivity of the masses. His theory posits that the masses mechanically
emulate the standards of conspicuous consumption and waste practised by the leisure class. Yet it is relatively easy to show that,
historically speaking, many social formations have been hostile to
the social standards of the rich and wealthy. For example, Yeo
(1976) and Gray (1981) argue that skilled workers in the nineteenth
century founded trade unions, and developed collectivist forms of
leisure and self-improvement, which were critical of the values of
both the ruling class and the unskilled working class. Similarly, within
consumer culture advertising, film, theatre, literature and popular
music have long traditions of attacking both the establishment and
the values of mass society. Examples include the 'angry young men'
of British theatre and fiction in the 1950s and 60s and house and
techno music of the 80s and 90s. Popular culture is more reflexive
and internally divided than Veblen allows. Its articulations do not
simply reinforce the ruling order of things. They pose criticisms
and challenges to the monotony and predictability of everyday life
(McGuigan 1992, 1996).

The third criticism of Veblen is that he does not grant enough
importance to the seductions of corporate capitalism in his account
of the logic of emulation. Veblen assumes that the commodity form
buttresses class rule. What this ignores is the separation between
the main representational codes in consumer culture from reciprocal exchange relationships, alluded to earlier. Through advertising
and design, corporate capitalism made the commodity form seductive so that consumers forgot the exploitation that underpinned
commodity transactions. This forgetfulness is the reason why
Benjamin (1970) treated advanced consumer culture as riddled with
fantasy and false values. The consumer never exchanges like with
like, but is caught up in a kaleidoscope of surface appearances.
Living life on the surface contributes to a sense of depthlessness

in one's personality. Paradoxically, the coarse materiality of ever-changing exchange values breeds an affinity to life with others which characterizes all relationships as immaterial. Simmel (1978) writes of the difficulties that people in modern culture experience in making lasting commitments and dedicating themselves to solid objects. The work of Lasch (1979, 1984) on the cult of narcissism and the psychology of anxiety, and Baudrillard's (1975, 1983) cartography of the illusions of modern consumer culture, can be read as belonging to the same tradition. Yet, by the same token, the colonization of the public sphere by the commodity form introduces a fundamental ambivalence into cultural relationships. The sober fact that it is the duty of Advertising to present the commodity in question in representational codes which suggest an excess of pleasure and excitement over and above the experience derived from the trans-action of consumption, makes ambivalence a standardized charac-teristic of consumer culture. Despite recognizing the larger part that representation played in consumer culture through advertis-ing, promotion and public relations, Veblen never succeeded in conveying the intrinsic ambivalence of modern consumer culture because he never understood the many-sided character of the com-modity form and commodity relations. His work suggests that people are tied together by solid bonds of emulation, whereas in fact these bonds are looser and more frayed than he suggests.

IS THERE A LEISURE CLASS TODAY?

Discussions of the leisure activity of the richest people in society today must overcome the strong puritan streak in the sociology of stratification and cultural studies. The absolute gap in wealth is so staggering that disapproval of wealth is understandable. A UN Human Development Report published in 1996 estimated that the com-bined wealth of the top 358 billionaires in the world is equivalent to the annual income of the 2.3 billion people who make up the poorest 45 per cent of the world's population (see Table 2.1 for a listing of the top ten billionaires in the world in 1996). As Blackburn (1997: 4) observes, the notion of millionaires is now out of date. The seriously rich measure their wealth in billions. In contrast, the average income in the European Union is £12 000 per annum (Eurostat 1998). Apart from eastern Germany, Britain includes the only two 'poor' regions in northern Europe: South Yorkshire and

Merseyside. Each has a per capita income of £8400 as against £11 400
for the rest of Britain. According to *Social Trends* (1997) the mean
disposable income per household in Britain is £16 170.

Calculating the real wealth of the poor is relatively simple. Their
assets tend to be limited and therefore tangible since they directly
support the continuation of human life. Similarly, their income stream
derives from taxable wages or state entitlements, both of which
belong to state registered wealth. Even allowing for the black
economy of unregistered income, the economic wealth of the poor
is quite easy to measure. In contrast, calculating the wealth of the
richest people in the world is an inexact science. Estimates vary
from year to year. Different sources, such as business magazines
like *Forbes*, *Fortune* and the *Sunday Times* give conflicting estimates
of wealth. Some forms of wealth are easily measured, notably if
they are held in company shares for which the price is always quoted.
But most other forms of wealth – whether because of the nature
of the asset or the way in which it is owned – are a matter of
guesswork. The rich have strong incentives to disguise their personal wealth in corporate forms and bank in different countries
around the world so as to enjoy beneficial variations in tax rates.
Offshore trusts also operate to distort the real level of wealth. The
rich also employ tax advisers to minimize their tax liabilities.

All of these features combine to mask the true level of wealth
among the richest people in society. A paradox of Veblen's (1899)
discussion is that even though the rich engage most prominently in
conspicuous leisure and conspicuous consumption, their real level
of wealth is screened by a variety of devices. Even so, that there
exists an immense gap between the rich and the poor in Western
society is incontestable. For example, Frank and Cook (1995: 67–8)
report that in 1993 America's most highly paid executive, Michael
Eisner, Chairman of the Disney Corporation, earned $203 million,
roughly 10 000 times that of the lowest paid Disney worker. In 1993
the financier George Soros earned $1.1 billion (£724 million). This
income was greater than the GDP of 42 countries and exceeded
the profits of the McDonalds chain. Only 36 US companies achieved
higher profits in the same year (*Guardian* 17.6.1994). In 1997 the
38-year-old Nomura banker Guy Hands received a salary of £48m.
Sandy Weill, head of the Travelers Group, was the world's highest
paid executive in 1997, with a salary of £140m. The income of the
highest paid is increasingly tied up with performance-related pay
bonuses and severance pay. In 1997, the Chief Executive of EMI,

Table 2.1   The *Sunday Times* Top 20 Rich List (UK), 1999 (figures in £m)

1.	Hans Rausing (Food packaging)	3400
2.	Lord Sainsbury and family (Retailing)	3100
3.	George Soros (Finance)	2000
4=.	Joseph Lewis (Finance)	1750
4=.	Duke of Westminster (Property)	1750
6=.	Lady Grantchester (Stores, mail order, pools)	1500
6=.	Garfield Weston and family (Food)	1500
8=.	Bruno Schorder and family (Banking)	1300
8=.	Richard Branson (Travel/Entertainment)	1300
8=.	Sri and Gopi Hinduja (Trading/Finance)	1300
10=.	Lakshmi Mittal (Steel)	1200
12=.	Terry Matthews (Electronics)	1100
12=.	Tony O'Reilly and Chrys Goulandaris	
	(Food, media and inheritance)	1100
14=.	Mohamed al-Fayed (Retailing)	1000
14=	Viscount Rothermere and family (Media)	1000
14=.	Sir Adrian and John Squire (Shipping/Aviation)	1000
18.	Robert Miller (Retailing)	975
19.	Sir Anthony Bamford and family (Construction)	950
20=.	Bernie and Slavica Ecclestone (Motor racing)	900
20=.	Ken Morrison and family (Food retailing)	900

Jim Fifield left the company with an astonishing £12m pay-off. Similarly, valued staff receive share option deals. For example, partners in Goldman Sachs each hold between 0.25 per cent and 1 per cent of equity in the company. Plans for stock market flotation in 1999 were set to raise £130m for senior partners and £22m for junior partners (*The Observer* 19.04.1998).

The *Sunday Times* 'Rich List' of the wealthiest 500 people in Britain in 1997 suggested that the 500 richest had an average wealth of £173.7m, up £33.7m on the 1996 average of £140m. The top 500 were worth £87 000 million, an increase of 23 per cent on 1996 figures. The list of Britain's top 20 for 1999 is reproduced above (see Table 2.1). The rich in Britain appear to have enjoyed a dramatic enlargement in their wealth in the period between 1979 and 1997, the years of the Thatcher–Major Conservative administrations. In 1976 the poorest fifth of the population received less than 1 per cent of the national income, while the top fifth received 55 times as much. By 1986 the bottom three-fifths had all experienced a fall in their share of national income, whereas the top fifth had increased to 169 times that of the bottom fifth. Hutton (1996: 57)

Table 2.2　World's Top Ten Billionaires (1996) (UN Human Development Report)

1.	William Henry Gates III ($18 billion)	Founded Microsoft, the world's leading PC software manufacturer; now Chairman and Chief Executive.
2.	Warren Buffett ($15.3 billion)	Chair of Investment, Insurance holding company Berkshire Hathaway. Also has a 10 per cent stake in American Express.
3.	Paul Sacher ($13.1 billion)	Entrepreneur with the pharmaceutical company Roche. Now honorary member of the board.
4.	Lee Shau Kee ($12.7 billion)	Based in Hong Kong. Chairman of Henderson Land and Henderson Investment.
5.	Tsai Wan-Lin ($12.2 billion)	Founder of Taiwanese insurance company, Cathay Life.
6.	Li Ka-Shing ($10.6 billion)	Founder of Cheung Kong (Holdings) and Hutchinson Whampoa Ltd. Made his money by building up property around his Hong Kong flowers company.
7.	Yoshiaki Tsutsumi ($9.2 billion)	Property investor and speculator.
8.	Paul G. Allen ($7.5 billion)	Co-founder of Microsoft and second biggest shareholder. Also has interests in several software, on-line, entertainment and sports companies.
9.	Kenneth Thomson ($7.4 billion)	Son of the late Lord Fleet, the Chairman of Thomson Corp. Owns newspapers, academic and professional publishing companies, electronic publishing and the Hudson's Bay Company.
10.	Tan Yu ($7 billion)	Head of real estate empire stretching from Philippines, Taiwan and China to San Francisco, Las Vegas and Houston.

estimates that the real wages for the bottom 10 per cent have fallen by about a third over the last 20 years. The privatization of public utilities swelled the salaries of top executives. Two and a half years after privatization of the water industry, the median salary for water board chairmen increased by nearly three times. The highest rise was 290 per cent and only Northumbria (28 per cent) had not doubled. The top salary was still relatively modest by the established standards of private industry. The top salary for water board chairmen was £160 000 (with share options this rose to £400 000). The salary for the chairman of privatized British Gas was £500 000.

Yet these salaries are almost modest compared with the rewards earned in long-standing private industry. For example, the *Independent on Sunday* (26.7.1992) estimated that David Sainsbury of the supermarket chain received an income of £30 million in 1992; Tiny Rowland of Lonrho pocketed £12.6 million; William Brown of Walsham, £9.2 million; the theatrical impresario, Cameron MacIntosh, £8.3 million; and Stephen Rubin of Pentland's, received £4.8 million.

The scale of inequality supports the cliché that the rich live in a different world. Outlandish inheritance settlement, massive executive perks, bonuses, severance settlements and share deals are the stuff of the daily press. Added to this there is no shortage of sociological treatments of inequality which remind us of the excesses of the wealthy (Scott 1982, 1991; Frank and Cook 1995; Marshall 1997).

It does not require a great leap of imagination to consider the benefits to health, the environment, education and welfare that a redistribution of wealth along more equitable lines would produce. The World Health Organization report for 1996 indicates that over a billion people – one-fifth of the world's population – live in conditions of extreme poverty. One-third of the world's children are undernourished; 12.2 million children under five die each year, 95 per cent from poverty-related diseases. The UN Human Development Report (1996) estimates that 1 per cent of global income would be sufficient to eliminate poverty. According to the *Guardian* the combined wealth of the seven richest men would be enough to transform the lives of 25 per cent of the world's population living in greatest poverty.

IS CLASS THE REAL ISSUE?

Few issues produce more divided opinions than class. For example, Pakulski and Waters (1996) argue that class distinctions have been undermined as social inequalities have been progressively structured by patterns of consumption rather than production. They draw upon recent theoretical work in postmodernism, to propose that hypercommodification has led to patterns of consumption organized around the capacity to differentiate between the semiotic meanings of goods rather than the use-values of goods. They emphasize the fluidity of identity, the proliferation of taste cultures and the erosion of traditional categories of solidarity by 'imaginary communities' of consumers. This suggests that leisure and culture are neglected categories in which distinction is registered and for which wealth is not necessarily the primary criterion for participation. Pakulski and Waters argue that corporate capitalism has stripped control from ownership. Thus, the managers who run the world's major companies do not own them, although they may have substantial holdings in shares.

Beck's (1992) discussion of risk society and reflexive modernization is often seen as supporting the end of class argument. Beck (1992: 87, 91) argues that in the 1950s stable life experience mediated by the market began to fragment. Consciousness of social inequality became 'individualized'. We began to think of ourselves as personally unequal to others, rather than as subjective expressions of an objective class. The new technocultures of leisure and consumption encouraged people to think in terms of multiple identities, lifestyles, opinions and subcultures. Mobility in the labour market, and the contraction of work as the central life interest, further weakened class bonds. Ethnicity, gender, age and nationality became the basis for new lifestyles and value attachments.

Other commentators are more sceptical about the end of class argument. Marshall (1997: 18) dismisses the postmodernist tone of Beck (1992) and Pakulski and Waters (1996) as 'in large part programmatic and rhetorical'. Class, he contends, is a central category in the organization of contemporary societies. Rumours of its death have been much exaggerated. Scott (1982, 1985, 1991) has produced some of the best recent research into the question of class in Britain. He argues that it is still appropriate to speak of a ruling class in Britain which has 'distinct and opposing interests to those of the other classes' (Scott 1991: 7). Following the work of Domhoff (1967) into changes in the composition of the American upper class, Scott allows that there has been a tendency to transfer wealth from personal ownership into more 'impersonal' forms such as Trust Funds and corporate holdings. As already noted, this has complicated the task of identifying the true levels of wealth accumulated by the very rich. Nonetheless, he argues that a ruling class can be identified and that their interests are based in shaping the system of private property to maximize their own personal wealth. The fulcrum of upper class integration is common collective wealth. This is reinforced by the social networks organized around education, family and leisure experience. Scott (1991: 142) argues that the ruling class exercises direct political power through their disproportionate decision-making power in the key economic and political institutions of the state.

Savage *et al.* (1992) mount an analogous reading of class. Interestingly, they argue that the emergence of the new service class may have been so dramatic that it has blinded us to the continuing relevance of class divisions and interests. For them, private property remains the most significant basis for class formation since it can be accumulated, stored and transmitted with ease. The intermediate class do not constitute a singular group of property owners. Rather they are a mix of the *petite bourgeoisie* in which share capital and *rentier* assets form the foundation of wealth; organizational strata, in which capital and power derives from positions in public and private bureaucracies; and cultural strata in which symbolic, rather than real, capital underwrites the power of individuals. Several commentators have argued that the intermediate classes have disproportionate cultural influence in society (Lash and Urry 1987, 1994). Their position in the knowledge and leisure industries give them a highly visible presence in everyday life. Moreover, their influence has strategic consequences for the development of the knowledge and leisure industries. The values of this class tend to give steering power to developments in these fields.

Yet Savage *et al.* (1992) counsel caution in taking the argument that power has switched to the intermediate class too far. Indisputably, the numerical size of the intermediate classes has grown this century. Routh (1987) shows that between 1911 and 1981 in the UK, the number of white collar (professional, managerial, supervisory and clerical workers) expanded from 14 per cent to 43 per cent of the salaried population. Commenting on the US experience, Gilbert and Kahl (1987) report that the growth in the white collar sector rose from 17.5 per cent to 52 per cent of the salaried population. Yet, because the intermediate class is internally divided between the *petite bourgeoisie*, organizational and cultural strata, it is misleading to think of this class as having common class consciousness. Indeed, the elasticity and variation in collectivist consciousness among these strata is one reason why postmodernist

arguments about the end of class have enjoyed such wide circulation
recently. Savage *et al.* argue that the power of each stratum in the
category is also unstable. Recession has cut into the assets of the
petite bourgeoisie; the Thatcher–Reagan, Major–Bush, years imposed
severe restrictions on the growth of state bureaucracies; while the
cultural strata are notoriously prone to changes in fashion and taste.
Savage *et al.* conclude that there are strong pressures within the
intermediary class category militating against solid class formation.
This makes talk of their alleged class consciousness and action
problematic. In summarizing the literature on the continued
significance of class, Edgell (1993: 60–61) writes:

> in contrast to managerialists who subscribe to an industrial soci-
> ety model of societal development, anti-managerialists claim that
> capitalism has not been transformed beyond recognition, although
> it has changed. Ownership has been depersonalized, not abol-
> ished. Strategic control (i.e. long-term planning) has been retained;
> only operational control (i.e. medium and short-term implemen-
> tation of basic long-term goals) has been relinquished. The profit
> motive, the motor of capitalist development has not become
> less important. The economic power of the capitalist class has
> increased as a result of the growth of international corporations,
> and continuity is achieved by a combination of the monopoliza-
> tion of wealth and educational privileges.

The proposition that capital ownership has become more globalized
is confirmed by the UN Human Development Report (1996). Of
the ten top billionaires identified by the UN in 1996, only five are
based in North America and Europe; the rest are situated in South
East Asia. Moreover, the corporate nexus is common to all ten which
reinforces the argument that personal wealth is now typically
accumulated in more impersonal holdings.

Interestingly, the *Forbes* (April 1998) list of the world's richest
top 20 in 1998 produced a very different list in which three of the
UN top ten billionaires are absent (see Table 2.3). According to
Forbes in 1998, five of the world's richest billionaires are American
citizens, two are Europeans and the rest are citizens of Brunei,
Saudi Arabia and Kuwait. The *Forbes* list underlines the prominence of American dominance, which is perhaps unsurprising since
it was composed after the economic crash in South East Asia in
1997–98. It also points to the twin importance of the corporation
in wealth generation. Traditional rich families, like the Middle Eastern

Table 2.3   World's Richest 20 (1998)

1.	Bill Gates	America	Software	£28.81bn
2.	Robson Walton & family	America	Retailing	£25.25bn
3.	The Sultan of Brunei	Brunei	Oil	£23.75bn
4.	King Fahd & family	Saudi Arabia	Oil	£19.37bn
5.	Warren Buffett	America	Investments	£18.68bn
6.	Paul Allen	America	Software	£11.18bn
7.	Johanna Quandt & family	Germany	BMW Cars	£10.06bn
8.	The Emir of Kuwait	Kuwait	Oil	£9.37bn
9.	Paul Sacher & Hoofman family	Switzerland	Pharmaceuticals	£11.37bn
10.	Pierre du Pont & family	America	Chemicals	£8.75bn
11.	Forest Mars & family	America	Sweets	£8.12bn
12.	Peter Haas & family	America	Jeans	£7.68bn
13.	Karl and Theo Albrecht	Germany	Supermarkets	£7.18bn
14=	Curt Engelhorn & family	Germany	Pharmaceuticals	£2.25bn
14=	Kenneth Thomson	Canada	Media/oil	£6.87bn
16.	Lee Shau Kee	Hong Kong	Property	£6.32bn
17.	Barbara Cox and Anne Cox Chambers	America	Media	£6.25bn
18.	Steven Ballmer	America	Software	£5.93bn
19.	Si and Donald Newhouse	America	Publishing	£5.62bn
20.	Li Ka-Shing	Hong Kong	Retailing/Property	£5.14bn

(*Source*: *Forbes Global Business and Finance*, April 98 *Sunday Times Rich List* 1998, April 98)

dynasties (The Sultan of Brunei, King Fahd family, Emir of Kuwait) ultimately derive their wealth through inheritance. But Bill Gates, Warren Buffett, Paul Allen and Paul Sacher are all self-made men who developed their personal wealth through the aegis of corporate operations.

Beresford (1997: 4) seizes upon the same trend to argue that 'old money' is declining in significance to be replaced by a genuine enterprise culture. Commenting on the *Sunday Times* listing of the 'Top 500' in 1997, he notes that only 155 of the 500 received their wealth through inheritance. This is 31 per cent of the total, compared with 35.5 per cent of the total in 1996. When the first 200 list was compiled in 1989, the wealth of 57 per cent of the entrants derived from inheritance. However, Beresford may be underestimating the extent to which personal inherited wealth is now clustered in impersonal holdings such as 'Trust Funds' and Charitable Bonds. Thus, Blackburn (1997: 7) emphasizes the continuity of class inequalities in Britain. Citing the *Sunday Times Report* (10.5.1992) on the Top 300 personal wealth holders in Britain, he notes that over 30 per cent were titled. Some received titles in their own lifetime as a further reward for their business achievements. Yet Blackburn insists it would be foolish to believe that hereditary wealth has 'withered away'. The Top 300 share common education characteristics. Twenty per cent had been to Eton, 3 per cent to Harrow. Nineteen per cent were Oxbridge graduates. Only 7 per cent of the top 300 were women.

Regional inequalities within the UK are also apparent. Most of the top 300 live in London and the South East. In 1992 45 per cent of the top 300 lived here, and by 1997 this appears to have increased to 51 per cent. The regions with the fewest super rich were Wales, Northern Ireland and East Anglia. Together these regions accounted for the homes of 6.7 per cent of the top 1000 (Blackburn 1997: 8).

The evidence supports the view that class inequality continues to be fundamental in modern (and postmodern!) societies. On the whole the rich have been extraordinarily adept at protecting and growing their wealth. Leisure continues to be a badge of membership to the richest class. Holiday homes, private yachts, jets and luxury cars are prestige leisure accessories. Social gatherings like Ascot, Henley, private fashion shows and operas are all common leisure events for the rich. Membership of gentlemen's clubs, luxury ski and health resorts, yacht clubs, hunting clubs all serve to further identify the richest in society. By contrast the conditions of leisure for the poor are marked by a lack of money, a lack of personal space, low geographical mobility and a homologous range of activities.

While popular culture repines the excesses of 'the filthy rich', there is a strong correlation today between wealth and personal invisibility. In 1899 Veblen could refer to the Rockefellers, the Vanderbilts, the Whitneys and the Astors, with a high degree of confidence that his readers would know who he was referring to. The same confidence cannot be expressed today in respect of figures like Paul Sacher, Paul Allen, Lee Shau Kee, Tsai Wan-Lin and Yoshiaki Tsutsumi. For most of us, these people are faceless and we would not recognize them if we passed them on the street. It is a paradox that the richest people in the world are among the most invisible. This says much for the corporate character of successful business and its global dimensions. It also underlines how segmented the lifestyles of the rich are from the rest of us. Moreover, the success of Bill Gates, Paul Allen and Warren Buffett in accumulating huge fortunes in their own lifetimes underlines the transformation in the new dynamics of wealth creation. The dynastic families of industrial capitalism such as the Fords and Fortes, have been less successful in growing wealth through the new opportunities offered by the new technologies and finance capital. The entry of Gates, Allen and Buffett into the richest echelons of world society confirms Harvey's (1989) thesis that 'flexible accumulation' is the key to business success in the contemporary world economy.

Perhaps one can criticize the anti-managerialist writers who insist on the continued salience of class for underestimating the corporate dimension. In Veblen's day the rich gathered as family members in their clubs and exclusive mansions. Leisure events, such as debutante balls, hunting trips, world cruises and a variety of prestige sporting fixtures, served to integrate class membership. Moreover, these common leisure interests drew on educational experiences which were basically uniform, being based either in the system of private tutors or training in elite boarding schools. Many of these features remain today. However, the increased mobility and globalization of the rich mean that they are likely to have exclusive homes in several continents and dual nationalities enabling them to maximize personal mobility and shelter from harsh fiscal regimes. They may continue to belong to clubs, but they share membership with self-made entrepreneurs and may even look down on the old aristocracy for its failure to adapt. As we have seen, leisure events, such as Cowes Yachting Week or the Royal Ascot races continue to perform integrating functions. However, these events are no longer the semi-sequestered gatherings that they were in Veblen's time. Furthermore, they are likely to involve corporate sponsorship and corporate leisure appointments. The involvement of 'old money' in these gatherings is often itself contingent upon corporate duties. Aristocrats lend their name to a corporation and sit on its board for a fee. The old aristocratic disdain of pecuniary activity has been replaced with an ethic that aristocratic patronage of industry, commerce and charity is almost a duty. In Britain the extensive involvement of the Royal family in charity work and Prince Charles's interventions in environmental issues, architecture and farming, are signs that the aristocracy is becoming more engaged in business and community relations.

In the final analysis, the thesis that a leisure class can be detected in Western society is not verified. Although the rich have more wealth than the rest of us, they do not necessarily choose to spend it in conspicuous leisure activity. The rich, especially those whose wealth derives from corporate affiliation, in business and politics often make no distinction between work and leisure. Surprisingly, the achievement of immense personal wealth is not generally the pretext for stopping work. Paradoxically, idleness is not a charge that one can lay at the door of most of the self-made rich. Buffett and Gates often work 16-hour days and allow their work to spill over into their weekend and vacation time. Veblen's leisure class were also not lazy. Rather, they devoted themselves to activities which symbolized their distance from the need to earn a living. Of course, evidence can be found that the aristocracy still follows suit today. Yet on the whole, the rich are no longer distanced from the world of commerce. Dodi Fayed had sufficient personal wealth not to work. There is no doubt that he spent some of his wealth in entertaining, holidays, luxury cars, private yachts and luxury homes on several continents. However, he also worked as a film producer gaining success with *Chariots of Fire*. Critics of the Rich ignore the persistence of the work ethic in this stratum at their peril. It shows a degree of self-consciousness about wealth creation which does not follow from the standard image of the leisure class.

THE CELEBRITY CLASS

The importance of the celebrity class has grown in direct proportion to the growth in significance in wealth creation of the business corporation. The celebrity class is often directly involved in mediating corporate products to the consumer. The involvement of Bruce Willis, Cindy Crawford or Claudia Schiffer in endorsing a product through advertising personalizes the commodity. In terms of emulatory power, the celebrity elite is far more important than the economically richest class. People may change their buying habits after being subject to an advertising campaign involving a leading film or pop star, whereas they do not give a fig for the purchasing choices of Bill Gates, Paul Allen or Warren Buffett.

Hence the celebrity elite is important in moulding consumption choices in leisure time. They function as a reference group for the consumer. Film stars like Michael Caine, Sean Connery and Jack Nicholson and rock stars like Noel and Liam Gallagher, George Michael and Mick Hucknall, came from working-class backgrounds. They are constantly in the public eye. They therefore seem to be more tangible role models.

There is no doubting the immense wealth of the celebrity elite.

In 1997 *Premier* magazine reported that John Travolta, Harrison Ford and Tom Cruise command a fee of $20 million per movie. Eddie Murphy receives $16 million, Demi Moore $14 million, Julia Roberts $13 million, Meryl Streep $8 million and Goldie Hawn $5 million. Frank and Cook (1995) report that in 1988 Arnold Schwarzenegger received $11m for his role in *Total Recall*, and in 1990 Michael Douglas received $15m for *Basic Instinct*; in 1994 Schwarzenegger got $15m (plus a percentage of gross receipts) for *True Lies*, Bruce Willis received a similar deal for *Die Hard 3*; in 1993–94 Steven Spielberg earned $330m. Advances and earnings are escalating quite rapidly. As an example, Frank and Cook (1995: 63–5) examine publishing advances for top authors. In 1968 Fawcett paid $410 000 for the rights to Mario Puzo's *The Godfather*. In 1972, Avon paid $1 100 000 for the rights to *Jonathan Livingston Seagull*, by Richard Bach. Colleen McCulloch's *The Thorn Birds* received $1 900 000 from Avon in 1976. Since then advances have rocketed. In 1990 Stephen King received $40m for the rights to his next four books, and in the same year Delacorte secured the next five novels from Danielle Steel for approximately $60m. Noel and Liam Gallagher of the pop group *Oasis* were jointly worth £40 million in 1997 and were 461st on the *Sunday Times Rich List*. Similar trends are evident in sport and television. Nor is Britain immune. Premier league soccer stars like Alan Shearer, Paul Ince and David Beckham, can expect to earn weekly wages of £30 000–40 000, to say nothing of the additional money to be earned from advertising and product endorsement. A table of Britain's top 20 highest earners in sport (1997) is reproduced in Table 2.4.

What emerges powerfully from this list is the close connection between personal wealth and corporate sponsorship. Top sportsmen and women may earn vast purses in the sports ring or the tennis arena, but a substantial part of their wealth comes from endorsing commodities.

Because the celebrity class are so closely enmeshed with leisure pursuits their lifestyle and wealth might be expected to have a particularly strong influence on mass audiences. Their lives do not have the degree of invisibility associated with leading business figures. As reference group models for emulation they stand out prominently.

Since Veblen's day, the rise in the significance and importance of the celebrity class in the politics and dynamics of emulation has been one of the most important changes in hierarchy. One hundred years ago it would have been impossible to think of a dramatic

Leisure and Culture

Table 2.4   Britain's 20 Highest Earners in Sport

		Sponsors	*Income*
1	Lennox Lewis (Boxing)	*Le Coq Sportif*	£6.4m
2.	Naseem Hamed (Boxing)	Adidas, *The Sun*, Al-Rabie (Dairy Company), Mahmoud Saeed (perfumes), *The Middle East Newspaper*	£5.8m
3.	Damon Hill (Motor Racing)	Whirlpool, Adidas	£5.3m
4.	Alan Shearer (Soccer)	Umbro, McDonald's, Lucozade, Braun, Jaguar, BT, Regency Plastics	£3.5m
5.	Nick Faldo (Golf)	Pringle, Bridgestone, Jaguar, Mzuno, Florsheim	£3.4m
6.	Johnny Herbert (Motor racing)	Sauber	£2.5m
7.	David Coulthard (Motor racing)	McLaren	£2.0m
8.	Colin Montgomerie (Golf)	Pringle, Calloway, Toyota, Titleist, Valmed, Marriott, Ebel, Pearson Videos	£1.8m
9.	Ryan Giggs (Soccer)	Reebok, Fuji, Cellnet, Coca-Cola	£1.6m
10.	Paul Ince (Soccer)	Adidas, Pepsi	£1.6m
11.	Les Ferdinand (Soccer)	Adidas, Kickmaster, Marks & Spencer, Eidos Games, Headline Books, Green Umbrella Videos, Mulberry, Harry Brown	£1.6m
12.	Greg Rusedski (Tennis)	Nike, Rover, Wilson, Austin Reed, Nestlé	£1.6m
13.	Teddy Sheringham (Soccer)	Nike	£1.4m
14.	Colin McRae (Motor racing)	None	£1.4m
15.	Stephen Hendry (Snooker)	G de Z Venture, Capital Fast Sandwich, EJ Riley	£1.4m
16.	Tim Henman (Tennis)	Adidas, Mercedes, Slazenger, Midland	£1.4m
17.	David Beckham (Soccer)	Adidas, Brylcreem, Sondico, Electronic Arts	£1.3m
18.	Stan Collymore (Soccer)	Diadora	£1.3m
19.	Henry Wkinwande (Boxing)	None	£1.2m
20.	Eddie Irvine (Motor racing)	Ferrari	£1.2m

Source: *The Guardian*: 18.11.1997

Table 2.5 Music Millionaires (UK 1998)

		m
1.	Sir Paul McCartney	£500
2.	Lord Lloyd-Webber	£480
3.	Sir Cameron Mackintosh	£350
4.	Robert Stigwood	£175
5=	David Bowie	£150
5=	Sir Elton John	£150
7.	Mick Jagger	£140
8.	Chris Blackwell	£125
9=	Phil Collins	£105
9=	Keith Richards	£105
11.	Chris Wright	£90
12.	George Harrison	£87
13.	Sting	£80
14.	Ringo Starr	£78
15=	Eric Clapton	£75
15=	Rod Stewart	£75
17=	Dave Gilmour	£60
17=	Charlie Watts	£60
19=	Tom Jones	£50
19=	Mark Knopfler	£50
19=	George Michael	£50
19=	Brian May	£50
19=	Mickie Most	£50
19=	Robert Plant	£50
19=	Jimmy Page	£50

(*Source*: *Sunday Times Rich List* 1998)

actor entering the White House. Ronald Reagan's success in the 1980s is a measure of the rise in cultural significance achieved by the celebrity class.

As with the business and political classes, the celebrity class is highly mobile and their activities follow global rather than national dimensions. The highly personalized nature of celebrity must make it doubtful that they think of themselves as belonging to a class. Rather they are more likely to think of themselves as brilliant individuals or outstanding performers. The top earners in sport and in the music industry in Britain (see Table 2.5) have a self-image of being competitors engaged in a fickle market.

This reinforces the tendency to define themselves as outstanding individuals rather than as representatives of a class. This is reinforced by the cultural tendency to present their activities in heroic terms.

Nor are the links with the business and political classes obvious. Most are passive sponsors, lending their faces and bodies to product endorsement without playing a serious part in company ownership or management. While the celebrity class undoubtedly uses business advisors and may court politicians, the evidence that they constitute an overarching ruling class is weak.

WHAT DO THE RICH DO IN THEIR LEISURE?

Available evidence about what the rich actually do in their leisure is scarce. The invisibility of the wealthiest, means that their 'free time' choices are often hidden from public view. Moreover, since their wealth is generally tied up with corporate finance there is a natural resistance on the part of their employees to vouchsafe information. In short there is an occlusive veil which surrounds the activities of the rich, which critics of class often miss in their ferocious assaults on inequality.

However, information does exist in the form of newspaper reports and biographical material. In what follows I want to briefly consider the leisure patterns of the two richest men in the world, Bill Gates and Warren Buffett, and then go on to examine the leisure of one of the leading businessmen in Britain, Richard Branson, the airline and leisure tycoon. These three cases are hardly exhaustive. For one thing, all of the individuals are self-made tycoons. But they challenge common-sense perceptions about the insidious and flagrant displays of wealth that are said to identify the lifestyles of the super-rich.

Bill Gates

Bill Gates is the Chairman and Chief Executive of Microsoft. He founded the company with Paul Allen in 1975. In 1997 his personal wealth was reported to be £18 billion. In 1998 it was thought to have risen to £28.81 billion. Despite this immensity of wealth, Gates shows no sign of fleeing from work or engaging in profligate leisure habits. He regularly works over 100 hours per week. 'I work hard,' he (1995: 275) writes, 'because I love my work. It's not an addiction and I like doing a lot of other things, but I find my work very exciting.' Gates displays a strong adherence to the work ethic. This is not surprising since he is working for his own company and is therefore the direct recipient of the rewards achieved by his labours. Even so, why should a man worth over £28 billion continue to work over 100 hours per week? Gates has redefined the work ethic. He does not see it as merely involving discipline, sacrifice and deprived gratification. For Gates, work is an extension of the play form in which competing and winning against one's peers is ultimately more important than the size of the purse.

This emphasis on work as 'fun' is common to much of the new managerial literature of the 1990s. The organizational guru, Tom Peters, is one of its chief advocates. Along with sport, work is the arena, *par excellence*, for testing oneself against others and discovering one's mettle. It is not enough for today's tycoons to succeed, they have to be more successful than any of their other competitors. This intense commitment to competition is understandable, given that the economic reward typically accrues to the tycoon. In Gates's case the technology expands exponentially. Engineers working in the micro-chip business refer to 'Moore's law'. In 1965 Gordon Moore, co-founder of Intel, predicted that the capacity of the computer chip would double every two years. Since 1965 the law has been verified with chip capacity doubling, on average, every 18 months. If Moore's law holds good for another twenty years, a computation that now takes a day will be more than a 100 000 times faster, and therefore need only a few seconds (Gates 1995: 33). Gates clearly sees himself as a voyager working on the frontier of enormous transformations in society and culture. In itself this is a source of attraction. He can keep work and leisure together so closely in his mind because he feels propelled by the dynamics of technocultural change which impacts upon all aspects of life. At the same time, Gates is acutely conscious of the attrition rate of businesses in his own sector of computer technology. He (1995: 275) notes ruefully, that there has never been a business leader in the sector from one decade to the next. It is a pregnant observation, for the reader is left in no doubt that Gates sees himself as the first to break the trend.

When he is not working, Gates watches movies (at least once a week), plays bridge and poker (often via the internet), travels and supervises the building of his home in Seattle. The last activity seems to dominate his leisure. This is particularly revealing because it demonstrates his fascination with living on the frontier of technoculture. Gates sees his home as a sort of personalized EPCOT centre, in which all of the cutting edge technologies unavailable elsewhere in society will be installed and fully functioning.[2] The house will be equipped with the latest computer technology. Lighting, heating, music and video equipment will be controlled by an electronic pin clipped to one's buttonhole and hand-held remote-control units. Gates (1995: 221) wants to realize the design principle of a house that tracks its occupants in order to meet their particular needs. He doesn't see the controlled environment as being oppressive because the technology is ultimately at the service of the householder. Gates has no sense of technology producing standardization and performativity. Instead he (1995: 221) equates technology with fulfilment and liberation:

> An object can authenticate you. It can inform people that you have permission to do something such as open a locked door, get on an airplane, or use a specific line of credit – yours – to make a purchase. Keys, electronic entry cards, driver's licences, passports, name badges, credit cards and tickets, are all forms of authentication.

Gates's account of his own leisure does not recognize a gap between work and leisure. Rather both spheres are subordinated to the wider goals of expanding personal choice and social control. His view of leisure in the era of the 'information highway' is based in the assumption that social actors control their own destinies. He pays lip-service to the excluded but implies that their condition can only improve by the expansion and improvement of information technology. His identification with Microsoft means that his work and much of his leisure is tied to endorsing the company. Corporate responsibilities are taken seriously by Gates and the corporation is the foundation of his lifestyle. The prevailing impression one receives is that Gates will not allow his lifestyle to step out of line with the corporate image of Microsoft.

Warren Buffett

Gates's self-discipline, relatively modest leisure habits and attachment to work as fun are shared by his friend, Warren Buffett. Buffett is Chief Executive of the investment company, Berkshire Hathaway. He began his career as an investment broker in 1956 with $10 000. Since then, he has consistently outperformed other investment analysts. In 1996 his personal fortune was estimated to be $15.3 billion. In 1998 it was thought to have grown to £18.68 billion.

Buffett has made a virtue of being parsimonious with his personal wealth and lifestyle. He still drives his own modest car, a blue Lincoln. His home is comfortable, but vastly undervalued compared with what he could afford. He deplores conspicuous consumption and the lifestyle of the super-rich (Lenzener 1993). His biographer reports that, in a recent two-week vacation he left his modest beach house only three times – twice to see movies and once to have lunch (Lowenstein 1995: 421). Like Gates, Buffett is fond of bridge. The sense of risk and gambling which is essential in the business sphere is clearly a self-sustaining source of pleasure which he plays out in some of his leisure. Again, like Gates, Buffett seems to make no distinction in his mind between work and leisure. Work is fun, a chance to outwit the other fellow. Again, the most revealing parallel is sport, rather than the quest to accumulate for its own sake.

He doesn't have Gates's fixation on technology. The one concession to technological ostentation that he has made is to purchase a personal jet. However, he justifies this as avoiding airport queues, and Lowenstein (1995: 336) reports that he rarely uses it for pleasure. The biographical material on Buffett gives no indication that he values vacation time or travel. Instead he seems to look to work for his primary source of excitement and stimulation. Buffett's moral philosophy mirrors Benjamin Franklin in his respect for self-reliance and austerity. This extends to his role as a father. Lowenstein (1995: 336) reports that he refused to give his daughter a bank loan to cover home improvements. Instead he advised her to negotiate a loan from the bank like everyone else.

Buffett is a folk hero in the US. Berkshire Hathaway meetings are glutted with admirers who have grown rich on his investment advice and his plainsman style of business dealing. His popularity rests on three additional reasons. Firstly, he is a fantastically rich man. The immigrant appreciation of the value of money looms large in the American psyche, and Buffett's self-made wealth is an automatic sign of status. Secondly, he has refused to allow his head to be turned by his own wealth. He gives Americans the impression that the true recognition of the value of money is to realize its ultimate shallowness. Thirdly, he has made a habit of being his own man. He has avoided building a coterie of professional experts around him and he is often contemptuous of market opinion. This has a high approval rating among most Americans because it reinforces the ethic of rugged individualism which was associated with the pioneers.

Buffett's attachment to work as fun eclipses the need for independent leisure. He spends his life making money, but there is little evidence that he is alienated from his fellow men and women by so doing. He is aware of the importance of money in the social order, but he is no adherent of the cult of mammon. Buffett's pleasure derives from outwitting competitors in what is, perhaps, one of the most competitive games in the world: investment brokerage. Buffett's uneasiness with the concept of 'free time' or 'time-off', suggest that he holds a feeling that the division between work and leisure in which society at large is enmeshed, is a false division. Buffett is integrated around the goal achievement of profit maximization. To him, the rest of us, who stop work at 5.30 and go for a beer, watch TV, or spend the evening reading a good book, must seem like profoundly ambivalent characters. In fetishizing our leisure-time we seem unable to grasp the opportunities for wealth which lie right in front of us.

Richard Branson

The closest comparison that Britain has to a populist folk-hero like Buffett, is Richard Branson. Yet as soon as the comparison is made it seems to break down. Buffett is a sober personality who dresses in a business suit and avoids personal danger; Branson is a business impressario, who favours casual clothing and courts danger by participating in cross-Atlantic boat races and assaults on the round-the-world hot-air balloon record. He is estimated to be worth £1700m. His wealth derives from a range of businesses: Virgin Atlantic Airlines, Virgin Cinemas, Virgin Financial Services, Virgin Radio, CDs, cola and the Virgin Megastore outlets. Like Gates and Buffett, work is the centre of his existence. He does not seem to hold a clear distinction between work and leisure. The love of risk is common to both. Floating a company or flying a hot-air balloon seem to be equivalent in his mind. As with Buffett, one has the impression that Branson regards the work/leisure distinction that applies in the larger society as irrelevant. His biographer, Tim Jackson (1995: 6–7) writes:

> He needs his eight hours of sleep a night, but is nevertheless able to put in very long hours without rest – keeping himself awake when necessary by snatching naps during the course of the day or even en route between one business meeting and the

next . . . Branson seems oddly detached from the outward details of his life. It does not bother him that the paint is flaking off the back of his house in Holland Park, or that the swimming-pool filter no longer works . . . He has always eschewed the ostentatiously high living of the music industry.

Branson is different from the other tycoons discussed here. Buffett is a genuinely private man who flinches from the spotlight; Gates tilts at privacy but ensures that his own name is closely associated with the fortunes of Microsoft; Branson is a flamboyant, inexhaustible and highly unorthodox self-publicist. In 1985 and 1986 he made well-publicized attempts to break the Atlantic speed record. In 1987 he made a perilous and closely followed attempt to cross the Atlantic in a hot-air balloon; and in 1990 he flew the Pacific by the same method. Each time he launches into sea or air, he ensures that Virgin's sponsorship of his activities is reported, thereby earning the company millions in free advertising.

Buffett and Gates shrink from vacations, but Branson has a luxury home in the Caribbean and is an ardent devotee of family holidays. He may see work and leisure as shading into each other, but he is also committed to short intense bursts of escape through balloon racing or retreating to his holiday hideaway. He adopts a playful stance to both work and leisure. This probably reflects the origins of his business wealth which derived from starting a cut-price record shop in London's Oxford Street.

Cynic or *ingénu*, he has kept the public second-guessing with his non-proft-making business to supply cheap condoms as part of a public health campaign to combat AIDS, and his brief interlude as the voluntary 'Minister Against Litter', under the Conservatives' 'Clean-Up Britain' campaign. Like Gates and Buffett, he insists that work should be fun. As an impressario of leisure, he appeals to populist sentiments and quasi-radical posturing, as his unsuccessful campaign to run the British National Lottery revealed. Virgin is presented as a company which consistently breaks the mould. It has profited by marketing itself as being against the establishment. The financial services wing advertises that its 'Personal Equity Plans' cut through the red tape and do away with charges that other competing countries treat as standard fixtures. Similarly, Virgin's dispute with British Airways over fair trading for air fares was symbolically a battle between old and new money. Branson presented himself as the outsider intent on giving a fair deal to the public. He alleged that the British Airways board approved sharp practice in selling tickets and that they were out of touch with consumers.

Branson has contrived to present a blokish innocence to the public. Business analysts see this as the secret of his success, since the public perception of his diversified businesses is that they are all run by Richard Branson. Actually, Branson has gone as far as Bill Gates in crafting a range of top-flight managers to run the various segments of his business empire. However, final control rests with him. He remains the last stop for all significant business decisions relating to the Virgin portfolio.

Although there are many important differences between the three figures discussed above, significant common themes are evident. They are all self-made men and inheritance has played no significant part in their accumulation of wealth. All three head powerful corporations and subscribe to the view that work should be fun. They hold a weak distinction between work and leisure. They go to the movies for escape, but interestingly risk and competition feature prominently in their leisure. Gates has persuaded Buffett to play bridge electronically; and Branson takes a boyish delight in his ballooning exploits. Business is seen as a form of sport and the thrill of competing is as important as accumulating wealth. The division between work and leisure which the rest of society observes is not recognized by them. Buffett's biographer suggests that he is awkward in family leisure events and finds it difficult to relax. The same seems to be true of Gates. None of them see themselves as driven by work or the need to make money. Their biggest pleasure appears to be outwitting their competitors and achieving success for their multinational corporation. The corporation is the key to their lifestyle. Veblen presented the rich as using their wealth to enhance the interests of themselves and their families. The families of Gates, Buffett and Branson gain benefits, but the orientation of the three tycoons is overwhelmingly towards the multinational rather than the family. Growing the business is the heart of their lifestyle. For these individuals, work has adopted the characteristics of a play form, so that institutionalized play possesses less attraction than for most of us.

This sketch of the leisure patterns of three leading international businessmen is not intended as a universal statement of the leisure

patterns of the rich. That would only be possible by means of detailed questionnaires and interviews. These methods are not possible
in a study of this type. Nor does it follow that the patterns of the
wealthiest people in the business sector are replicated in the aristocracy or the political or celebrity sectors. As I argued in the last
section of the chapter, the rich do not follow standard rhythms of
life. Mobility, globalization and corporate loyalties make it dangerous to attribute the designation of a 'ruling class' to them. Nor are
they immune from the cares and worries that affect the rest of us.
Like all of us, the rich worry about losing their assets. They have a
clear tendency to be unable to relax. The hyperactivity of their
work leaves its mark on their leisure patterns so that their work
adopts a play form.

LEISURE AND THE CURSE OF SUCCESS

Not unreasonably, the sympathies of sociology have traditionally
been with the powerless and the exploited. This has resulted in
quite a strong archive of literature on the leisure of the working
class, the poor, and working women. By the same token, it has left
a gap in knowledge of the wealthy. We know very little about the
psychology, hopes, fears and leisure activities of the top one per
cent in our societies. Conspicuous wealth may equate with conspicuous consumption, but there is no iron law which states that it
will occur as night follows day. Nor should we assume that the rich
form a universal object for emulation. Despite the impact of cultural studies, there has been very little empirical research on the
construction of objects of emulation in popular culture. Billig's (1992)
qualitative study on the cultural significance of the Royal family in
Britain, suggested that the Royals had a significant effect in order-
ing people's lives. Ordinary people did not aspire to emulate their
wealth, but they had a strong tendency to organize their collective
memories around Royal events, such as the Royal jubilee, Royal
weddings and Royal births. Ang's (1985) study of the audience for
the television series, *Dallas*, also made an interesting empirical
contribution to our understanding of how the subjectivity interpellates
around the celebrity class. However, generally the effects of emulation have been argued out at the level of theoretical ideas and
propositions. As Ang (1996: 13–14) complains, too often this research
has resulted in the construction of,

a too abstracted, generalized 'we'. After all, for whom does all this apply? And how do different people in different places, living in different conditions and under different circumstances, with more or less semiotic skills and familiarity with postmodern aesthetics, actually attach meanings to the images they encounter, whether or not they are of their own choosing?

Although Ang's remark is formulated in the context of theories of popular culture, it applies just as well to theoretical perceptions of the rich.

What we do know is that success does not necessarily produce pleasure. As we saw in Chapter 1, Schor's (1992) study of the American worker concluded that the quest for success leads to overwork and exhaustion. American workers seem obsessed with the need to get ahead and find that their leisure fails to provide adequate rest and relaxation. Schwagger's (1992) interviews with successful Wall Street traders confirms Schor's argument. Bill Lischutz, who is estimated to have earnt Salomon Brothers profits of one and a half billion dollars in eight years, and enjoys a salary commensurate with his achievements, told Schwagger (1992: 64):

> Some professional traders may claim that they separate their personal life from their business life and are able to completely turn-off on the weekends. I don't believe that for a second. I think that when they're relaxing in their sailboats, at some level they're still focused on the market.

Another super-trader, Monroe Trout, confessed to taking only three days off in a year and a half (Schwagger 1992: 174). This level of work involvement is only possible if the domestic divisions of labour support it. Neither Schor (1992) or Schwagger (1992) provide much ethnographic material on the consequences of super-success on family life. But it seems logical to propose that it requires women to do the bulk of child-rearing and home-care and also involves reduced parental contact with children. Peter Ingram Walters, in 1987 head of British Petroleum, confessed that his work produced difficulties in rearing his three children:

> My poor wife. I'd quite often leave her when I had to go off abroad somewhere. There were real strains on the nuclear family (in Ritchie and Goldsmith 1987: 158).

Another leading British executive, David Plastow, who in 1987 was managing Director and Chief Executive of Vickers complained that in one particularly stressful period, overwork took its toll:

> My judgement was losing its edge. There was no sense of values.
> The balance had gone out of my life. My relationship with my
> wife and children had become very brittle. Even more frighten-
> ing was the discovery that my senior colleagues had been following
> my example and had health or emotional problems (Ritchie and
> Goldsmith 1987: 141).

Comments like these are not uncommon. Yet they rarely reveal
the true extent of sacrifice required of wives and children to support great business success.

One sociologist who adroitly revealed how the tendons of success in the labour market are connected with the domestic division
of labour is Ray Pahl. His (1984) emphasis on *divisions* of labour
did much to increase the visibility of the division of labour within
the home for sociologists of work. Recently, Pahl (1995) has been
conducting interviews with successful people. His aim is to determine the lifestyle values that follow the acquisition of power and
material achievement. The ethnographic character of his study, makes
it particularly valuable for us in exploring the leisure patterns of
the rich.

Pahl's (1995: 83) interviews found 'insecurity and a vague appre-
hensiveness' in the majority of his respondents. The successful people
with whom he talked expressed guilt as well as surprise at their
achievements. The 'undeserving rich' may seem a curious formula-
tion. Yet Pahl's work supports the proposition that many rich people
feel a degree of personal worthlessness about the level of material
assests and power that they control. The successful also worry about
losing the self-discipline and drive that made them successful in
the first place. Pahl's research paralleled Ehrenreich's (1989: 15)
finding that 'even the affluence that is so often the goal of . . . striving
becomes a threat, for it holds out the possibility of hedonism and
self-indulgence'. This contrasts sharply with the stereotypical picture of the rich as power-mad and indifferent to the needy that
one sometimes finds in the sociological literature. It also suggests
that there may be important limits in Britain at least, in redefining
the work ethic to adopt a play form.

A concrete reason for insecurity and anxiety is a lack of cer-
tainty about the future. This was also the finding of the American
research into status anxiety conducted by Ehrenreich (1989). She
argues that the American middle class is benighted with 'a fear of

failing'. There is no doubt that the 'freeing up of the market' in the 1980s and 90s left most people less certain about their personal future. The girdle of support provided by the welfare state may not have been removed, but it was considerably relaxed. In Britain, welfare payments for the unemployed and pensioners have been progressively cut in real terms. Standards of public education and health care have deteriorated as people have been encouraged to switch to private health insurance and education schemes. Rather insidiously people have 'grown used' to the idea that a state and occupational pension scheme is unlikely to support them in their old age. In the 1980s and 90s many have started their own private pension schemes to back up state and occupational arrangements. Nor does 'New Labour' show much sign of intending to restore welfare cover to levels offered in the 1960s and 70s. On the contrary, in its first three months in office, it followed the Dearing Report (1997) recommendation to introduce fee-paying for university students, and it continued the Conservative policy of reviewing the state pension scheme with a view to transferring contributions from the public to the private sector. Similar developments are evident in most countries in Western Europe as well as the USA, Canada, Australia and New Zealand. Pahl's (1995) study reflects the decomposition of security that has followed the contracting out, downsizing and de-layering of the 1980s. His respondents found themselves strongly constrained by economic and political factors. They felt trapped by changes which they could not control. Giddens (1991) and other commentators on the 'new identity politics' argue that new identities are characterized by high levels of reflexivity and autonomy. Pahl's (1995: 154) interviews suggest that the connection between reflexivity and autonomy cannot be assumed for successful people. The successful are only too well aware of the threats that surround them, and their wealth does not immunize them from the fear of failure.

Generally speaking, Pahl's respondents did not draw a hard and fast line between work and leisure. Some followed instrumental workers in centring their real lives on leisure experience. However, most were oriented to work as a source of fun and excitement. They worried about the social consequences of a society which was unable to produce rewarding work for the majority. Most took it for granted that the consequence of the new technologies and efficiency savings is to exert downward presure on work time. Most do not expect this pressure to lead to a new Gorzian 'politics of time' in which labour will be reduced for all. Rather, they view the downward pressure on work time to be spread unevenly with manual labourers facing the greatest threat of prolonged unemployment. For themselves, many foresaw an increase in work demands as the struggle to compete and acquire material wealth intensifies. The famine in leisure time that Schor (1992) discovered in relation to successful workers in America seems to be echoed in British experience. Part of the uncertainty about the future is expressed in the anxiety about the lack of a clear social and economic strategy to cope with effects of reduced working time. For example, one of Pahl's (1995: 70) industrialists complained that people did not have the right education to cope with more leisure so that 'we might end up with destructive leisure time rather than constructive leisure time'. A difficulty in being able to relax in leisure was a common response. Leisure was valued, even longed for, but once accomplished individuals complained of feeling trapped or anxious about work issues.

A strong finding of Pahl's research was that the successful often have a feeling that their lives are out of balance. They wish to find a way of matching success at work with success with their partners, friends and children. This often has the effect of condemning them to an onerous existence, since they feel that they are never successful enough in all of these areas. Pahl's study verifies the stock sociological proposition that material values are not sufficiently satisfying to people. His respondents seem to spend much of their time wondering if success is worth all of the effort. The industrialist's remark that people are not educated for more leisure, seems to apply to the leisure patterns of the successful – at least as they are represented in Pahl's book. In general, his research shows people who do not know how to appreciate free time. They snatch at contrasting experience by going to the opera, watching movies, attending sports events, but there is no seam connecting their leisure to make a coherent whole.

Pahl (1995: 194) concludes that, 'when identity is not securely fixed by either community, class, kin or gender, widespread anxiety is to be expected'. Again, this is broadly in line with the American research conducted by Ehrenreich (1989). This is the situation of the successful today. They do not so much resemble a class as a collection of isolated individuals who occupy a broadly similar wealth and income bracket. They do not act as a class but as individuals. They are internally divided. Their pursuit of private interests brings them financial rewards, but it also drives home the lesson that uncoordinated societies are dangerous societies. Paradoxically, the people who have gained most from the market also have most to fear from the market turning against them. The evidence confirms Giddens's (1990, 1992) hypothesis that 'ontological insecurity' is a characteristic of contemporary life. Of course, the rich do not have the terrifying material worries that afflict the poor. But it does not follow from this that they are without worries or terror. Ontological insecurity affects all levels of society because the conditions of life are not fixed or certain.

If the leisure class no longer unequivocally sets the emulatory standards of behaviour for the rest of society, what are the new axes of emulation? What shapes our leisure choices and planning decisions? These are the questions that I will take up in the final sections of the chapter.

HABITUS AND THE NEW LEISURE CLASS

Unquestionably, Bourdieu's (1984) work on stratification and culture has emerged as a key reference point in discussions about culture and stratification. Bourdieu does not so much invent new concepts and approaches as revitalize old ones. For example, his work on culture, status and distinction is deeply indebted to anthropological accounts of primitive classification; while his use of the concepts of 'taste', 'taste communities' and 'distinction' take over notions that would have been familiar in the court of King Louis XIV, and gives them a new twist.

At the core of his analysis is the belief that neo-Kantian aesthetics have no part to play in understanding contemporary cultural practice. There is no 'pure' judgement of cultural value and no 'objective' means of prioritizing one form of leisure practice over another. Instead Bourdieu argues that judgements of taste and distinction can only be satisfactorily studied as social constructs. A person's response to a painting by Matisse or an opera by Verdi is not conditioned by the 'sublime' quality of the art, but by the social position occupied by the person and the background knowledge, values and prejudices mobilized in reacting to the experience. Bourdieu argues that a person's response to culture is in part an expression of the 'cultural capital' that they possess. The term 'cultural capital' refers to the understanding of and competence in the classificatory codes and conventions of cultural forms. Bourdieu (in Bourdieu and Passeron 1977: 133) acknowledges that the work of Basil Bernstein on 'elaborated' and 'restricted' linguistic codes and schemes of knowledge, influenced his own approach to the operation of systems of classification and codes of interpretation and transformative action in modern culture. Bernstein (1975) argues that the capacity of the individual to interpret culture, to express it and to act upon it, is shaped by parameters of the socio-cultural-economic stratum to which he or she belongs. Bourdieu agrees, but replaces Bernstein's emphasis on class as the decisive predisposing structure shaping a person's sense of taste and outlook on culture with the more flexible concept of 'habitus'.

Bourdieu (1977: 95) defines habitus as 'an acquired system of generative schemes objectively adjusted to the particular conditions in which it is constituted'. The term is intended to sum up the entire 'way of life' and 'social and cultural orientation' of a given stratum of people. Bourdieu means it to apply to the conscious and unconscious prejudices, native beliefs, priorities and values common in the stratum in which the person is situated. For example, members of Veblen's (1899) leisure class would have automatically 'understood' the correct repertoire of performance in culture. That is, the correct way to dress in public; the appropriate form of address to use with individuals from the same and different classes; the necessities of 'good' carriage and bearing in the body; the approved way of conducting oneself at the dinner table; the appropriate and inappropriate forms of amusement; and in short, what is important and relevant in cultural life and what is unimportant and irrelevant. This 'understanding' would not be fully shared by the other classes in society. And this is one reason why these forms of practice were so attractive to them. This is the sense in which Bourdieu (1984) believes that the accoutrements of habitus confer 'distinction' upon personal articulations of culture. They enable an individual, as it were to size up 'in a glance' an encounter or a setting for interaction and to judge 'what is going on' (Goffman 1967).

Habitus is more flexible than the concept of class because it allows for status variations and other divisions within class categories. It also provides a critical counterpoint to the philosophy of, for example, the rational recreationist's or moral majority, that there are objectively valid and invalid categories and forms of leisure practice. Bourdieu's approach identifies leisure as a category of culture and further insists that the socially constructed nature of leisure and culture makes it impossible to appeal to neo-Kantian absolutes of correct and appropriate behaviour. It infers that standards of elite and mass culture have no absolute reference points but are themselves socially constructed. If this is correct, the notion that a dominant leisure class is in a position to set trends is made dubious, because the standards of this class are vulnerable to the criticism that they are socially and historically constructed rather than 'immemorial' and 'objective'. A logical implication of Bourdieu's argument is that culture is becoming less regimented and hierarchical and that canons of taste are more changeable and porous than, for example, Veblen's (1899) theory of the leisure class would allow.

However, Bourdieu's critics maintain that this loosening of cultural analysis is more apparent than real (Savage *et al.* 1992; Chaney 1996). They note that Bourdieu's (1984) model of taste differentiates between 'legitimate', 'middle brow' and 'popular' taste and that this inferentially reproduces the division between 'upper', 'middle' and 'working' class which is so familiar in conventional class analysis. Theoretically, the concept of habitus supports a richer analysis of how groups experiment with culture and test conventional attitudes and mores. But practically, Bourdieu locates these 'habitus wars' in the familiar terrain of class society. Moreover, as Chaney (1996: 66) observes, Bourdieu's reading of habitus does not acknowledge the self-reflexivity and transformative capacity of social actors. For Bourdieu insists that the conduct of social actors derives from the habitus in which they are situated. Bourdieu is accused of failing to escape the prescriptive determinism which he claims to have transcended.

On the other hand, Bourdieu does succeed in revealing the complexity of performative culture in contemporary society. His approach rejects the hierarchical model of class domination found in Veblen's (1899) study and the work of others, operating in different traditions who espouse a version of the dominant ideology thesis (Clarke and Critcher 1985; Tomlinson 1989; Green *et al.* 1987; Bialeschki and Henderson 1986). Bourdieu's approach allows for trend-setting behaviour in culture to emerge from classes who do not hold the balance of economic power. In this respect he (1984: 310–11) follows many other commentators in emphasizing the significance of the new intermediary classes as the new trend-setting agent in leisure practice (see also Lash and Urry 1987, 1994; Savage *et al.* 1992). The expansion of the 'service' and 'knowledge' classes, based in the new digital information industries, advertising, mass communications, public relations, higher education and fashion, is held to have contributed to the aestheticization of everyday life. As Featherstone (1990) notes, the emergence of these intermediary classes is bound up with the vast expansion in consumer society in the postwar years. The volume and flow of data have produced new ways of presenting information, new images and new codes of representation. Symbolic capital has become a more prominent and insistent part of lifestyle and culture. Bourdieu (1984) sees this development as involving a switch from the ascetic behavioural codes which regulated lifestyle and leisure in the early and middle stages of industrial capitalism to a variety of codes organized around hedonism. Interestingly, he traces this shift to the economic level. As he (1984: 310–11) puts it:

> The new logic of the economy rejects the ascetic ethic of production and accumulation, based on abstinence, sobriety, saving and calculation, in favour of an hedonistic morality of consumption, based on credit, spending and enjoyment. This economy demands a social world which judges people by their capacity for consumption, their 'standard of living', their life-style, as much as their capacity for production. It finds ardent spokesmen in the new bourgeoisie of the vendors of symbolic goods and services, the directors and executives of firms in tourism and journalism, publishing and the cinema, fashion and advertising, decoration and property development.

An important corollary of the new class thesis is that a variety of significant cultural changes have been introduced as a result of the rise of the service and information classes. These range from arguments that the new stress on appearance and the new reliance on digital technologies has resulted in the emergence of 'post-scriptural' economies in which interpersonal exchange is organized around the exchange of images and signs, to the proposition that the cybernation of culture is transforming the human body as body modification interventions, such as facelifts, hair transplants, suction surgeries and implants become more common and acceptable (Rheingold 1994; Featherstone and Burrows 1995).

If these arguments are correct they have deep implications for our understanding of leisure. For the sake of easy and direct comprehension it may be helpful to list some of these implications in notational form:

Body Modification and the Life Cycle

Bio-technologies focused on youth-enhancing body modification, cloning
and spare parts surgery challenge our traditional notions of the adult
life-cycle. Hedonistic culture places an extreme emphasis upon youth
and this is reinforced by a range of images and symbols which associate youth with sexual attractiveness, energy and cultural relevance.
The extension of youthful appearance until advanced middle age, *in
vitro* fertilization, the development of cloning techniques (which in
1997 had already produced 'Dolly', a sheep cloned from its mother's
cells) and the possibility that the Biblical three score years and ten
will soon be a redundant description of life expectancy, is full of implications for family life, sexual relations, morality, work career plans,
housing requirements and insurance and pension arrangements. Women
in particular, will have the choice to start a family much later in life
which will impact both on the structure of the labour market and
the provision of leisure activities throughout the life cycle – while
cloning technologies present the possibility of infinite serial reproduction. As an aside one should note that cloning represents the
greatest challenge to our conventional understanding of 'society'.

Post-Fordism and Lifelong Learning Arrangements

The replacement of primary and secondary jobs with occupations
based in the tertiary sector is associated with a move from Fordist
to post-Fordist economic and cultural patterns. The traditional
concept of primary, secondary, further and higher education concentrated in the first 21 to 30 years of life will cease to be tenable.
Already, further and higher education systems in Western societies are developing the concept of 'lifelong learning'. In Britain
this has been reinforced with the move towards semesterized, modu-
larized teaching in the 1980s and 90s. The idea of developing a
personal education menu to suit changing job requirements is gradually being established. The increased importance placed upon
certification in the job market is likely to blur the boundaries between
education and the rest of life.

Further Erosion of the Work–Leisure Divide

Flexitime, homework and the professionalization of standards in
many leisure activities, have already eroded the division between

work and leisure. Career patterns under post-Fordism do not correspond to the 'job for life' pattern enjoyed under Fordism. On the contrary, interrupted work patterns, career retraining, periods of unemployment and travelling are all now common features of the labour market. As digitalization grows through the spread of home computers and the internet, domestic space is likely to include workspace. Of course, homes already include kitchens and toolsheds in which unpaid labour is routinely practised. Digitalization will further encroach upon the living and relaxation areas of the home by establishing workstations in which working for money will be concentrated. For many forms of paid work in the information and knowledge areas, it is already unnecessary to leave the home in order to work. The spread of the internet is likely to increase this tendency by enabling instantaneous, low-cost, high-quality communication between producers and consumers. The evidence suggests that people do not want to flee work. Rather they want customized work and leisure patterns which enable them to work when they want to and to have time off when it suits them. The flexible accumulation patterns of the new information industries have gone some way to accommodating to these desires (Harvey 1989).

Privatization of Leisure

The privatization of leisure has been one of the most prominent trends of the Industrial Revolution. Radio, hi fi, television, video, computers and playstations were instrumental in enhancing the leisure uses of domestic space. The electronic revolution in home entertainment has sliced away many traditional family leisure pastimes. Playing board games, musical ensembles, nature trails and even time and space for family conversations have generally been replaced with the more solitary pursuits of watching television, playing computer games and listening to tapes or CDs. Satellite and cable television allows one to shop from the privacy of one's own home. The new technologies of reproduction and virtual reality that will become commonly available in user-friendly formats in the next two decades, will push the privatization of leisure still further. For example, in 1990 Polaroid announced the introduction of a new process for creating 'museum quality reproductions'. The technique uses large-format photography and advanced digital image processing to reproduce life-size copies of original works of art. It increases access to artworks and decreases the need to visit museums and art galleries. As the Polaroid promotional literature put it: 'Imagine having the opportunity to own and actually live with works of proven importance by artists like Monet, Cézanne, Sargent, Homer and more. Each day will bring new discoveries in nuances of colour and technique.' As for virtual reality, Rheingold (1990) speculates confidently on the emergence of 'teledildonics' as a form of domestic leisure which will be equivalent to watching television or listening to the radio. Teledildonics, predicts Rheingold, will utilize a soundproof chamber with a head-mounted display and a lightweight body suit. The body suit will be fitted with thousands of tiny effectors which, under the computer's control, would simulate the feel of any object. The teledildonic unit will be plugged into the phone network, enabling you to download and interface with a limitless number of synthetic experiences.

The proposition that emerges from this material is that by shaping the content of mass communication the service class have leverage to influence leisure practice in society as a whole. There is not enough empirical research to either confirm or deny this. One might just as well posit that the rise in body piercing among youth groups is evidence of a new leisure class. Facial chains, studs, multiple rings and other mechanical adornments have the general effect of diminishing power in the labour market. For it is less likely that facially pierced or tattooed people will be offered jobs. One can extrapolate and regard this as evidence of a new class emerging in society which does not want to submit to the routine of full-time paid labour. However, this is to engage in pure speculation. To repeat: there is insufficient empirical research to decide one way or the other about this or about the effect on leisure practice of the new service class.

However, as Savage *et al.* (1992) sound a cautionary note about the more effusive claims being made on behalf of the social influence of the service class. They remind us that the emergence of the new service class may have been so dramatic that it blinds us to the continuing power of established class divisions and interests. They argue that property remains the most significant basis for class formation since it can be accumulated, stored and transmitted with ease. The intermediate classes do not constitute a singular group of property owners. Rather they are a mix of *petite bourgeoisie* in which share capital and *rentier* assets form the foundation of wealth; organizational strata, in which capital derives from middle-ranking power in public and private bureaucracies; and cultural strata, in which symbolic capital underwrites the power of individuals. The numerical size of the intermediate classes has clearly grown in this century. Routh (1987) shows that, between 1911 and 1981 in the UK, the number of white-collar (professional, managerial, supervisory and clerical workers) swelled from 14 per cent of the salaried population to 43 per cent. Commenting on the American scene, Gilbert and Kahl (1987) report that the growth in the US white-collar sector rose from 17.5 per cent to 52 per cent of the salaried population. Yet as the distinction between *petite bourgeoisie*, organizational and cultural intermediate class members made by Savage *et al.* (1992) makes clear, it is highly misleading to think of the growth in white-collar workers as advancing unitary class consciousness. Leaving aside the question of the nuances and power differentials between the three divisions, Savage *et al.* (1992) also point out that the power of each level in the intermediate category is unstable. Recession cuts into the value of the property assets of the *petite bourgeoisie*. The Thatcher–Reagan attempt to roll back the state clearly diminished the power and real incomes of individuals located in the public sector intermediary class occupations. For its part, the members of the cultural intermediary class deal in symbolic capital which is notoriously vulnerable to fashion. This year's thing may be old hat and forgotten within twelve months. The instability of organizational and symbolic capital intensifies competitive pressure within the intermediate classes to outbid one another. The result of this is that the intermediate classes carry strong inherent tendencies to fragment. This makes talk of their alleged class consciousness and action problematic.

LEISURE AND COMMODITY CULTURE

Bourdieu's (1984) work emphasizes that, questions of taste, distinction and trends in culture and leisure cannot be satisfactorily explored by applying a trend-setting class model. There are indeed historical reasons for supposing that this was the case even in Veblen's day. Even at the height of the rational recreation movement, the working class sought to develop their own political organizations, leisure associations, play and relaxation forms which were defined as being separate from the bourgeois values of rational recreation reformers. Yeo's (1976) study of voluntary working-class organizations in Reading and Gray's (1981) exploration of the work and leisure of 'the aristocracy of labour' (skilled workers) in the nine-teenth century, powerfully conveys working-class pride in making their own, distinctive forms of recreation which were often critical of ruling-class values. Veblen's (1899) theory of the leisure class tended to assume an active model of ruling-class action and a pas-sive model for the working class. It underestimated the power struggles and status contestation that occurred between the classes and exaggerated the domination of leisure-class values in society as a whole. These critical points have become more evident in the postwar years with the enlargement of the categories of commod-ity culture. For many commentators, the explosion of commodity culture in the postwar years is the key cultural phenomenon of the times rendering the divisions between high and low culture, elite and mass values obsolete (Foster 1985; Huyssen 1986). Corporate capitalism has replaced class as the key influence in popular leisure. The calculated advertising campaigns developed by Nike, Levi Strauss, Jack Daniels, Disney, Calvin Klein, Nicole Fahri and the other leading commodity manufacturers shape our leisure choices. They trade in status goods. It is the coolness or cultural cachet of owning these goods which is at stake in the consumption process. This is why, in the last ten to fifteen years, designer manufacturers have taken to placing designer labels prominently in their merchandise. It is no longer enough to own the commodity, one also needs to be able to advertise ownership in the technology of commodity display.

The extraordinary power attained by commodity capitalism in the postwar period has altered the exchange process. Trading in the cultural value of goods means that the exploitation which is at the heart of capitalist exchange processes has been masked. We do not feel exploited when we buy goods by Nike, Calvin Klein, Dis-ney, and so on, rather we feel culturally deprived if we do not own these goods. Exploitation has been rendered invisible by the hedo-nism of processes of commodity consumption. It is now very difficult to repeat the established Marxist critique of consumer culture, because the commodities of consumer culture have become such an integral part of lifestyle. Criticisms of the culture tend to be recommodified in the system. For example, Plant's (1992: 143–7) analysis of the punk movement in the 1970s drew out its links with the French situationist movement of the 1960s, but it also demon-strated how these links were reconfigured to reinforce commodity capitalism. She argues that punk was a mixture of calculated entrepreneurial zeal and spontaneous working-class rebellion.

Impressarios like Malcolm McLaren and designers like Jamie Reid recycled situationist ideas about the banality of commodity culture, the emptiness of leisure and organized recreation and the monotony of everyday life. They connected these ideas to the growing disaffection of post-60s youth culture, economic decline and the return of mass unemployment. The result was a cultural moment in which the frustration and disgust of working-class youth with royalty, the culture industry and organized politics erupted onto the streets. However, as Plant (1992: 144) notes, the symbols of working-class youth rebellion, such as safety pins, ripped jeans and mohican haircuts, were rapidly recommodified. Punk became assimilated into consumer culture and lost its spontaneity and edge. It became a commodity to be bought and sold in the market place just like any other.

The glamour and value of escape activity makes it an object of investment for entrepreneurs. Leisure activity which begins as a spontaneous attempt to deny social boundaries becomes commodified. Thornton (1995) brings this out clearly in her analysis of how rave culture developed from dance clubs. Raves use unconventional venues such as derelict warehouses, municipal swimming pools and tents in farmers' fields. In principle they operate an 'open door' policy which theoretically maximizes egalitarianism and classlessness. In practice, only those 'in the know' can locate the party. Knowledge is exchanged through a variety of routes. Regular participation in the club scene, which is itself segregated by doormen and bouncers, is one of the central sources of knowledge. Blacks and gays tended to see rave culture as a straight, white activity (Thornton 1995: 56). Indeed, both the dance and rave cultures which Thornton examines maintain an imaginary freedom from the commodity world. Escape experience is centrally organized around music and, to a lesser extent, drug-taking (especially Ecstasy and LSD). These are assimilated as 'leisure goods' involving a complex world of merchandising and cash payment. The commodity form is integral to rave and dance cultures. Of course, the taste cultures organized around these leisure forms are aware that it is money which oils the machinery of their escape activity. But they support the myth of being bracketed from the dominant values of the straight world of consumer culture because it affords opportunities for fantasy work and self-expression which are typically denied in the 'real world' order.

In fact most of the symbols of escape and the escape routines used by taste cultures are usually profoundly unoriginal. Reading the latest novel by Will Self or Martin Amis; listening to the latest

CD by Oasis or the Chemical Brothers; watching the latest movie
by Quentin Tarantino or Martin Scorsese; relishing the latest screen
performance by Johnny Depp, Bridget Fonda, Minnie Driver or
Brad Pitt; following the latest soccer match involving Manchester
United or the latest exploits of the LA Lakers, may seem to be
highly personal experiences. In reality they are mass-produced commodity forms which are ultimately controlled by the leisure industry.
This is not to say that within them there is no room for a wide
variety of experience or that varieties of personal experience are
negated by the commodity form. Rather, I wish to draw attention
to the structured, calculated quality of these escape activities in
commodified culture. They depend upon marketing, packaging and
they involve cash payments for 'objects' of potential experience.

Plant echoes Greil Marcus (1989) in regrading punk to be the
last significant confrontation between the values of the street and
formal culture. The same theme is prominent in the work of Hebdige
(1979; 1987). However, he stresses the links between punk and black
urban working-class music. For Hebdige the crucial opposition in
British postwar culture has been between the values of the black
diaspora and those of the host community. His work prioritizes
colonialism and postcolonialism over class in approaching postwar
culture. For Hebdige, postwar black immigration provided a critical counterpoint to the hegemony of white culture. The point is
that all of the classes in white culture were wrapped up in the
values and assumptions of white hegemony. In this respect, aristocratic beliefs in the immemorial sanctity of the 'Country' and
working-class insistence that 'British is best' are part of the same
system of domination. In Hebdige's view the physical presence of
the black subordinate classes in the major cities of 'the mother
country' exposed the insoluble contradictions of white hegemony.

TASTE CULTURES AND LEISURE

Hebdige's work is already moving towards a position in which questions of distinction and taste no longer automatically invite
considerations of material class background as the starting point
for analysis. Instead it suggests that social distinction is a function
of the capacity to interpret and manipulate cultural codes. While
material circumstances may be a factor in this, they are not the
determining factor. Interestingly, Thornton's (1995) recent study

of the 'taste cultures' generated around rave and acid house dance clubs, emphasizes the *classlessness* of the events. 'It is relatively common,' writes Thornton (1995: 91) 'for upper middle class Londoners to adopt working class accents during their youth and vice versa. However, in pursuit of classlessness, they are still interested in being one step ahead.' Thornton (1995: 163–8) goes on to criticize the focus on 'resistance' and 'hegemony' in the work of Hebdige (op. cit.) and the Birmingham School (Hall and Jefferson 1975; Willis 1978). According to Thornton, this work is faulty because it oversimplifies and overdramatizes cultural relations by positing class struggle as the axis of all cultural life. In contrast, she draws heavily on Bourdieu and the older tradition of the Chicago School to propose that the motor in subcultures is not driven by class opposition but by the assertion of difference through taste cultures. As she (1995: 10) puts it, the discourse of subcultures must be studied

> not as innocent accounts of the way things really are, but as ideologies which fulfil the specific cultural agendas of their beholders. Subcultural ideologies are a means by which youth imagine their own and social groups, assert their distinctive character and affirm that they are not anonymous members of an undifferentiated mass.

Her focus is on youth subcultures, but the principles apply to taste cultures throughout the life-cycle. For Thornton (1995: 163–8) subcultural formation is a reflexive process of representing difference through dress, language, body culture and musical taste. Crucially, it involves an imaginary dimension. Again, following Bourdieu (1984), she argues that subcultures construct 'elaborate scenarios' whereby the practices of other taste culture groups are distinguished from their own real and imagined 'subcultural capital'. Subcultural behaviour is therefore a matter of acting out difference 'as if' the subculture is independent of the rest of society. Thornton avoids the common conflation of subculture with *ethnie*. The 'popular' quality of subcultural values and ritual does not stem from the etymological root of being 'of the people' or from the sense of being 'common' or 'prevalent' in the behaviour of the people. For Thornton it derives from the conscious choices of value made by members of the subculture. This is why she favours the term 'taste cultures' to describe subcultural activities. The term italicizes the omnipresence of reflexivity in the actions of the group. Interestingly, Thornton deals with the question of the influence of the media in the behaviour of taste cultures by insisting that the media is an ingrained, continuous presence in the activities of the group. It is not a question of the media standing 'above' subcultures or 'pushing' them in determinate directions. Rather, the media is an essential component in the material culture of subcultures providing novelty, stimulation, reassurance and, in general, access to cultural data. The judgements that taste cultures make about 'hip', banal, honourable and trash culture correlate with the media's exposure of these forms. The parallel that Thornton draws is with the educational curriculum which also prioritizes some forms of culture and implicitly and explicitly dismisses others. The media operate to set a sort of informal curricula, which taste cultures use to reinforce, negotiate and amend their own cultural judgements. Since media influence is primarily concentrated in leisure time and space, Thornton identifies leisure as a key focus of taste culture practice. It is through relations of leisure that taste cultures formulate a self-image and develop judgements about cultural form and subcultural practice.

Bourdieu and Thornton have been criticized for overstating the freedom of taste cultures to set their agendas. For example, other studies provide good reason for linking some subcultural formations with *ethnie*. Jenkins's (1983) study of working-class youth lifestyles on a Belfast housing estate identified 'common' and 'prevalent' values relating to masculinity, family, honour and respectability which derived from property and correlative social position. Jenkins distinguished between the lifestyles of 'the lads', 'the ordinary kids' and the 'citizens' in order to convey a sense of structurally differentiated lifestyles. His work suggests that a weakness of Thornton's approach is that it over-emphasizes the roots of subcultural formation and differentiation in consumption and leisure tastes and underestimates the effect of property. Davis (1990) makes a similar point in his analysis of gang subcultures in Los Angeles. He (1990: 268–316) argues that the conflict between the two hostile super-gangs, the 'Crips' and the 'Bloods', and the subcultural formations nested within this division, turns on questions of property and territoriality rather than questions of taste. Cultural capital is a vital means through which these questions are articulated and nuanced. But it is not the heart of the matter.

Bourdieu and Thornton are also relatively silent about the influence of corporate capital in structuring the choices made in taste cultures. The idea that taste cultures set the agenda, conflicts with studies of the shaping influence of corporate capitalism through its manipulation of advertising and the mass media (Fiske 1989; Ewen

1988). Thornton's imaginative and useful work, tends to exaggerate the autonomy of taste cultures in setting generative schemes.
Thompson's (1995) work on the media and corporate capitalism
balances the picture by showing the effect of the media in altering
time and space consciousness of individuals beyond their immediate *locales*. To take only one example, Thompson (1995: 168) notes
that in 1989 the Sony Corporation bought Columbia Pictures and
Tristar pictures for $3.4 billion. Sony already own CBS Records,
so their move into film production represented an enlargement of
their influence in the culture industry. Shortly after the Sony takeover,
Matsushita acquired MCA for $6.9 billion. MCA's interests included
Universal film studios, record, publishing and leisure activities.
Matsushita is the leading Japanese producer of domestic electronic
goods. Thompson notes these points in connection with his thesis
that the media exert increasing global influence over individual
practices. But the parallel point to make in connection with the
leisure industry is the concentration of power that these purchases
represent. Sony and Matsushita sit at the centre of webs of control
which include the planning, production, design, marketing and consumption functions. The people who buy Sony Discmans or
Matsushita video recorders also buy CDs and videos produced by
the Sony and Matsushita corporations. All of this points to much
greater levels of corporate control of taste cultures than emerges
from Thornton's account of taste cultures. Thompson's discussion
highlights the significance of corporations in establishing and dis-
seminating taste cultures.

Nonetheless, the emphasis on weaving identities around real and
imaginary forms of difference, which Thornton derives from Bourdieu,
is a very useful way of conceptualizing and studying leisure subcultures. Corporate capitalism is of axial importance in establishing
the context in which taste cultures are generated. But the formation of taste cultures is always a question of the interplay between
consumers and corporations. It can never be merely understood as
a reflection of either consumer taste or corporate manipulation.
Focusing on interplay delivers five analytical advantages.

In the first place, it emphasizes that leisure choices are made for
the purposes of identity distinction. Joining a taste culture or locating
oneself with the 'lads' or 'ordinary kids' on a housing estate, lays
down a marker which distinguishes the individual from the mass.
Joining a taste culture should be interpreted as a conscious attempt
to transform one's given relationship with the rest of society. It

challenges one's assigned social status and provides one with a sense of self-worth. Even joining a neighbourhood gang lays down markers about personal identity and its relation to the immediate and general social context.

Secondly, it emphasizes that taste cultures are primarily organized around leisure forms. It is unsatisfactory to regard taste cultures as the simple expressions of corporate logic. Taste cultures in leisure involve a high degree of reflexive maintenance by actors. References to work are banished from taste cultures. Instead personal identity is focused on the activity in question. The rest of society is bracketed out of consciousness. This reflects the general move away from work towards leisure as the central life interest in society. As Gorz (1982, 1983) and others have argued, in mature consumer cultures 'real life' tends to be identified with non-work experience; and work is practised as a means to achieve the necessary financial resources to maintain oneself and to participate in the non-work spectrum of activity.

Thirdly, the focus on interplay underlines that the fantasies of identity generated and supported in taste cultures are a central source of *pleasure*. There is a potent imaginary quality involved in seeing yourself and the taste culture to which you are attached, separated from the rules of ordinary society. 'Make believe' elements are a vital part of leisure taste cultures because 'make believe' activity provides outlets for capacities and desires which are capped in the rest of life. Hence the enduring popularity of dance clubs, theatre, cinema, television and fiction. It is far easier to engage in make-believe differences which define one's autonomy from the mass, than to take steps to change the character of mass society. In this sense leisure participation in commodity cultures is relatively passive, since it depends heavily on production and design issues already determined by corporate capital. Yet the reflexive capacity of actors prevent them from assuming the conformity proposed in Frankfurt-type analyses of popular culture.

Fourthly, focusing on interplay allows for dynamic, multiple identities in the practice of the individual. To reinterpret Marx's famous statement about communism, one can be a student in the morning, a soccer player in the afternoon and attend a rave in the evening, without any of these identities dominating the others. The approach allows for much higher levels of 'drift' between identities and the reflexive switching of identities in different social contexts than is recognized, by, for example, orthodox Marxist or feminist approaches.

Indeed the narrational space of taste cultures is conceived of as being multidimensional rather than as the expression of 'folk' or gender' cultures.

Fifthly, interplay treats the media as a layer of material culture. Rather than 'standing above' culture as in the Frankfurt-style of analysis, it is regarded as a part of the narrative space through which we make sense of the world. As such it is equivalent to the family, education and the community in accessing information and building identity formation. The media is not something which is 'brought in' to everyday life once the more tangible face-to-face relationships with others have been worked through and negotiated. On the contrary, the media is an immanent resource in face-to-face encounters and in the personal construction of the lifeworld.

Bourdieu and Thornton highlight the capacity of taste cultures to make their own leisure forms. As I have noted, in this respect they are open to criticism since their work gives a false picture of individual and group autonomy. Be that as it may, in their analysis, the people that they study are consciously trying to use leisure to escape from the restrictions of ordinary life while at the same time secretly acknowledging that genuine escape is impossible. For example, the youth groups that Thornton interviews are conscious of both segregating 'ordinary life' from the context of leisure and also that segregation will be compromised once they become too old to fit in with the youth category and start to pay mortgages, develop a career structure and have children (Thornton 1995: 90–91).

Looking beyond the stage of youth in the life-cyle, there is reason to believe that the need to invest some forms of leisure experience with an imaginary break from the rest of life remains constant. Thus, business executives treat a round of golf as an antidote to the cares of work and the responsibilities of family; we go on long week-ends and vacations to 'get away from it all'; in working-class life the pub features as an intimate, relatively secure leisure environment in which private worries can be forgotten for a few hours or shared with others outside the immediate circle of family and work; and the cinema and television provide loopholes from the routine and predictability of everyday life by allowing the audience to vicariously participate in fantasy escape experience. In most cases, imaginary separation from the mundane order does not become an end in itself. The need to experience the contrasting, reassuring tempo of mundanity, the requirement to pay the bills, maintain contact with partners and family and make sure that the place where you live isn't falling down, intrude into the imaginary bracketing of escape experience and ordinary life. For most of us, escape experience is a means of managing the ordinary tasks of maintaining stable relationships and keeping a job (Cohen and Taylor 1993). However, there are categories of actors in bohemian and criminal counter-cultures which adopt the goal of escape as the compass which guides lifestyle.

The point that emerges most unequivocally from the discussion is that most of the popular leisure forms today can be understood more accurately through the prism of culture rather than class analysis. Of course, the significance which we attach to these leisure goods is a consequence of the interplay between global stimuli (through advertising, merchandising and reviews), the character of the local taste cultures in which we are situated and our personal interpretations. Commodity culture is not completely controlled by corporate capitalism, because that would be to deny all autonomy to the consumer. On the other hand, corporate capitalism produces the range of commodities which consumers sift through in making their leisure choices. It also commodifies leisure forms and taste cultures which emerge through life with others. In this sense they structure leisure conduct. Their gross influence over mass communications suggests that corporations have replaced the leisure class as the main trend-setting agent for emulation. Moreover, while resistance to corporate capitalism is an ordinary feature of everyday life, escape activities are subject to surveillance and recommodification. Constructing a viable escape enclave is most easily handled by the richest strata since they have the means to avoid the monitoring processes that regulate behaviour for the rest of us. However, the evidence relating to the leisure practices of the rich does not support the cliché that they are driven by conspicuous consumption and an abhorrence for pecuniary labour. A generational element evidently comes into play. The three millionaires studied in this chapter, Bill Gates, Warren Buffett and Richard Branson, made their money themselves. The practices of self-discipline and ascetisim which I identified in their leisure may not be transferred to their children. Even so, these are men who do not need to work and who can live the rest of their lives in a condition of pure hedonism. Yet all three elect to work regular long hours and to devote themselves to business. The British Royal family is also conditioned to engage in public works rather than simply to remain idle. To be clear, I am not denying that the lifestyles of these individuals are ostentatious or that conspicuous consumption plays no part in their existence. Royal palaces, Richard Branson's homes in Notting Hill and his holiday retreats in the Caribbean, Bill Gates's house of the future and Warren Buffett's personal jet plane are luxuries that nearly everyone reading this book will see as representing an almost unimaginable lifestyle. However, this does not legitimate Veblen's view that the rich devote themselves to chronic conspicuous consumption. The habits of asceticism and work discipline which are drilled into the rest of us through the socialization process also encompass them. The feelings of guilt and worthlessness when there is no work are also shared by the wealthy. The objects of desire which they covet are the same objects that we covet. The argument suggests that Veblen was wrong to identify class as the most significant context in which to situate the study of leisure. Commodity culture and taste cultures of resistance played a more important part than he recognized. The next chapter aims to go deeper into the subject of the relationship between culture and leisure desire, practice and resistance.

3 The Cultural Context of Leisure Practice

The debate in the study of leisure about the proper context in which to locate leisure practice continues. In the postwar period there have been three moments, or phases, in which different competing claims have expressed themselves strongly. In the 1950s and 60s, as the study of leisure began to be established in the university system, and the professionalization of leisure services began to develop quite rapidly, the functionalist model was ascendant. This reflected the position in sociology where functionalist theories and propositions set the tone of the discussion. Functionalism in leisure studies began with the concept of the free individual, and attributed choice in leisure practice to individual determination. The arena of leisure policy was identified with the nation-state. Transnational and global relations were undertheorized. The object of policy was to maximize the freedom and choices available to individuals while maintaining social and political order in the nation-state. Governments and leisure planners saw leisure as the reward for work and a mechanism for increasing social integration. Funds were allocated to parks and recreation departments and public and voluntary cultural agencies, with the object of maintaing and, wherever possible, enhancing the quality of leisure.

After the mid-1960s, with the rise of counter-cultures, functionalism came under a period of sustained attack. Public and voluntary leisure provision was castigated as a method of social control. Individual freedom and choice were denigrated as treacherous concepts, since they ignored the structural dimensions of social action. Where the system demanded paid labour, the restriction of women's participation in the labour market and the oppression of ethnic rights as conditions for its survival, the questions of freedom and choice were seen as highly problematic. The emphasis switched from system maintenance to creating a social order in which human capacities could be fully expressed. Initially, counter-cultures confined their ambitions to changing conditions in the nation-state. However, it was soon argued that changing the nation-state was beside the point. For nation-states are part of wider systems of power. The Cold

War, environmental risks, economic destabilization all pointed to the need for a wider canvas in which critical policy must operate. Increasingly, the focus of criticism moved from the nation-state to global capitalism and 'the West'.

The counter-cultures constituted an amorphous web of activity which was loosely attached to a broadly conceived liberationist politics. They emerged from the combination of economic affluence which enlarged the service, communication and knowledge sectors of society, the baby boom of the postwar years which levered an expansion in the university system and a growing disquiet with the inevitable limitations of nation-state management. One of the leading figures in the counter-cultures, Timothy Leary (1990: 252–3), expressed the essential structural conditions well:

> For the first time in our history a large and influential sector of the populace was coming to disrespect institutional authority, not as members of organized dissident groups but as intelligent individuals, highly selective political consumers who demanded responsive and effective leadership, which no exisiting party, no religion, no labour union seemed able to provide. Thus a conflict between the old industrial society and the new information society was to be played out in the new arena of power – the media. Those who understood this would create the future.

Leary's identification of the media as the new crux of cultural and political power is revealing. The communications revolution enlarged people's imaginations by providing them with a richer diet of news and entertainment. It also overdramatized political and cultural relations and overstimulated ambitions of collective transformation. Spontaneity and being at the centre of the action were crucial to the self-image of the counter-cultures. However, politics and culture soon became an extension of the movie set or television studio, with gesture and impression-management taking precedence over the planning and administration that was required for successful oppositional politics based in effective solidarity. Leary himself resorted to the clichés of the movie business to drive home his liberationist message. As he (1990: 257) famously declared to a radical meeting in the Santa Monica Civic Auditorium in the summer of 1966:

> Turn On, Tune In and Drop Out. Now's the time to flick on the inner switch to full power! Listen, you'll either spend the rest of

your life as a badly paid extra in someone else's low-budget black-and-white documentary/training film. OR. You become the producer of your own movie. Direct it, script it, cast it, choose the locations for the greatest reality flick ever made. Why settle for less?

Looking back, it is easy to deride many aspects of counter-cultural criticism. Jerry Rubin's advice to kids to kill their parents, Leary's ill-conceived efforts to form an alliance with the Black Panthers, the inflated championing of psychedelic experience and drug culture, Abbie Hoffman's efforts to levitate the White House through an act of collective meditation, all seems decidedly cranky from the perspective of the post-Thatcher–Reagan years.

In the UK, the anti-psychiatrist R.D. Laing, emerged as a leading figure of the counter-culture. Laing was a powerful critic of the irrationality of the modern nation-state. He argued that madness should be seen as a realistic response to dehumanizing social structures. He also advocated a liberationist overturning of the system. He based his ideas on his clinical observation. In the ferment of counter-cultural radicalism it was a short step to regard the mentally ill as the worst victims of the capitalist police state and the family as the root of cultural malaise. In a speech delivered to the Congress on the Dialectics of Liberation delivered in 1967 to an audience at the Roundhouse in London's Chalk Farm, Laing (1968: 27) declared:

> The *normal* way parents get their children to love them is to terrorize them, to say to them in effect: 'Because I am not dropping you, because I am not killing you, this shows that I love you, and therefore you should come for the assuagement of your terror to the person who is generating the terror that you are seeking to have assuaged' (emphasis in the original).

To an audience of baby-boomers who had no children yet, and older middle-class liberals who feared for the future, the references to terror and killing must have been multiply resonant. After all, this was the era of the Vietnam war in which the exhaustion of nation-state politics was thrown into stark relief by the American programme of napalm bombing. However, Laing's words now read as unjustified and irresponsible hyperbole. Not unreasonably, the same complaint can be made about much of the written output of the counter-cultures (Carmichael 1968; Cooper 1974).

Yet to remember the counter-cultures only with derision is to give a false and one-sided picture of their social consequences. Together with the New Left, who had their roots in the oppositional socialist and beat cultures of the 1950s, they created a phalanx of agitation and criticism which undoubtedly expedited the retreat of American military forces from Vietnam. This was perhaps their most concrete achievement. The other actions and consequences are harder to specify because they refer to what might be called different ways of being. The communes, housing collectives, health groups, auto repair and carpentry collectives, alternative publishers and women's groups that emerged in the 1960s changed the relationship between the individual and the state. In the 1950s, sociologists spoke of 'mass society' and 'mass culture'. Governments managed 'the people' through a system of hierarchical negotiations with organizations which nominally represented the masses, most notably the trade unions and private and voluntary sector associations. The counter-cultures transformed this by dramatically exposing the striated character of society and culture. They showed that the masses could no longer be conceptualized as a homologous collection of people with broadly the same interests, wealth and potential. Instead society and culture had to be reconceptualized as a collection of cluster formations with ambiguous, changing alliances and goals. In a sense, the counter-cultures were the catalyst between the transition from mass society organized around classes to critical pluralism organized around the identity politics of today. This is not to imply that classes cease to be important in economic, political and cultural life. The New Left played a pivotal role in the cultural criticism of the 1960s. In Britain, the *New Left Review*, which involved Robin Blackburn, Perry Anderson, Stuart Hall and a variety of other charismatic left-wing intellectuals, acted as a mouthpiece of left-wing radicalism.

Hall acted as the vital catalyst in filtering New Left thinking through to leisure studies.[1] Through his Directorship of the Centre for Contemporary Cultural Studies in Birmingham University, he developed a wide-ranging and sophisticated analysis of British culture. Hall was perhaps most influential as a theoretician. However, he also participated in important studies on youth cultures (Hall and Jefferson 1975), policing (Hall *et al.* 1978) and media and culture (Hall *et al.* 1980). The ideas of the Marxist philosophers, Gramsci and Althusser, formed the intellectual matrix for the work in Birmingham. The Centre's importance to the study of leisure was twofold. First of all, it examined the ways of life of working-class people as significant cultural expressions. Up until the 1960s, the

study of culture was shot through with elitist assumptions relating
to high and low culture which derived from the work of Arnold
(1869), Ruskin (1903–12), and T.S. Eliot (1948). The Centre was
instrumental in breaking this mould. Hall and his associates launched
a series of research projects and discussion groups which examined
urban working-class culture, youth cultures, race relations, policing
and culture and the media. By turning the spotlight on popular
culture they inevitably led to the question of the character of popular
leisure. Clarke and Critcher's (1985) analysis of leisure in Britain
clearly bore the stamp of the Centre's theoretical position.

The second important effect of the Centre on Leisure Studies
was to produce a stream of graduates who developed research into
popular culture and leisure. Their number included Paul Willis,
whose studies of working-class schooling (1977), motor bike and
hippy cultures (1978) and youth cultures in Wolverhampton (Willis
(1990b) provide a rich ethnographic inventory of non-work activity
in the working class; John Hargreaves (1986) who examined sport
in Britain; Dick Hebdige (1979, 1987) who investigated youth subcultures and music; Tony Bennett (1986) who provided an early
Gramscian reading of tourist space; Angela McRobbie (1978, 1994)
who worked on popular media for girls, fashion and feminist cultural
theory; and Larry Grossberg (1983, 1984, 1986) who investigated
the cultural consequences of Cultural Studies and rock music.

Leaving aside Clarke and Critcher (1985), who wrote the most
systematic application of the Centre's approach to leisure, the
Centre's research agenda and theoretical assumptions are evident
in much critical work in leisure studies in the 1980s and early 90s
(see Wimbush and Talbot 1988; Green *et al.* 1987; Tomlinson 1989,
1990; Henry 1993). The Gramscian/CCCS approach provided the
first important critical counterpoint to the functionalist tradition
in leisure studies and leisure policy. From the late 1970s to the
late 80s, its members organized a series of discussion groups, conferences and publications which attacked capitalist hegemony and
functionalist analysis. This coincided with the expansion of leisure
studies degree courses and the growth of leisure as a module option
in sociology and cultural studies courses. The institutional context
of expansion was important in spreading the influence of this
approach throughout the field of leisure. Yet by the mid-1980s, there
were already cracks in the Gramscian/CCCS ascendancy. Feminist
writers, like Deem (1986) and Wimbush and Talbot (1988), were
clearly sympathetic to some aspects of Gramscian/CCCS theory and

research. However, they also criticized the 'male-stream' of assumptions and ideas which they detected in both the functionalist and Gramscian/CCCS traditions. As we will see presently, feminism emerged as the third 'moment' in postwar leisure studies. What other cracks existed in the Gramscian/CCCS ascendancy? For one thing, the tone of arguing and the peremptory dismissal of other 'bourgeois' positions, were reminiscent of many of the worst aspects of counter-culturalism. For example, Clarke and Critcher's (1985) refutation of functionalism perpetuated caricatures of the writings of functionalists like Parker (1983) and Roberts (1978, 1981), which exaggerated the 'break' offered by Gramscian/CCCS theory. Tomlinson (1990) did the same with ill-considered jibes and groundless speculation about a 'Leicester–Glasgow axis' in respect of figurational sociology. The advocates of the Gramscian/CCCS position in leisure studies seemed to approach other competing positions in the field, except feminism, with open hostility. The exception was interesting because while feminism undoubtedly constituted a rising perspective in leisure studies, it did not obviously fit with the class-based analysis of the Gramscian/CCCS school. Brundson (1996) reveals something of the tensions by emphasizing the *pluralisms* within the study of culture which cannot be reconciled by positing a neat equation between class and patriarchy. She is also extremely critical of Stuart Hall. She (1996: 279) recalls Hall's 'profoundly shocking' description of feminism in the Centre which he (1992: 282) uttered at a conference in the USA as 'the thief in the night (which) broke in; interrupted, made an unseemly noise, seized the time, crapped on the table of cultural studies'. Not unreasonably, Brundson uses this to air some reservations about the genuine openness of the 'malestream' to feminist thought.

Harris (1992) has also pointed to difficulties with the form of analysis developed in the Gramscian/CCCS tradition. In particular, he (1992: 152) refers to the 'evasiveness' and 'circularity' of many of the arguments and the 'self-confirming' character of the concept of hegemony. Harris (1992: 152) writes:

In skilled hands, any activity which looks as if it reveals choice, or autonomy, or political innocence, for example, is liable to be reinterpreted by some underlying articulation to show that its very autonomy is a source of its usefulness in hegemonic unity. Hegemonic cultures can reveal traces of dominant and subordinate cultures, united by either alliance or struggle, wither in some sort of temporary equilibrium or in an immanent state of disequilibrium; pretty well everything can be explained by the term hegemony.

The criticism is particularly apposite in respect of Clarke and Critcher's (1985) discussion of leisure in Britain. Confusingly, they see leisure as both a way of changing and reinforcing capitalist hegemony. There is a lack of specificity about their argument. In part, this is general and intrinsic to the field. Leisure activity is both reinforcing and critical of existing ways of being and rules of conduct. The problem with the Gramscian/CCCS tradition is that in insisting on the contested, conditional nature of hegemony it provides no way of predicting changes, so that actual change either comes as a surprise or is assimilated retrospectively as 'wisdom after the event'. This is particularly evident in Hall's controversial 'new times' thesis (Hall and Jacques 1989). The thesis appeared to embrace many aspects of postmodernism and therefore constituted a major 'slippage' from Hall's earlier work which kept faith with a neo-Marxist programme of theory and change. There have, to date, been no major works in leisure studies which attempt to apply Hall's more recent work on post-colonialism and hybridity. However, in the field of cultural studies these developments in Hall's thinking are widely interpreted as evidence of more slippage in the basic programme of research (McGuigan 1992; 1996; Storey 1995). Hall's insistence on producing relevant theoretical work for the problems of the times, leaves him open to the charge of being too fashionable in his intellectual concerns. Certainly, the constant extensions and tunnellings in his work over the years make it very hard to know what he is actually saying. Elsewhere, I (1998) compared Hall to a master-builder who, over time, added so many rooms and dividing doors to his house that he can no longer find his way around the premises. While this is not yet true of the Gramscian/CCCS 'diaspora' in Leisure Studies, who have remained wedded to the central task of welding class analysis and feminism together, adding on the latest innovations from 'post-colonialism' and 'hybridity theory' is a logical next step. If they do this they will find that the conceptual clarity of their analysis of leisure is fatally compromised. For the concept of hybridity inevitably produces an analytical ambivalence and relativism that is not present in class analysis. The question of ambivalence and relativism is certainly frequently raised now in connection with Hall's recent work.

The influence of feminism in Leisure Studies dates from the mid-1980s. In Britain the main figures are Deem (1986), Talbot (1988), Scraton (1993) and Green, Hebron and Woodward (1987). In North America Henderson *et al.* (1989, 1996) and Shaw (1985, 1994) have produced influential work; while the best overall assessment of the feminist leisure studies is to be found in Wearing (1998).

The main achievements of feminism have been to pinpoint the links between the domestic division of labour and the general division of labour; to expose male control of public leisure space; to examine how patriarchy represses women through the family, education, the media and popular culture. This has reversed the position of two decades ago when feminism was marginalized in the study of leisure. In Britain the two main leisure studies training centres, in Leeds Metropolitan University and North London University, clearly demonstrate the influence of feminist ideas. Similarly, the main British journal in the field, *Leisure Studies*, includes prominent feminist representatives on the editorial board.[2] In 1988 Wimbush and Talbot (1988: 177) complained that women had been dismissed as 'extraneous noise' by the functionalist tradition. That claim is no longer sustainable. As Wearing (1998) demonstrates, feminism is central to the field of Leisure Studies. It would be going too far to claim that it has eliminated sexism and prejudicial beliefs against women. However, there can be no doubt that any study or policy in the field of leisure which fails to take account of women's experience and needs will leave itself open to criticism on grounds of relevance and value.

Having said that, the particular trajectory that feminism has taken in Leisure Studies is not without difficulties. Dialogue with men and with other women who criticize some aspects of feminism, remains more elusive than elsewhere in the social sciences. Feminism in leisure studies has adopted a permanent seige mentality and too often presented women automatically as victims. The feminist case is driven by an evangelical crusade against 'male power'. Criticisms of any kind from men or other women, tend to be automatically branded as 'swipes', so debates tend to get bogged down in defensive counter-retractions rather than productive exchange (Aitchison 1996).

One aspect of siege mentality is the auto-rejection of new positions in social theory which hint at 'post-feminism'.[3] These positons derive from poststructuralism and postmodernism. Aside from Wearing (1998), I know of no approach in feminist leisure studies that has sought to think through the implications of these positions for feminist work in the field. The position is strikingly incongruous with the rest of social science where poststructuralist and postmodernist ideas have been sifted and, wherever possible, integrated, into the feminist tradition. Writers like Ann Game (1991), Elizabeth Grosz and Elspeth Probyn (1995), Judith Butler (1993), Nancy Fraser (1989) and Donna Haraway (1991) are all recognizably feminist, without being stuck in a 1970s problematic of 'liberating the collective subject'. The latter problematic remains the dominant one in leisure studies. It is evident in the work and political interventions of Talbot, Deem, Scraton, Brackenridge, Green, Hebron, Woodward, Bialeschki and Henderson. Besides hindering dialogue, it produces a high degree of repetition in argument, as is perhaps most evident in the recent writings of Henderson *et al.* (1989, 1996).

The 'circularity' and 'self-confirming' characteristics which Harris (1992) identified in respect of the Gramscian/CCCS position is also evident in feminist leisure studies. For men, or other women, to present these criticisms is to invite the counter-criticism that they exemplify the intolerance and insensitivity to women that is typical of patriarchal culture. All that one can say in response to this is that the debate elsewhere in the social sciences has gone beyond this level of defensiveness. One hopes for the same in the feminist study of leisure. Certainly, in terms of the realized and potential contributions to the field it goes beyond the Gramscian/CCCS tradition. However, the potential will only be achieved if it reaches out positively to the genuinely creative work on identity, the body, technoculture, citizenship, rights, work and social and cultural theory and loosens its seige mentality. Criticizing feminism is not the same as being unsympathetic to feminist argument.

CULTURE MATTERS

Interestingly, the three moments in the study of leisure all treat the concept of culture in unsatisfactory ways. In the functionalist tradition, culture is the mere neutral, 'life-stuff' which individuals use to exercise choice and self-determination in leisure. Functionalists differentiate between high and low culture and to that extent, hold an evaluative position. Functionalist strategy in policy in leisure can be read as pruning the worst features of low culture through appropriate public investment in sports, parks, the arts and the countryside. This is to treat culture as a dependent variable of society which is amenable to rational thought and action. It does not offer a self-reflexive treatment of culture. It is therefore open to the criticism that it reproduces cultural bias because it treats market, patriarchal, class-based culture in normative terms.

For their part, both the Gramscian/CCCS and feminist positions in leisure studies are more sensitive to cultural considerations. Indeed, the Birmingham School appears to predicate its entire programme of enquiry in the concept. However this is deceptive. Culture is given little autonomy in the Birmingham School literature because it is viewed as the reflection of hegemony which depends ultimately upon class struggle. Analogously, feminism treats culture as the reflection of patriarchy. Of course, feminism produces cultures which struggle against the rule of hegemonic force, but patriarchy precedes culture in the feminist scheme of things.

None of this should be surprising. In fact, the differences between the three positions match the general treatment of culture in Western thought. Eco (1994) has helpfully divided Western interpretations of culture into three main categories: aesthetical, ethical and anthropological:

Culture 1 compares culture with science, politics, economics and work. It privileges the formation of aesthetic taste according to the standards of the dominant class. Culture is associated with distinction. The aesthetic version rotates around a strong division between high and low culture. However, the division is primarily expressed in terms of taste. It follows that what has low cultural value at one point, may possess high cultural value at another point in time. Epistemology is interpreted as a feature of taste cultures.

Culture 2 also reproduces the divisions between high and low culture. However, it primarily expresses them in terms of intrinsic superiority. The 'cultured person' is a person who is better in terms of knowledge, skills, language and appreciation. The cultured person is, in short, a better person. The ethical view demands a certain detachment from everday life. One cannot cultivate culture in the midst of the staple transactions of mundane reality. For this reason, Eco argues that the aesthetic idea of culture entails a degree of idleness as a necessary condition for cultural growth.

Culture 3 is the anthropological attempt to invest objectivity and value neutrality into the concept. As Eco (1994: 119) puts it:

It comprises the complex of institutions, myths, rites, laws, beliefs, codified everyday behaviour, value systems and material techniques elaborated by a group of humans.

The anthropological position is associated with a high degree of tolerance and relativism. For other cultures are not viewed as superior or inferior, but as merely involving different complexes of myths, rites, laws and so forth.

The proposition that I want to develop here is that there never has been an anthropological version of culture in leisure studies. The main positions in the field have adhered to a mixture of aesthetic and ethical judgements about the relation of culture to leisure. The three main positions have treated culture either as a dependent variable of individual choice or as a reflection of class and patriarchy. They propose that culture proceeds either from the actions of individuals or the structural influence of class or patriarchy. My proposition is that exactly the opposite is the case. Culture, in the anthropological sense described by Eco, precedes individuals, class and patriarchy.

There has been a long tradition in sociology and philosophy which stresses the ambivalence of meaning and the mobility of attachments. It includes the work of Simmel, Schutz, Goffman, Rorty, McIntyre, Kristeva, Eco, Bauman and Levinas. Regardless of the important differences which separate these writers, all follow the idea that there can be no privileged reading of culture because culture is an 'open work', constantly developing and constantly requiring new ways of conception and interpretation. Implicitly, this approach is critical of the 'univocal' readings of leisure found in functionalist, neo-Marxist and feminist approaches.

Following Eco (1990), culture may be usefully thought of as conforming to Peirce's notion of 'unlimited semiosis'. That is, cultural signs have no essential meaning. Their meaning is only intelligible in relation to other signs. Since these relations are not fixed, no privileged reading or intepretation is possible. However, as Eco (1990) insists, one can speak of 'limits to interpretation' and preferred interpretations. In semiotics, these limits and preferences are defined by correctly locating the meaning of a sign in relation to other signs in the sign system. This requires a close interpretation of the place of the sign in the immediate sign economy. Hence, the emphasis in Eco's work on encoding and decoding techniques.

I am not about to embark upon a semiotic analysis of leisure. My concern here, is to pursue the collateral line of analysis which Eco (1990) argues is essential in providing an accurate reading of signs. That is, to examine the cultural context in which leisure is situated. Basic to my enterprise is the hypothesis that culture precedes patriarchy and class in the organization of behaviour. This is not the general view in either leisure studies or cultural studies. Whether it be expressed from the functionalist, neo-Marxist or feminist camps, the general view is that the *Homo Faber* model is the starting point for enquiry. Culture, as it were, is read off from what is taken to be the primordial need to work. It is this need that is regarded as the ultimate seat of human motivation and, from a more critical standpoint, it is the need to work which promotes property relationships which are the ultimate basis for class and sexual exploitation. Despite the recent interest in postmodernity and reflexivity in the organization of everyday life, the *Homo Faber* model remains dominant in cultural and leisure studies. So essential is it to the study of leisure that many researchers assume that leisure has no meaning except in relation to work. My argument is that what researchers have taken to be a primordial need, is, in fact, an historically specific expression. Human culture did not begin with the need to work, it began with language, dancing, laughing, acting, mimicking, ritual and a variety of play forms. The argument supports the position of Huizinga (1947), Bakhtin (1968) and Mumford (1967, 1970) that play rather than work is the formative element in human culture.

This argument has deep consequences for the study of leisure. So before attempting to set it out in more detail, let me briefly run through the main consequences. The proposition that play is the basis of culture challenges the dominant assumption that self-discovery and self-transformation are accomplished through work. Sayers (1987) and others have argued that leisure is a problem in contemporary society. For many people, it is unfulfilling and meaningless. In addition, it is suggested that people do not have the education to know how to use their free time to best effect. The solution is to 'get people back to meaningful work'. Sayers (1987) notes approvingly that this is also the solution offered by the trade union movement and implies that this is the most realistic route to provide meaningful leisure. Similarly, Stebbins's (1992, 1997) work on 'serious leisure' demonstrates the organic benefits to the individual and community of leisure activity which is rooted in the concept of a career and self-development. These concepts derive from the sociology of work and Stebbins applies them to the sphere of leisure in ingenious and interesting ways. Nonetheless, by emphasizing their importance he reinforces the work-centred *Homo Faber* model. This is evident above all, in his (1993) view that distraction activity, or 'non-serious', leisure is morally inferior to serious leisure. Stebbins's view is that worthwhile, 'serious' leisure involves the harnessing of individual capacities to trained and measurable outcomes that add value to the individual and the culture by developing a sense of career in the individual and progress in the community. I think that this misunderstands the meaning of the culture of leisure and also misreads what is happening in industrial culture today. The logic of Stebbins's position is that society should aim at a condition of full employment and further, that resources should be switched to promoting serious leisure, either through central, federal or voluntary mechanisms. It is the 'back to work' argument all over again. The difficulty with it is that the emerging pattern of work in industrial culture is not moving in that direction. Post-Fordist work regimes are moving in three simultaneous directions:

1) *The transfer of manufacturing industry from the core to the periphery.* The de-industrialization of cities, and the concomitant strain on community life and leisure relations, have become familiar themes in the sociology of industrial life. The rust belt of Middle and North-eastern America stretching from Detroit to Pittsburgh, and the collapse of traditional manufacturing industries like shipbuilding, heavy engineering and textiles in the UK, are evidence of the evacuation of manufacturing jobs from the heartlands of Western capitalism to the newly emerging, low-wage, low-cost economies of South East Asia. Pahl (1995: 192) estimates that no more than 15–16 per cent of manual workers are now employed in manufacturing industry. In Britain more people are now employed in television and film than in the automobile industry. Old work has not been replaced by new work. Communities organized around traditional industries have suffered an absolute decline in the labour market.

2) *The increasing market significance of a flexible workforce.* Lash and Urry (1994) note that post-Fordism involves greater volatility in consumer preferences; increased market segmentation; the

development of new products, each of which has a shorter shelf-life; and a shift to non-mass forms of consumption. These requirements make the notions of a 'mass labour force' and 'a job for life' redundant. The individuals who are most likely to get jobs today offer flexibility in their skills and a high degree of adaptability.

3) *The feminization of work.* One of the most tangible effects of the feminist movement has been to increase the number of women working in paid jobs. The development in the postwar period is dramatic. Hochschild (1997: 6) reports official US statistics which show that in 1950, 12.6 per cent of married mothers with children under 17 worked for pay, by 1994, 69 per cent did so; and 58.8 per cent of wives with children under the age of one or younger were in the workforce. A similar trend is evident in Western Europe (Finch and Mason 1993). However, British research cautions against the conventional feminist view that this expansion has been concentrated in part-time work. Buck *et al.* (1994) provides evidence to demonstrate that women often have multiple employment statuses in a calendar year, from part-time to full-time, or from self-employment to employment, or between employment and unemployment. This supports the proposition that work patterns in the economy as a whole are becoming more flexible. It also, of course, carries, the corollary that work experience for women, as with men, is increasingly 'discontinuous' and irregular. Yet because of the weaker position of women in the labour market, they are likely to suffer the worst effects of these conditions.

Employment policies in Western Europe and North America have, on the whole, rejected the 'back to work' demands of the trade union movement. Instead, they have sought to take practical measures to habituate the workforce to the new conditions of flexibility, discontinuity and irregularity. These have involved retraining programmes and encouraging relocation. The decision of many governments in the West to encourage workers to contract out of state pension schemes into private arrangements, looks like a tacit admission that the Western economy is unable to deliver full employment for the foreseeable future. The trend is to throw people back upon their own resources and, in the case of right-wing governments, to present this move as a 'liberation' from the 'nanny state'.

There may be rhetorical value in appealing to full employment as an ideal standard, but there seems little reason to believe that it can be achieved in the foreseeable future. The West seems set on a course between the discontinuous and irregular labour patterns of the majority and Schor's (1992) 'overworked worker' which applies to a minority, albeit a sizeable minority.

It is timely then, to consider the limitations of the *Homo Faber* model especially from the point of view of its evasions with regard to the balanced use of time and the place of leisure in healthy lifestyle. In this, I will rely primarily on the work of Lewis Mumford. The strange neglect that Mumford has endured in sociology, let alone the sociology of culture and leisure, is surely a comment on the astounding breadth of his interests. Like his mentor, Patrick Geddes, Mumford decided at an early age to become a generalist. It was a decision that allowed him to stray over the course of a long life between studies of the American photographer Alfred Stieglitz, Herman Melville, the condition of architecture, the value of aesthetics, urban planning, the history of cities, the shape of utopia, the consequences of technology and the fate of civilization. But it left sociology, and the Academy as a whole, mystified as to how and where to categorize him. Mumford was a considerable thinker. His work on technics, civilization and play suggests a new way of conceptualizing culture.

For Mumford, play, not work, is the key to human development. It is a view that he shares with the Dutch hisorian, Huizinga (1947). Yet Mumford went much further in substantiating the hypothesis by recourse to detailed historical analysis of civilizational change. While he did not choose to pursue the consequences of his hypothesis for understanding leisure, those consequences are compelling and I will try to draw them out in what follows.

TECHNICS, CIVILIZATION AND LEISURE

Mumford (1967: 9) begins by rejecting the *Homo Faber* model of civilization. He (1967: 9–10) rationalizes his position in a preliminary way, thus:

> The evolution of language – a culmination of man's more el-
> ementary forms of expression and transmitting meaning – was
> incomparably more important to further human development than

the chipping of a mountain of hand-axes. Besides the relatively simple coordinations required for tool-using, the delicate interplay of the many organs needed for the creation of articulate speech was a far more striking advance ... spoken language was infinitely more complex and sophisticated at the dawn of civilization than the Egyptian and Mesopotamian kit of tools. To consider man, then, as primarily a tool-using animal is to overlook the main chapters of human history. Opposed to this petrified notion, I shall develop the view that man is pre-eminently a mind-making, self-mastering, and self-designing animal; and the primary locus of all his activities lies first in his own organism, and in the social organization through which it finds fuller expression. Until man had made something of himself he could make little of the world around him.

Leaving aside the sexist use of the term 'man' – one should note perhaps that Mumford was born in 1895 and in this respect was a male of his times – Mumford is claiming that the origins of civilization lie in the symbolic and communicative capacities of human beings and not in their tool-making abilities. Indeed, the capacity to create tools for work is treated as a subsidiary feature of human development. Long before the turn towards the body in sociology, which one can trace roughly to the 1980s and especially Bryan Turner's (1984) influential book, Mumford was arguing that the 'primary locus' of human activity is one's 'own organism'. In making these claims, Mumford does not intend to disparage the significance of technology in human development. On the contrary he (1967: 9) recognizes that 'technics' 'supported' and 'enlarged' the capacities for human expression. Like Bachelard (1968) and Goudsblom (1992) he recognizes the importance of technically controlling fire in the development of civilization. However, and this is crucial, Mumford conceives technics as being secondary to the primary influences of self-consciousness and communicative capacity. Language is the key. It enables humans to treat their self-consciousness as an object and to transmit their thought and learning to others. Language stops life from being experienced as a private universe and enables private experience to be shared and stored in collective traditions. To put it concisely, language makes culture possible.

Mumford's use of archaeological and anthropological evidence is necessarily speculative. His canvas is the origin of the human

species and the role of culture in human development. Doubtless
he can be accused of drawing insupportable inferences and making
faulty deductions in many details of his argument. Yet the general
argument is utterly compelling. Mumford proposes that the neural
capacity of *Homo sapiens* reached its present size and composition
some 50 000 to 100 000 years ago. Consciousness was a characteristic of the primordial nomad, but thousands of years passed before
the current of thoughts, dreams and fancies passing through the
brains of *Homo sapiens* was harnessed in symbols and words that
could be communicated with others. Once this happened, the rate
of human development accelerated. Culture, Mumford proposes,
nourished the brain.

In pondering how language develops Mumford is perhaps at his
most speculative. He (1967: 48–65) traces language back to dreams.
The dreamlife of primitive nomad furnishes them with images and
creative impulses. 'From the dream,' writes Mumford (1967: 54),
'man got his first hint that there is more to his experience than
meets his eye: that there exists an unseen world veiled from his
senses and his daily experiences, as real as the food he eats or the
hand he grasps.' Culture satisfies the incessant energy of the brain
by acting as an arena for the expression of ideas. Yet precisely
because human development became so rapid and volatile after
the development of language, it is also necessary for culture to
perform a soothing, containing function. Ritual is the cultural expression of this soothing function. It established regularity and
predictability in the expanding world of *Homo sapiens*. The repeated
rite gave security to human existence. Tribal rituals revolved around
play forms such as dance, music and drugs. They formed the social
cement necessary for the re-enactment of group life. Eliade (1957),
Sahlins (1985) and other anthropologists have described the connections between repetitive rites and the elaboration of the realm
of the sacred. Mumford (1967: 64–9) painted a similar picture. He
proposed that rituals acted as an essential component in renewing
tribal cosmology. He also recognized the obstructive effect of ritual
in limiting the application of intelligence and corking innovation
and change.

Mumford's discussion of the transition from tribal society to
kingship is complex and the details are not strictly relevant to his
conception of *Homo ludens*. Expressed strategically, the crux of the
story he tells is the increasing centralization of power in fewer and
fewer hands. Tribal warriors grabbed more and more territory through

gaining victory in battle and power gradually became concentrated in kingships. Mumford's account parallels Elias's (1978; 1982) discussion of the emergence of the monopoly mechanism in Europe which describes how kings slowly emerged through competitive struggles with others to control the legtimate use of physical force and taxation. Yet in accounting for the rise of kingship, Mumford assigns greater significance to the alliance between tribute-exacting hunting chieftans and religious leaders. Without this alliance, argues Mumford (1967: 170), the King's line of ascendancy to God or a group of gods could not have been legitimated. The important point to make is that physical force by itself was not sufficient, it required the supernatural authority vested in kings by religious figures in the tribe to make kingship secure.

Mumford's account of the social consequences of kingship echo many aspects of Veblen's (1899) description of the leisure class. Thus, Mumford (1967: 213) holds that the rise of kingship divided civilization into two main classes: a majority who must work for their immediate and communal needs and a 'noble' minority who denigrated manual and pecuniary labour and devoted themselves to ostentatious consumption. If anything, Mumford (1967: 206) is more dismissive than Veblen of the wasteful practices of the nobility:

> in times of peace, kings and nobles lived by the pleasure principle: eating, drinking, hunting, playing games, copulating, all in ostentatious excess . . . The boredom of satiety dogged this economy of surplus power and surplus goods from the very beginning: it led to insensate personal luxury and ever more insensate acts of collective delinquency and destruction. Both were means of establishing the superior status of the ruling minority, whose desires knew no limits and whose very crimes turned into Nietzschean virtues.

Veblen's discussion of the leisure class focuses particularly on the psychological addiction of the lower orders to conspicuous consumption. Mumford differs by considering the effects of the leisure class in the area of performativity rather than consumption. He (1967: 226) argues that psychologically balanced people do not engage in fantasies of absolute power or seek pleasure through risk-taking activity. The weakness of industrial civilization is that it is chronically over-regimented. Over-regimentation does not produce psychologically balanced and healthy individuals. The rigid division of labour and the establishment of segregated status hierarchies 'produce nbalanced characters, while the mechanical routine normalizes – and rewards – those compulsive personalities who are afraid to cope with the embarrassing riches of life.'

Mumford's dismay at the prevailing psychology of modern life stemmed from his belief that economic and emotional relations were becoming increasingly mechanized. Mechanization is the presiding metaphor for his critical account of industrial civilization. The human machine of specialized labourers which the Pharaohs developed to erect the pyramids at Giza, provided the pretext for the engines of steam and electricity which eventually powered the Industrial Revolution. The pyramids were built by labour-intensive means, the Industrial Revolution sought labour-saving means through the transformation of human labour into mechanical power. For Mumford, in both cases the effects were the same. The inflexible, dictatorial structures of Ancient Egyptian society are mirrored in the over-regimented, hierarchical structures of the industrial age. People are imprisoned in both systems in narrow and ultimately unfulfilling and self-mutilating tasks. The rise of *Homo Faber* fetishizes technics as the engine of progress. Technics breaks free from culture. There is no doubt that Mumford regards this to be a calamity for civilization. He contrasts the degraded stage of industrial culture, in which technics plays a free-loading role in driving human endeavours, with the condition of culture in Ancient Greece. As Mumford (1967: 9) points out, the classic Greek term *tekhne* made no distinction between industrial production and 'fine' or symbolic art. There was a unity between art and craft in Ancient Greek society which does not exist in industrial culture. Mumford maintains that this unity existed for the greater part of human history (see also Applebaum 1992). It is only with the Industrial Revolution that the extreme division of labour confines workers to specialized technical or artistic functions; and the deleterious effects on community become evident. Mumford regards industrialization as a period in which technics for technics sake is glorified. Leisure ceases to provide balance or enlightenment and instead becomes a mechanism of social control. Yet the roots of this mechanization of everyday life reach back much further to the Middle Ages. Mumford (1967: 263–72) submits that mechanization did not start with the steam age of James Watt. Instead he traces it to the devotions of the Benedictine monks in the Middle Ages. The first primitive clocks were introduced in the medieval monasteries to control the ringing of bells which regulated the pattern of work and prayer. The forerunner of bourgeois timekeeping, was the religious desire to ensure that monks assembled and dispersed in an orderly fashion in order to obey their devotional duties. Timekeeping was an essential catalyst for the emergence of science. According to Mumford it led to the obsessions with weighting, counting and measuring that characterize the scientific worldview. Forms of life which could not be calibrated and quantified tended to be dismissed as 'unreal'. Measured life became arranged into precise, regimented units, destroying the organic connection with community, nature, art and craft that the Ancient Greeks protected in their concept of *tekhne*.

BATAILLE AND THE PROBLEM OF 'THE SURPLUS'

In making this case, Mumford plumbs a line of argument which is also to be found in the work of the anarchist and libertine, French writer, Georges Bataille (1988, 1991). According to this, the main problems of post-tribal economies do not derive from issues of scarcity but from issues of surplus. In industrial society considered, *sui generis*, it is not that we do not have enough wealth and resources, it is that we have too much. Mumford (1967: 40) quotes a passage from the psychologist, William James to support the point:

> Man's chief difference from the brutes lies in the exuberant excess of his subjective propensities – his pre-eminence over them simply and solely in the number and in the fantastic and unnecessary character of his wants physical, moral, aesthetic, and intellectual. Had his whole life not been a quest for the superfluous, he would never have established himself as inexpugnably as he has done in the necessary . . . Prune down his extravagance, sober him, and you undo him.

James is repeating a point made in the poetry and mysticism of William Blake which argues that 'energy is pure delight'. The attempt to curtail *Homo ludens* from playing, from philosophizing and subverting the established rules and practices of the day is intolerable to human beings. Bataille (1988: 27) elevates the point into a general principle of animate life:

> As a rule an organism has at its disposal greater energy resources than are necessary for the operations that sustain life (functional activities and, in animals, essential muscular exercises, the search for food) . . . Neither growth nor reproduction would be possible

if plants and animals did not dispose of an excess. The very principle of living matter requires that the chemical operations of life, which demand an expenditure of energy, be gainful, productive of surpluses.

Bataille (1988: 29) goes on to argue that the immediate limit upon offloading surplus energy is culturally given. 'What goes' in the community as the 'appropriate' standards of behaviour is what the individual is prevailed upon to internalize in the socialization process. Cultural limits must always leave energy 'in reserve' or in a volatile state. For human energy is prior to, and greater than, cultural energy. As Bataille (1988: 29) notes, 'the terrestrial sphere (to be exact, the *biosphere*), which corresponds to the space available to life, is the only real limit'.

I find this line of argument extremely suggestive in thinking about leisure. After all, most of the problems that leisure theorists and policy-makers struggle with revolve around the question of limits to human behaviour. These are defined in innumerable ways, from the budgetary restrictions that prevent a council from building a neighbourhood swimming pool to the moral objections which derive from burning the national flag at a rock concert. The orthodox way of dealing with these matters is to examine the character of the rule which prevents counter-factual behaviour. The line of argument that James, Mumford and Bataille sketch out is quite different. It requires us to consider the character of human energy in terms of a surplus which will always exceed the delineated rules of culture and is therefore bound to act as a cultural irritation and source of destabilization. In addition, it urges us to see this state of affairs not as something that must be negated, but as something which is indispensable to the vitality of human development.

I propose that these issues are pivotal to the study of leisure. Leisure may not be free and self-determining, but it is time and space bound by more relaxed levels of compunction than other bounded spheres of human life, such as work, family life, politics and so on. In the time and space allocated for leisure we have greater liberty to objectify the rules of ordinary life and to challenge them. We can, as it were, be more 'boundless' or 'without boundaries'. By the term 'objectify', I mean the practice of turning the received, 'common-sense', 'taken-for-granted' motifs of life that guide 'common culture' and turning them into objects for critical speculation and analysis. It is not to be inferred that I am proposing that objectification occurs solely in leisure. In our ordinary school-ing, family and work practices we encounter taken-for-granted motifs and rules which we challenge and try to transcend. Nonetheless, because leisure is the space and time in which our energy is least subject to the compunction of others, it is the segment of human life in which objectification can go furthest without external detec-tion or censure. This is to claim a more subversive and destabilizing role for leisure activity than is generally allowed in the literature. Of course, it is not to claim that leisure time and space are only devoted to subversion and destabilization. I quite accept that much leisure activity is concerned with the emotional and moral remak-ing of collective life, just as Durkheim (1915) hinted in his submission that leisure would replace religious life in collective reaffirmation in a secular age. By the same token, I maintain that the subversive and destabilizing effect of leisure in human development has been grossly neglected in the literature. The dominant critical positions in the field have tended to reinforce the *Homo Faber* model over the *Homo ludens* model, by either failing to imagine a world with-out work or preventing themselves from considering what the *Homo ludens* model fully entails. In other words, despite its legitimate and illuminating criticisms of the functionalist positions in leisure studies, the critical literature reinforces a fairly narrow and limit-ing conception of 'appropriate', 'correct' human behaviour in leisure time and space.

Decadence and deviance are not subjects that have been exten-sively investigated in the study of leisure. This is surprising, for as Wagner (1997) notes, problems arising from concupiscence, promiscuity, pornography, drugs, alcoholism, cigarette-addiction, over-eating are hardly marginal in our cultures. These activities are overwhelmingly concentrated in leisure time and space. In accounting for the lack of interest in these areas in the study of leisure one cannot ignore the moral fastidiousness and judgementalism that runs through the traditional dominant critical traditions. Critical positions in leisure studies scorn the middlebrow view of 'normal-ity' enunciated in functionalist writers like Roberts (1978) and Parker (1983). However, they have been exceptionally naive in the posi-tive views of leisure in the future society of 'the associated producers' or the 'women only' enclaves of contemporary society (Clarke and Critcher 1985; Talbot 1988).

In much of the rest of the book, I want to do what has not, I believe, been done in leisure studies. I want to take the implications of the *Homo ludens* model seriously. By current standards that prevail in the field, some of what I will have to say will be construed as being 'amoral'. By considering the role of leisure in serial killing, gangsterism, drug abuse and other forms of deviant practice I am pointing to 'the dark side' of leisure. In part, my object is to highlight the narrow and limiting standards of current moral culture in respect of the expenditure of human energy. I am also concerned to argue that these questions have tended to be 'over-medicalized' in the literature. That is, they have been categorized as the preserve of medical practitioners as if the culture of leisure has nothing to do in explaining them. In this discussion I take issue with the medicalization of deviance. I propose that the culture of leisure is essential in understanding the rhythm and intensity of deviant practice.

Questioning the standards that prevail in the field of leisure studies does not lead to the moral universe inhabited by a Nero or a Saddam Hussein. One can disapprove of many forms of deviant behaviour, while at the same time insist that students of leisure and culture have much to learn from them. It is hardly necessary to make the point in the fields of criminology and the sociology of deviance where moral degradation is not attributed to researchers who look into the subject. Because leisure studies is so riddled with the judgemental value that leisure is a positive characteristic in human life, the same concession cannot be made of students working in the field of leisure. Elsewhere, I (1993) argued that leisure is bound up with the Enlightenment ideal of 'the good life'. This has bedevilled serious enquiry into the subject because one is always battling against presuppositions that leisure is intrinsically a social benefit. To attribute costs, or bad effects, to leisure is *ipso facto* to collide with this ideology.

Before taking up the themes of abnormal leisure in more detail I want to summarize the contribution of Mumford to the analysis of leisure and culture and return to the question of the unique characteristics of the cultural context of contemporary leisure practice.

Mumford provides arguably the most detailed and tenable basis for regarding *Homo ludens* rather than *Homo Faber* as the crux of human civilization. Huizinga's (1947) classic work was the first to argue that ritual, mimesis, sport, games and drama release man from his 'animal attachments'. Mumford (1967: 8) alleges that Huizinga's thesis was toned down in translation so that play was redefined as an aspect of culture, rather than *vice versa*. Mumford restores the radical component of Huizinga's original thesis by insisting that all culture is a form of play; and he enlarges this thesis by showing in great anthropological and historical detail how play related to the emergence of power and industrialization. For Mumford, the symbolic form of language and communication is the primordial state of being. Tools and technics are the result of a mental revolution. The argument rejects technological and economic determinism. The mental world of dreams, desires and fancies is identified as the crucible of civilization. Mumford also shows how technics became separated from culture to stand over and dominate human behaviour. He describes how play and leisure themselves became mechanized in the machine age and relegated to a subsidiary role. In the industrial age the lack of balance between work and art produces cultural malaise. Leisure becomes subordinate to work and typically assumes a passive form. The organic relation between work and art that Greek civilization achieved is replaced by harassed, overworked labourers who turn into couch-potatoes in their leisure hours. Mumford's moral indignation against mechanized culture and overwork is that it is unnecessary. Industrial technics produces too much abundance. Indeed, there is so much surplus production that industrialists frequently need to destroy it in order to keep prices stable. Mumford calls for a complete rethink in the central values of industrial civilization. We need urgently, he argues, to reassess how long we need to work per day and in the course of the normal life-cycle; we need to question if economic values are the most important stars by which to set our life-course; and we need a new politics of abundance. In developing this argument Mumford falls back upon some of the ideas of the French socialist, Charles Fourier, who was, of course, discredited as a dreamer by Marx (Marx and Engels 1968). In Mumford's (1970: 406) words:

> The economy of plenitude which now beckons suggests an entirely different approach from that of the old-fashioned division of labour. The new possibility was outlined more than a century ago by that singular if mad genius Charles Fourier. This is what Fourier called the 'butterfly principle'. Instead of working a whole day at a single occupation, still less a whole lifetime, Fourier proposed that the working day should be enlivened by moving at intervals between one task to another . . . As against the segregated activities, the regimented discipline, the bleak environment of the factory . . . the economy of plenitude, in achieving briefer work periods, would

make it possible to restore initiative on a voluntary basis in many forms of work now denied to the beneficiaries of affluence who are chained to the demands of compulsory consumption.

Mumford published those words in 1970. Now, nearly thirty years later, as Gorz (1982) Schor (1992) and Aronowitz and Di Fazio (1994) remind us, we continue to live in an age of overwork, generally alienated labour and unfulfilling, discontinuous leisure. Must we reject Mumford, in the same terms that Marx rejected Fourier, as a utopian dreamer incapable of recognizing the real character of his own times?

No-one can deny that there is an awful repetitiveness about the demand for reducing working hours and increasing quality leisure time. The indisputable twin trends in industrial development in the industrial age have been the replacement of labour-intensive functions with labour-saving functions through mechanization and the deskilling of labour (Braverman 1974). In many ways the cultural and economic conditions in the 1960s and early 70s when Mumford made his own case for a shorter working week were more propitious than they are now. In general, the advanced economies of the West were delivering full employment with growth. In addition, Keynesian demand management of the economy and the commitment to building an effective welfare state, created the basis for further state intervention into the organization of daily life. These conditions began to change in the mid-70s with the development of economic recession triggered by the oil crisis. The swing to the Right in the 1980s reinforced the trend. Most Western states introduced the delayering and franchising of welfare services. A public ideology of welfarism was replaced by an ideology of voluntarism. These conditions do not favour central intervention because they encourage the enlargement of individualism and market logic in the determination of resource distribution. On this basis there seems little to support Mumford's proposition that economic plenitude must be translated into a rational, equitable and healthy centrally controlled system of allocating time.

Yet something should also be learnt from the repetitiveness of the demand to rethink the work ethic and reduce working time. In recent years it has been made by Gorz (1978), Schor (1992), Aronowitz and Di Fazio (1994) and Hochschild (1982). The nub of their argument repeats Mumford's point, that the wealth of the economy is capable of supporting a shorter working day, a shorter

working week and earlier retirement for all, without any appreci-
able decline in living standards.

What is required is a cultural change which acknowledges that
the work ethic has outlived its day and recognizes the ethical virtue for the individual and society of more leisure. We need to think
deeply about the nature of life with others in post-work society.
Deep cultural changes of this type are not unprecedented in the
postwar period. The environmental movement has transformed public
attitudes to pollution and the eco-system; and the health movement has transformed public awareness of the harmful effects of
fatty diets and the addictive consumption of cigarettes and alcohol.
Displacing technics from our idea of progress would not be necessary, since technology is increasingly automated. What is required
is curtailing the notions that adult personal dignity and social well-
being derive from the 40-hour working week, and being employed
in full-time work until retirement at 60 or 65. The most powerful
way of achieving that is to develop an ethic of leisure which recognizes the organic, economic and cultural benefits of more free time.

TACKLING THE RESERVATION CULTURE

Attempts to pinpoint the defining characteristics of contemporary
culture are legion (Riesman 1950; Marcuse 1964; Bell 1976; Lasch
1979; Elias 1978, 1982; Harvey 1989; Ehrenreich 1989; Ritzer 1992;
Giddens 1990; Mestrovic 1997). A variety of contenders have emerged
from these ruminations: other-directedness, one-dimensionality,
cultural contradictions, narcissism, the civilizing process, postmodernity, class and status insecurity, rationalization, McDonaldization,
disembeddedness, media-saturation and post-emotionalism. Much
can be learned from these ideas. However, their common fault is
that they lack a convincing, general social-psychological concept to
underpin them. Therefore they often appear to be confusing and
contradictory in the eyes of students and researchers. I propose
that the concept of reservation is a helpful way of underpinning, in
social psychological terms, the various strands of argument associated with the debate around Modernity and Postmodernity. The
ideas of reserve and reservation are familiar from the history of
manners (Elias 1978, Gay 1994). In this context it is used to mean
a threshold of social diffidence in relations with others, especially
strangers. To be socially reserved is to pay respect to the status of

others, to apply formal means of address and practice caution and manners in face-to-face encounters. While this historical usage is still relevant, it does not exhaust the meanings that I wish to assign the concept. These meanings are threefold:

1) *Manners and Caution*. Reservation involves practising manners and caution in face-to-face encounters with others. In Freudian terms, it assumes high development of the super-ego function and the control of the id function. Reservation is often expressed as shyness and diffidence. However, these external appearances usually mask a strong sense of what the individual 'knows' to be proper in social relationships and with whom one should and should not consort.

2) *Withdrawal and Lack of Commitment*. Reservation assumes a constant tactical orientation to public life in which encounters are made on the basis of judgements about 'proper' conduct and 'suitable' contacts. The socially reserved person stands on the sidelines of social life and finds it difficult to make deep commitments to others. The mental attitude is similar to the long-distance traveller or hotel guest: one checks in and checks out of relationships; one looks for minimum standards and services and leaves if they are not manifest; one withholds personal commitment to others unless tactical considerations dictate otherwise; one maintains one's own face-saving devices in public circumstances; one accepts that life is driven by change and mobility.

3) *Identity and Tribe*. Reservation involves judgements about commonality and difference. In Britain, during the twilight years of the Thatcher adventure, the press became fond of using the phrase 'not one of us' to describe people with opinions and characteristics that Thatcherism automatically discounted as unsafe and dangerous. The definition is automatic because it is visceral rather than consciously considered. People who are sidelined in this way are not granted preferment in face-to-face encounters. They are treated with polite disdain. Judgements of commonality and difference are characteristics of all social groups. One thinks of the popular distinction that Nancy Mitford made in the 1930s between people who are 'U' and 'Non-U'. That is, people who are immediately recognized as 'one of us' or 'not one of us'. The distinction is ultimately tribal and on the individual level involves the identification of the self with the values of the tribe. Social groups develop elaborate

social protocols to cool-out people who are 'Non-U'. The details differ according to precise historical and cultural circumstances. This sense of social reservation connects up closely with the postmodern argument that contemporary culture has fragmented into an array of interest and identity groups which lack social cohesion.

Cultures do not proliferate and grow without good reason. The Reservation Culture, of which I speak, has its roots in the dramatic transformations wrought upon everyday life by the rise of Modernity. Elsewhere, I (1995) made the distinction between Modernity 1 and Modernity 2. I conceived of these as interdependent and sharing a mutual origin with the rise of science, industry and urbanization. Modernity 1 sought to lay down rational rules of order to govern life. Its accomplishments included training regimes for the government of the household and raising children; drills for schoolchildren; the division of the day into working hours and leisure hours; the association of rights and duties with citizenship; and the general enlargement of codes of practice in the public and private sphere. Modernity 1 aimed to provide rational shape to the bourgeoning and often alarming consequences of industrial-urban revolution. Modernity 2 is the reaction to the attempt of Modernity 1 to impose a rational grid-like structure on daily life. It focuses upon the anomalies and elisions of rational order. It emphasizes the exuberant, uncontainable character of life and the necessity of transgression for innovation and civilization. The interplay between these two faces of Modernity has produced bureaucratization and alienation in leisure; but it has also led to resistance against bureaucratization and the quest for more enriching, authentic forms of leisure.

Mestrovic (1997: 79–84) draws upon this distinction and gives it an interesting twist. He argues that the 'battle' between Modernity 1 and Modernity 2 has been 'won' by Modernity 2. The rational aspects of Modernity 1 have produced an emotional withdrawal both from the rational/orderly aspects of Modernity 1 and the transgressive potential of Modernity 2. We live in societies in which we are unable to commit to the rational order which governs our lives and unwilling to believe that any superior change is possible. In a highly original and important discussion, Mestrovic argues that the social psychological results are twofold. In the first place, we retract our emotions from daily life and meet the world with a face of neutrality and indifference. This is only possible because the machinery protecting the security of our own lives has become so efficient. Policing and self-discipline have given individuals in the West a hard outer skin so that they are unable to empathize with the plight of the starving, the tortured, the oppressed and the poor in their own societies. Mestrovic (1997) argues that post-emotionalism is magnified in relation to our empathy for conditions of suffering in other countries. Genocide in Bosnia and Rwanda, famine in Africa seem to be removed from us by chains of interrelations which are so complex and involved that we psychologically neutralize these conditions. We leave it to government departments and international aid agencies to bring relief, while we get on with the immediate, local matters of our own lives. The consequence is a general lowering of emotional valencies and the enlargement of the *blasé* attitude which Simmel (1971, 1978) analyzed with such power.

At the same time, there are other tendencies at work which transfer our emotional valencies to 'counterfeit' communities and surrogate primal relations. We may remain emotionally neutral about news of genocide in Bosnia, but we are perfectly capable of being moved to tears by the imaginary events portrayed in movies like *ET, Forrest Gump* or *Titanic*. The convulsive emotion which often follows the death of celebrities belongs to the same category. When Princess Diana died in a car crash in Paris on 31 August 1997 crowds massed outside her Kensington Palace home and Buckingham Palace, the home of the royal family, and left thousands of floral tributes; they queued for up to ten hours to write their names and messages in condolence books; the national radio and TV channels were given over to commentaries, tributes and constant news flashes. This apparently overwhelming wave of emotional belonging rested entirely on second or third order relationships with the Princess. The overwhelming majority of people who mourned her and found themselves tearful and distressed at her death had no direct connection with her. The order of relationships was largely conducted at an imaginary level, in which people assumed levels of intimacy and sharing with the Princess, which were not historically validated by face-to-face encounters. The same people skipped the other stories in the press on that day which dealt with the British failure to address violence in schools; the murder of a Sikh in North Yorkshire; the volcanic threat posed to life on the island of Montserrat and police moves to establish a register of paedophiles. These remained on the level of 'ordinary news' which we typically deal with by withholding our emotional involvement.

Princess Diana was not alone in being a charismatic figure whose death can trigger overpowering emotions. Similar public reactions met the deaths of James Dean, Marilyn Monroe, John F. Kennedy, John Lennon, Kurt Cobain, River Phoenix and Versace. Significantly, the web of these imaginary relations relies heavily on leisure time and space. It is in non-work time that individuals engage in the fantasy work and mind-voyaging that leads them to develop feelings of identification and belonging with celebrities. The media act as a catalyst to this type of psychological bonding by supplying audiences with a perpetual diet of images, news clips and other data. These imaginary relations cater to our need to feel connections with others. They lead to virtual forms of community and solidarity which are often more meaningful than one's relations with others at work or in the family. We can nourish reserved identities in social interaction with others because our fantasy lives are so rich.

The important point is not that cults of glamour exist or that they form a significant element in leisure time and space budgets. Rather, it is that contemporary society has developed huge reserves of emotional energy which can be roused more readily by counterfeit relations than by the real relations of injustice, poverty and suffering that we directly encounter in everyday life. Indeed, our typical response to the injustice and pain that we observe in immediate society is indifference.

Gitlin's (1995) work on political correctness deepens the picture. Recalling some aspects of Daniel Bell's (1976) analysis of the cultural contradictions of capitalism, Gitlin argues that the counter culture seriously weakened the tradition of common, national culture. It legitimated ideas of difference and diversity which eventually became expressed in the movement for multiculturalism. Gitlin recognizes that multiculturalism addressed many issues of injustice and prejudice associated with nationalist culture. He also acknowledges its role in supporting tolerance and the respect for difference. However, he (1995: 148) also points to the culture of 'exultation and victimization' that multiculturalism perpetuates. In particular, it supplies some feminist, Black Power and gay and lesbian identity groups with the rhetoric of 'rapturous marginality' and victim ideology (Gitlin 1995: 149). Isolated, often precariously situated and harassed by the Right, these identity groups developed a lifestyle of 'separatist rancour'. They withdrew their emotional support from the centre ground and forged a combative politics of attrition against the mainstream. Marginality became a passionate value to counterpose against the bureaucratic face of humanism. Gitlin (1995: 150) writes:

> For identity-based movements, the margin is the place to be. Within each margin there are always more margins to carve out. Postmodernist thought confirms that there is no centre, or rather that those who claim the centre – who claim a common truth or even the possibility that a common truth is attainable – are false universalizers, colonizers, hegemonists. The centre, if there is one, is the malevolent Other. But this false centre – so the argument goes – is only a margin in disguise. The margins are bastions from which to launch intellectual raids on a centre that has no right to be central, and has, moreover, lost confidence in itself.

Gitlin argues that the counter-culture exploded into a condition of chronic sectarianism. Emotional valencies became strongly attached to the task of protecting the integrity and difference of identity groups. One consequence of this was that moves between identity groups to build collective action became burdened by caveats and mutual bad faith which worked against compromise and encouraged reservations about non-identity groups. Gitlin (1995: 236) remarks that 'there is a lot of fantasy in circulation' with the result that 'dialogue today is inflamed and incoherent in part because the symbolic stakes are overloaded on every side'.

Gitlin is conscious of his position as a white, heterosexual, middle-aged male who has witnessed the disintegration of effective Left-wing politics. He sees himself as a target for sectarian criticism, that his position is nostalgic and authoritarian. His (1995: 172–7) condemnation of the Dinesh D'Souza's version of black history and his (1995: 149) criticism of campus-based militant feminist enclaves, leaves one in no doubt that he holds a dim view of the turn towards identity politics. Yet it is impossible to dismiss Gitlin as a reactionary figure who spouts prejudice and *resentment*. His credentials as a significant left-wing writer who has campaigned against prejudice and violence for over a quarter of a century are impeccable. Moreover, his criticism of sectarianism is not that militant feminists, black power groups and gay and lesbian rights agitators are wrong, but rather that they couch their criticism in rhetorical gestures which perpetuate polarization and scapegoating. His criticism points to the same kind of emotional distancing techniques that Mestrovic (1997) identifies in his account of post-emotionalism.

The reservation culture is the cultural expression of this psychological state. It involves the withdrawal of the emotions from everyday life beyond the family and the fantasy relations perpetuated by the culture industries. The family becomes the seat of overdeveloped emotional commitment. One's children and partner matter, society does not. The high emotional expectations of trust and respect within the family are frequently disappointed. Parents get divorced, children leave home and gradually become distant from their fathers and mothers. We all eventually die. The effect is to reinforce the psychological view that culture is based in low trust relations. Decisions not to invest too much emotionally in the lives of others is confirmed by these events. Simultaneously media saturation offers constant outlets for emotional blockage. It was not for nothing that Debord (1967) attributed prominence to the spectacle in the organization of contemporary culture. Sport, cinema, rock music, theatre, processions and exhibitions provide us with the opportunity to express our emotions vicariously without making deeper commitments. Of course, many are seduced so that a soccer team, film director or rock star become the emotional axis of their lives. Yet as Lefebvre (1991) argued, emotional commitment to these leisure forms is likely to be ultimately unsatisfying because they are mediated by ideologies of marketing and commodification. Emotional investment also becomes subject to bureaucratization which divorces the consumer from the heart of leisure experience and therefore contributes to the general sense of remoteness and distance in the rest of life.

Nearly fifty years ago, Riesman (1950) commented on the rise of the 'other directed' personality type. Following Lowenthal (1944), Riesman (1950) noted the decline in the popularity of heroes of science and industry in popular culture and their replacement with a galaxy of heroes drawn from sport and the movie world. He argued that this was symptomatic of the replacement of production values with consumption values in the organization of personal motivation and status hierarchies in everyday life. The craft ethic of the factory was being edged out by the more meretricious and mercurial images of consumer culture and the leisure industry. According to Riesman (1950) the basic character type in consumer culture was moving from an inner-directed to an other-directed type. The character of inner-directed types was formed through the internalization of adult authority models in the home and local community. In contrast, other-directed types drew their behavioural cues from more impersonal sources like advertising and the media. The character of the other-directed type, concluded Riesman, was increasingly influenced by the remote example of strangers, rather than the close examples of the immediate family.

Riesman's thesis presupposes atomized consumers, mass communications and the decomposition of *gemeinschaft* culture. He anticipates the humanistic discussion of metropolitan isolation, dissonance and *Angst* later found in the work of Slater (1971). There are also unacknowledged echoes of central themes in classical social theory in his work, notably in respect of Marx's (1844) discussion of alienation and estrangement and Simmel's (1978) account of the anonymity and superficiality of metropolitan life. The representative of the lonely crowd is only loosely connected with others, engulfed in conflicting information from the media, lacking a rigorous moral code, prone to the impression management techniques of advertising, looking for the next momentary exit from low-trust relations with others provided by film, magazines and popular music, and helplessly caught up with the massifying tendencies in urbanization, technology and the growth of the state.

The metaphors of 'the other directed personality' and 'the lonely crowd' worked so well because they captured the disintegration of small town values and their replacement with impersonal and standardized values of consumer culture. The 1950s, when Riesman wrote his book, accentuated the consumer culture of the 1920s and 30s. The crux of the new developments was the electrification of visual culture. Television was first demonstrated in 1926 by John Logie Baird. The first regular TV service was introduced in Germany in 1935; the BBC followed suit in 1936 and NBC in the US in 1939. The development of the service was interrupted by the war years. However, by the 1950s the expansion of television was rampant. Lhamon (1993: 14) reports that in 1950 about 10 per cent of homes in the US received TV broadcasts. Five years later the percentage vaulted to 64.5 per cent; and by the end of the decade it stood at a remarkable 86 per cent. Parallel trends were evident throughout Western Europe. The 1950s was the start of the television age. Colour was introduced in the late 1950s and 60s. Riesman's arguments were therefore formulated at the moment in which the first TV generation was emerging. Television offered a quantum leap in electronic mass culture. The perception of national and,

eventually, global co-presence and simultaneity was vastly enhanced.
Television is perhaps the key technoculture underpinning reservation culture. As McLuhan (1997: 245) puts it:

> Television is the most significant of the electric media because it
> permeates nearly every home in the country, extending the central
> nervous system of every viewer as it works over and moulds the
> entire sensorium with the ultimate message.

McLuhan's contention that television is an extension of the central
nervous system anticipates Baudrillard's (1983, 1998) proposition
that individuals have become the 'monitoring screens' or 'terminals'
in networks of communication which ignore time and space. Both
writers may be criticized for underestimating the autonomy of the
individual and, in particular, the capacity of the individual to with-
hold emotional attachment. Be that as it may, there is no gainsaying
the proposition that television revolutionized technologies of interpersonal communication. After television a mass audience with
common responses became something that individual consumers
could not only sense but could see with their own eyes and hear
with their own ears. Radio prepared the way for this. Adorno (1944)
wrote of the hypnotic and menacing effect of radio in stirring mass
opinion. Hitler's minister of propaganda, Josef Goebbels, understood the value of the radio in popularing Nazi ideology. He regarded
the medium to be 'by nature authoritarian' (Reuth 1993: 176). He
organized the mass production of an inexpensive '*Volk* wireless'
which he used as one of the main channels for getting the Nazi
message to the people.

However, because it combines moving images with sound, television is a far more insistent medium than radio. Television exacerbated
other-directedness and the reservation culture by promoting a diet
of news and entertainment that could be absorbed in the home.
The domestication of the medium meant that the messages from
television had equivalent power to the messages from parental
authority figures in the socialization of children. Also, because the
rise of television coincided with the growth of dual career families,
television became a more insistent presence in the socialization
process. The agonized debates about whether television is good or
bad that have been made from time to time in the postwar period
are beside the point (Fiske 1987; Gitlin 1984). Television has become
an indispensable part of cultural life and, as such, is a primary
source of leisure and opinion-formation.

Television is the most significant technological mechanism for
emulation and opinion-formation to emerge in the postwar period.
The essentials of advertising (Jhally 1990; McLintock 1995) and
film culture (Robinson 1973, Thompson 1995) were in place long
before 1945. Their power is not in dispute, but it cannot rival television, since television is situated in the home. In reservation culture,
the home is the sphere of intimacy and authenticity. It is the physical
space in which one can really be oneself, when all the defences
against the outisde world are down. The acceptance of television
as part of the domestic furniture greatly contributes to its power
to inform and seduce.

But, of course, it would be wrong to claim that television operates alone. The private lives of men and women today intersect
with the media complex. Our news, values, stimulation and view of
reality are enmeshed in the networks of communication and information supplied by film, radio, CDs, video and television. We depend
upon them as addicts depend upon their next fix. Virilio (1995)
comments on a revealing historical fact concerning the place and
meaning of the media in contemporary culture. Until the start of
the twentieth century, he (1995: 6) argues, to be *mediatized* meant
being stripped of one's immediate rights.

Napoleon mediatized the rulers of the countries that he con-
quered, by depriving them of their freedom to make decisions while
nominally, leaving them in charge. Today, the concept of being
mediatized has a double meaning. On the one hand it means to be
connected to the essential channels of communication. No-one can
function effectively any longer without taking account of the media.
On the other hand it means receiving the messages produced through
these channels. One is nominally free to decide, but private
consciousness is also caught in the undertow of media agendas and
considerations.

The media complex enlarges the element of fantasy in everyday
life. It does so by providing a multiple series of concrete images of
'otherness' which the other-directed personality consumes. No type
of human life is possible without fantasy. But the media complex
supplies such an abundance of images of otherness and difference
that the status of reality is rendered unstable. In their private and
public lives, men and women today may have strong convictions
but the world around them is more diversified, contingent and conditional than ever (Gitlin 1995). The media complex continuously
raises the question of who is speaking, from what background and

to which audience. It also raises the auxiliary questions of what is truth and what is fiction, what is a mirror of the world and what is distortion.

Riesman's (1950) discussion presupposed that manipulation operated on mass society. Whatever differences existed between other-directed personalities, their propensity to be influenced by external sources of emulation, beyond the circles of family, peer group and community. Today globalization and multiculturalism have contributed to disembeddedness and decentred the axis of manipulation. Class politics and the counter cultures of the 1960s made extensive use of personal pronouns to establish commonality and difference. Trade unionists referred to 'us', the workers, against the capitalists; feminists pointed to 'them', the demagogic patriarchs of contemporary society. In the days of the reservation culture we can no longer be sure who 'we' are, just as attributions of 'us' and 'them' are no longer simple. Precisely because of this, reservation culture contains a strong tendency towards self-reflexivity. We do not simply reproduce the values of the group, even though our experience of socialization has attached us very closely to those values. Rather we have the capacity to criticize and dissent and this capacity is exercised as an ordinary feature of everyday life.

Durkheim (1902) argued that the practice of criticism and dissent is the mark of specialization and individualization. He believed that the 'organic societies' in which specialization and individualization are practised are morally superior to the 'primitive' 'mechanical societies' in which criticism and dissent are repressed. Durkheim (1897) made a distinction between repressive and restitutive law which he intended as an external measure of social and moral development. He argued that repressive law which punished crime severely is the mark of societies bound together by a strong *conscience collective*. The punishment of the criminal is severe because it reinforces the shared values of the group and therefore confirms collective solidarity. In contrast, restitutive law seeks to govern reciprocal relations, to enforce contracts and restore imbalances in exchange relationships. It is indicative of a weaker *conscience collective* because it reflects a social condition in which the separatedness and distinctiveness of individuals are recognized by all.

Anthropologists and sociologists have criticized Durkheim's account (Taylor *et al.* 1973). They argue that Durkheim was being too ethnocentric in applying industrial concepts of law to tribal societies. Tribal reactions to transgression and crime have more to do with cosmologies which symbolize belonging and stigmatize difference. It is not clear that the concept of law is very useful in describing how these cosmologies work. In addition, he overstated the repressive character of the tribal *conscience collective*. Taylor *et al.* (1973) argue that the rise of repressive law has more to do with the emergence of private property than the power of the *conscience collective*.

Despite the validity of these criticisms, I want to argue that Durkheim's emphasis on the greater specialization and individualization of life which developed through modernization anticipates the enlargement of self-reflexivity and also the growth of reservation culture. Specialization and individualization separated actors from one another and reinforced the notion of limitations in rights and responsibilities. The concept of the psyche as ultimately atomized and isolated was reinforced.

However, the enlargement of self-reflexivity also produced a questioning orientation to the social construction of values and social categories. It contributed to the objectification of social forces. The expansion of leisure time and space contributed to this by giving individuals more freedom to reflect upon social limits and the construction of social values. Durkheim's sociology provides a useful entry into these questions. It also raises the subject of what is normal and pathological, healthy and morbid, in leisure practice. The next chapter takes up this subject and examines it in greater detail.

4 The Abnormal Forms of Leisure

In *The Rules of Sociological Method* (1895) Durkheim distinguishes between normal and pathological behaviour. The decisive characteristic of the normal form is that it is 'generally distributed' (Durkheim 1895: 55). That is, it is to be found in the majority of individuals; where variations of behaviour are evident they occur within 'narrow limits'. Thus, in principle, a simple head count of a population will establish normal characteristics. To the 'exceptional variations' in human behaviour, which he (1895: 55) avowed, 'most often do not persist throughout the life of the individual,' he proposed to affix the term 'pathological' behaviour. He inferred that normal characteristics must perform necessary functions for society. For, he (1895: 58) reasoned, 'it would be incomprehensible if the most widespread forms of organization would not at the same time be, *at least in their aggregate*, the most advantageous'.

As it stands, Durkheim's methodology is unsatisfactory and has been attacked by criminologists and sociologists (Taylor, Walton and Young 1973; Turner 1984). First, it presupposes a naive view of power. What is normal for one stratum in society may be viewed as deviant or pathological by another. We have already encountered this point in this study. The conspicuous consumption which, Veblen (1899) argues was a normal characteristic of the leisure class in the nineteenth century, was perceived by other strata, notably the intelligentsia, as 'morbid' and 'pathological', since its emulative effect threatened to bring about the collapse of the entire system.

Secondly, Durkheim was wrong to infer that the 'most widespread forms of organization' in society must be the 'most advantageous'. Racial and sexual oppression were widespread in the Western society of Durkheim's day, but they were certainly not the 'most advantageous' forms of organization for the health of society. For one thing they fuelled resentment and conflict which threatened to make the social system dysfunctional; and, in addition, they provided an arbitrary basis for squandering the talents and capacities of the racially and sexually disadvantaged groups.

Thirdly, postmodern authors now query the concept of normality.

For them, the attribution of a centre, common ground or a silent majority always involves the mobilization of power (Bauman 1992). Power confirms some values and marginalizes or excludes others. The textbook example is colonialism which presented the white order of things as normal. Post-colonial authors have done much to expose the partial, brutal and indefensible character of white 'normality' *vis-à-vis* the excluded (Said 1978; Dyer 1997). Their work concludes that it is a naturalistic fallacy to assume that what appears to be common in society is normal. The best antidote to this is comparative and historical analysis which soon establishes the distinctive features of our own time and place in relation to other places and times.

At all events, Durkheim was not consistent in applying his methodology in his sociological work. For example, in *The Division of Labour in Society* (1902) he drew a distinction between normal and abnormal forms of the division of labour. His discussion of the normal form had a utopian, idealistic ring about it, even to the ears of the audience in his own day. He regarded the normal division of labour as a general condition in which the aptitudes and skills of individuals match the social and economic requirements of society. As Durkheim (1902: 237) himself noted, this implies 'a harmonious development of all functions' and, in principle, 'the simultaneous growth of all faculties'. The normal division of labour moderates the egocentric ambitions of individuals by encouraging their activities to resonate with the whole. When this condition is met 'there is a maximum of happiness as well as a maximum of activity that cannot be surpassed' (Durkheim 1902: 238).

Durkheim contrasted the normal form of the division of labour with abnormal forms. These, he claimed, were of three types:

1. The *Anomic Division of Labour*, arises because the regulating rules of organic society are not yet *in situ*. This may be due to the over-rapid industrialization or the persistence of some residues of mechanical society. The solution is that the classes must be enjoined to follow clear rules and regulations in job selection, wage bargaining and industrial codes of practice. The state has a role in combating *anomie*. However, such is the complexity of industrial society that the state cannot be expected to intervene in every dispute and disagreement. Employers and occupational associations of workers must therefore play a voluntary role in ensuring that the division of labour obeys binding, impartial, just rules of conduct. Durkheim looked forward to the estab-

lishment of associative democracy in which relations would be governed by a binding code of civic morals. The development of professional ethics would constitute the basis for adjudicating between competing claims and settling disputes. The state would be called in to arbitrate only as a last resort.

2. The *Forced Division of Labour*, occurs when the task assigned to an individual in the division of labour is not fitting to his or her aptitudes and skills. 'Labour,' writes Durkheim (1902: 377) 'is divided spontaneously only if society is constituted in such a way that social inequalities exactly express natural inequalities'. Underlying Durkheim's description of the normal division of labour is a meritocratic view of society. Under organic society, the aptitudes and skills of individuals will be expressed truly in the character of their work and personal rewards. Thompson (1982: 81–2) argues that Durkheim recognized class inequality as the main impediment to the spontaneous division of labour. However, while it is true that the Second Preface to *The Division of Labour in Society* makes reference to the need for planning and reform and sketches out a managerial role for 'occupational groups', Durkheim's plea for eliminating inequality remains very understated.

3. The *Uncoordinated Division of Labour* is the result of rapid and uneven development in the division of labour. Where some aspects develop a spontaneous division swiftly and easily, others languish and require direction. The normal division of labour in society requires continuous spontaneity. Where this is absent, a combination of state, entrepreneurial and occupational group activity must be enacted to intervene.

Durkheim repeatedly refers to the three abnormal forms as 'exceptional'. In his (1902: 372–3) own words, the normal division of labour

> presumes that the worker, far from being hemmed-in by his task, does not lose sight of his collaborators, that he acts upon them, and reacts to them. He is then not a machine who repeats his movements without knowing their meaning, but he knows that they tend, in some way, towards an end that he conceives more or less distinctly. He feels that he is serving something... The economists would not have left this essential character of the division of labour in the shade ... if they had not reduced it to being merely a means of increasing the produce of social forces, if they had seen that it is above all a source of solidarity.

Durkheim's discussion is faulty on three counts. First, it failed to anticipate the challenge that leisure would mount to work as the central life interest. The feelings of harmony, resonance and growth which he attributed to the normal division of labour are now more 'generally distributed' in leisure experience. As Gorz (1982) notes, most people today do not gain intrinsic satisfaction from work. Instead they are instrumentally oriented to work as a means of acquiring the finance to support their leisure interests.

Secondly, the normal form of the division of labour was not the most widespread form in Durkheim's time, just as it remains a minority form today. Durkheim advanced his argument on deductive grounds. He believed that the normal form was logically necessary for the integration and health of society. Yet in fact, the three abnormal forms are, in aggregate, the most widespread in society. The result is that the majority feel 'hemmed-in' in their work; they feel that their work tasks do not reflect their aptitudes or skills; they feel that the rules governing work are often unclear and skewed to the interests of the employer (Braverman 1974). Durkheim's proposition has been falsified by the empirical evidence.

Thirdly, Durkheim failed to foresee the vast wealth that modern industrial processes are capable of achieving. Automation and computerization have contributed to immense productivity gains (Schor 1992; Aronowitz and Di Fazio 1994). It is no longer a question of determining how labour can be divided spontaneously in the work process. Rather, it is a question of developing social and economic policies for a post-work state. The immediate issues here revolve around drastically reducing the working week; bringing the age of retirement down; devising guaranteed income and pension plans; enlarging work-sharing schemes; and weakening the tenacious hold of the work ethic. However, the key issue is to educate people not to feel guilty or distressed if they are not engaged in paid labour. A deep change in education and policy is required which will support and popularize the concept of the leisure ethic. For the need to work will not disappear in the foreseeable future. What must change is the general association of self-worth and dignity with paid labour. This is the product of the work ethic and its effect is to devalue the experience of leisure. Changing this is no easy matter. The work ethic has been drilled into people's heads for many centuries and modifying it will be difficult. This is the lesson learnt from writings on leisure from Fourier to Mumford which have, for two centuries, drawn attention to the plenitude of wealth created by industrialization and advocated the reduction of the working week. On the other hand, it is difficult to see how society can absorb the massive freeing-up of labour which the new technologies of production have achieved, without serious social unrest. I will return to this critical question in the final chapter of the book.

THE MEDICALIZATION OF LIFE

In attempting to explain the medicalization of many issues of social behaviour and moral conduct, Bryan Turner (1984: 211–14) sketches an intriguing model of social development. He argues that, in pre-modern societies distinctions between deviance and sin are either non-existent or underdeveloped. Health and morality are united in theory and practice. Society is relatively undifferentiated so there is no professional specialization of lawyers, clergy and doctors. Reaction to transgressive behaviour derives from the tribal leader and the elders. Judgements about moral conduct and physical sickness are typically combined. This is one reason why punishments adopt the repressive form. Wrongdoing must be ritually exorcised from the system (Foucault 1979).

In transitional society differentiation and specialization are more advanced. Sins, crimes and diseases are classified and specialized institutions develop to manage them. Asylums, hospitals and prisons emerge and reactions to deviance begin to be sequestered from the public domain. The nineteenth-century practices of public hanging and allowing the public to view inmates of the asylum gradually cease. Moral questions are separated from physical and natural questions. The discovery of the tuberculosis bacilli by Pasteur and Koch adduced proof of micro-organic causes of disease which could be scientifically isolated and treated. The pre-modern association between disease and evil began to be demystified. Medical science undertook to produce objective accounts of disease which were independent of theological and moral considerations. The spurt of the professionalization of medicine was reinforced by the state which supported official definitions of health and disease. This in turn reinforced the professional concept of objective causes to disease and illness which are independent of personal subjectivity or moral judgement.

In modern societies the power of religious institutions is much diminished. Moral considerations became concentrated in the hands of specialized professionals, of which doctors and lawyers represent the most powerful groups. The aetiology of deviance is viewed as a question of science rather than a matter for theology or morality. The decriminalization of some practices, notably homosexuality and political dissent, occurs as science posits objective causes behind forms of behaviour which were previously labelled 'deviant' or 'pathological'. Traces of the pre-modern moral and social universe remain in the modern stage. For example, medical practice advocates moral asceticism as the main defence against sexually transmitted diseases, heart disease, cancer and stress. It was not so long ago that doctors preached about the harms of masturbation. Even today the medical establishment's moral censure directed against gays, bisexuals and prostitutes confuses scientific judgement with old-fashioned moralism (Wagner 1997: 90). Despite its self-image of objectivity and dispassion, medical science still attacks certain human practices largely on moral rather than health grounds. Even so, to return to the nub of Turner's argument, the general value system supports a secular reading of deviance. Scientific solutions are likely to be sought for aberrant and abnormal behaviour rather than resorting to superstition or magic. To this extent it is accurate to propose that a large-scale medicalization of human behaviour has occurred over the last two and a half centuries.

As with Foucault (1979, 1981), Turner's sociology is primarily concerned with exploring the normative institutions of coercion. He is interested in how the law, medicine and education regulate bodies and moral orientations. The story he tells is of the progressive medicalization and legalization of social and moral issues. The rise of science in explaining and managing human affairs sidelines the public. Turner speaks of predominant tendencies here. Consistent with his argument is the recognition that the public have, from time to time, challenged legal and medical advice and also that the juridical system retains the role of arbitration in public hands. All of this is allowed, without mitigating the force of the central point which is that, over the last 500 years, the predominant tendency has been for the determination of moral and ethical issues to be switched from the domains of theology and public debate into the professional ranks of lawyers and doctors.

This is certainly evident in Leisure Studies. By and large, practitioners here have accepted that the subject of abnormal leisure is the responsibility of criminologists and medical practitioners. This has contributed to the legalization and medicalization of abnormal leisure. Drug abuse, alcoholism, dangerous sexualities, violence and murder have been studied as arising from a mix of biological, psychological and political economic causes. The notion that leisure cultures are causally involved in explaining aspects of these behaviours does not flourish.

My argument is that leisure cultures are often significant causal factors in explaining drug abuse, alcoholism, dangerous sexualities, violence and murder. Further, in kow-towing to the legalized, medicalized model of deviant leisure we fail to see the continuities between deviant leisure practice and ordinary, 'normal' leisure practice. Leisure space and time allow forms of relaxed behaviour, free from the compunction of others, which can very easily tip over into criminal activity. I shall use case study material, drawn from secondary sources, to illustrate these arguments presently. Before doing so I want to contextualize my argument theoretically by drawing on theoretical work which, I believe, is essential to my general case. As will be clear presently, these strands mix and match a variety of sources. For the sake of clarity of exposition, I have organized them around three concepts, which also act as the subheadings to each section: Liminal Leisure; Moral Transcendence and Edgework; Surplus Energy.

Liminal Leisure

Victor Turner's (1969; 1982; 1992) anthropological work parallels and anticipates my own position. Namely, that one of the serious features of leisure is that it constitutes the time and space in which cultural values can be objectified and subject to reflexive investigation. As an example, it is, I think, no accident that many of the important political movements of the industrial period have their origins in taverns and public houses. It was in these leisure settings that the first trade unionists met and the adherents of free trade and anti-slavery developed their campaigns.[1] Even Hitler used alehouses and street-bars in his first speeches on National Socialism. The loosening of inhibitions in these leisure and recreational spaces led to questioning the values underpinning normality and posed the question of change. They raised the question of another order of things. Similar questions were posed in other recreational settings such as workers education groups, sports clubs, football crowds, film clubs, dance halls, walking groups and so on.

Of course, I do not mean to be understood as claiming that

recreational space is the sole generator of social change. Rather my aim is to submit that the political consequences of leisure and recreation are more significant than has generally been allowed; and further, that the relaxation of inhibitions in these spaces is one reason why they are attractive to people and often challenging to orthodox and official social values.

Victor Turner provides an interesting anthropological basis for explaining this phenomenon. He argues that modern leisure settings are analogous to the 'antistructures' of tribal societies. In these ritualized settings, participants engage in role playing which enables them to stand outside the structures of ordinary society and subject these structures to critical reflection. Bakhtin's (1968) discussion of the social consequences of the Medieval Carnival identifies the same phenomenon in the Middle Ages. The days of Carnival usually followed the intense work period of harvest time. Carnival was given over to hedonism and openly criticizing the social hierarchy and moral order. It was a time of sanctioned transgression in which the people were given licence to lampoon the main normative structures of coercion which regulated their lives in the rest of the year. Bakhtin follows Turner in emphasizing the heavily ritualized character of behaviour in these times and spaces.

Turner uses the term *liminal* to describe these settings. In tribal society, and in Medieval society, liminal time and space typically operated to reinforce the common value system of the tribe and reinforce social integration. However, the differentiation and specialization of modern cultures permits leisure in liminal settings to play a more independent role. By allowing, and encouraging, the individual to stand outside the ordinary flow of collective values, axioms and conventions, leisure in liminal settings is potentially culturally transformative. As Turner (1992: 57) puts it:

> Liminal phenomena ... are often subversive, representing radical critiques of the cultural structures and proposing utopian alternative models... Liminal and liminoid phenomena constitute metalanguages (including non-verbal ones) devised for the purpose of talking about the various languages of everyday, and in which mundane axioms become problematic, where cherished symbols are ... reflected upon, rotated, and given new and unexpected valences.

Examples of liminal leisure practices which transformed postwar society include the psychedelic drug culture of the 1960s and 70s;

the Beat Culture of the 1950s; the successive music and dance cultures between the late 1950s and the present day; and the anti-trespass walks of the 1970s, 80s and 90s. But more generally, I want to submit, that leisure and recreational space has a liminal quality. In the relaxation and informality associated with these spaces, people can objectify the order of everyday life and subject it to criticism or mockery. Following Bakhtin (1968), mockery often takes the play form. But it does not necessarily end there. In a word, recreational and leisure activities have the capacity to generate political and cultural changes which affect the whole of society.

Turner's work is important because it shows that deviant, abnormal leisure values and practices are expressed habitually as part of the ordinary relations of everyday life. They do not constitute a departure from, or break with, normality. Rather, they are a continuous part of everyday life which allow us to objectify and reflect upon the 'axiomatic' character of the laws and practices of normal culture.

Another significant contribution of Turner's work is that it demonstrates that leisure practice in liminal settings has transformative power over the entire culture. Leisure does not simply reproduce collective life as Durkheim (1915) argued in his theory of recreation and collective remaking and Stebbins (1992) suggests in his discussion of 'serious leisure', it challenges and overturns categories of normal identity, association and practice.

Work by criminologists and sociologists interested in youth culture parallels these findings. For example, Presedee (1994) and Stanley (1997) refer to the 'wild-zones' in urban-industrial culture in which space is deregulated. Examples include shopping malls, computer hacking, joy-riding and rave parties. Wild zones arise because the regulation of space logically implies deregulation. Rational-legal jurisdiction and the panopticon of modern regulatory culture cannot reach into every nook and cranny of everyday life. There are always surplus spaces which act as the habitat of transgressive behaviour. Crimogenic zones in cities, where prostitution and drug dealing occur are familiar examples. These no-go areas permit much higher levels of tolerance to 'deviant' and 'transgressive' behaviour. The association of these 'hot spots' with crime is a tourist attraction which is beginning to invite analysis from researchers working in tourist studies (Ryan 1991; Crotts 1996). What emerges most clearly from all of this literature is the elective affinity between crime and leisure. Much crime is concentrated in leisure settings such as shopping malls, sports crowds and beaches. More tellingly, much leisure involves testing the limits of escape experience. Presedee (1994: 182), commenting on consumerism writes,

> what it portends to offer the consumer is an escape from the realities of working life. But this escape – the comfort of home, car, video, television and travel – is only ever momentary and dependent on the money available to participate in the images and dreams. This is indeed a culture that literally 'plays at life' and where transgression, doing wrong, can become a leisure activity in itself. Not that leisure becomes a crime, but that crime itself takes on the characteristics of leisure.

Presedee is drawing attention to the continuum between ordinary escape experience (shopping, travel) and deviant conduct. His work, and the work of Stanley (1997), highlights how the fantasy content of ordinary consumer culture carries the compulsion to go beyond limits and obscure the moral prohibitions of legal-rational order. It is a point that I shall take up in greater detail later.

Moral Transcendence and Edgework

The second relevant theoretical strand refers to the elective affinity between liminal leisure and deviance. Katz (1988) has argued convincingly that a good deal of criminal activity is only understandable as a search for excitement, vitality, fun and sensuality. He directly relates deviance to leisure. Citing Wolfgang's (1958) classic study on the temporal distribution of criminal acts, Katz (1988: 21) notes that the rate of homicides increase as the weekend approaches, reach their height about midnight on Saturday and decline as the weekend comes to an end. Freeing up work time also frees inhibitions against the expression of aggressive instincts. The result is that leisure time is likely to be the time in which deviance is most likely to occur. It follows that leisure spaces are typically more crimogenic than non-leisure spaces. Leisure spaces vent repressed emotions. As Katz (1988: 22) puts it:

> Casual life, affectionate relationships, the weekend and Saturday night, or drinking and cruising Main Street – all the characteristic social settings for non-predatory homicide – are distinctively places of last resort for the pursuit of relaxed fun. If one cannot escape serious personal challenges then and there, it may seem as if there is nowhere else to go.

More generally, paralleling Mestrovic's (1997) view of modern society as post-emotional, Katz maintains that criminal action is an
attempt to release emotions that have been pressed down by the
standardization and timidity of the dominant moral order. Katz's
account breaks with the materialist accounts of crime favoured by
the Marxist and Mertonian traditions of criminology. It emphasizes the moral dimension in criminal conduct. For Katz, the central
feature of criminal activity is the desire for moral transcendence.
This derives from a variety of causes. Katz lists sentiments of
humiliation, righteousness, arrogance, ridicule, cynicism, defilement
and vengeance. Of course, he recognizes that these sentiments may
derive from material inequality. However, he maintains that the
key to explaining criminal conduct is the desire to transcend the
general moral restrictions and 'timidity' of the times.

O'Malley and Mugford (1991) recognize that Nietzsche is a seminal
influence in Katz's argument. The desire to transcend moral timidity recalls Nietzsche's discussion of the struggle between Apollo
and Dionysus (for an account of Nietzsche's relevance to leisure
see Rojek 1995: 80–83). This is where the elective affinity between
deviance and leisure becomes transparent. Nietzsche presented this
desire as a general characteristic of society which is repressed in
ordinary relations. Katz also recognizes that the quest for moral
transcendence is not confined to crime. In commenting on the thrill-
seeking component in criminal activity, he (1988: 77) notes the general
character of seeking excitement and escape which lies in:

> fundamental contrasts between experience in mundane activities
> and in various alternative 'worlds' such as those of theatre, night
> and day dreams, and jokes or laughter. Experience in the mun-
> dane worlds of practical reality is confined by time, space and
> social boundaries . . . Dreams, fantasies and (similar experiences) . . .
> do not respect these limitations.

O'Malley and Mugford (1991) develop this point by referring to
Lyng's (1990) study of edgework. We know that large numbers of
people in their leisure devote themselves to risk-taking activities.
By risk-taking activities is meant behaviour which deliberately places
their physical or mental well-being or sense of an ordered existence in danger. Lyng argues that pushing oneself to the edge of
limits is pleasurable. It elicits feelings of self-actualization and self-
realization. Lyng (1990: 858–9) writes:

The archetypal edgework experience is one in which the individual's failure to meet the challenge at hand will result in death or at the very least debilitating injury.

Examples include sky-diving, skiing, speed racing, mountain climbing, sea diving, excessive drinking, drug and solvent abuse.

O'Malley and Mugford (1991) contend that many aspects of modern leisure practice should be analyzed as an attempt to go beyond moral boundaries and the pacified physical standards of everyday life. In this sense, edgework may be thought of as a form of liminal leisure because it involves testing and challenging routine moral and cultural boundaries. Indeed, how could it be otherwise? We know from Foucault's (1975, 1981) work that contemporary life is experienced as a series of limits. Foucault himself was interested in 'limit-experience' (Miller 1993). Miller (1993: 30) writes of Foucault's interest in

> certain forms of Passion, implicitly linking a shattering type of 'suffering-pleasure,' the lifelong preparation for suicide – and the ability, thanks to potentially self-destructive yet mysteriously revealing states of intense dissociation, to see the world 'completely differently'. Through intoxication, reverie, the Dionysian abandon of the artist, the most punishing of ascetic practices, and an uninhibited exploration of sado-masochistic eroticism, it seemed possible to breach, however briefly, the boundaries separating the conscious and the unconscious, reason and unreason, pleasure and pain – and, at the ultimate limit, life and death – thus starkly revealing how distinctions central to the play of true and false are pliable, uncertain and contingent.

Foucault's work developed the concept of 'limit experience' in two major lines of pursuit. First, his (1961, 1975, 1981) studies on madness, punishment and sexuality emphasized the mute Dionysian dimension of human behaviour. It was almost as if civilization had gone out of its way to repress human pleasures and allow them tame, periodic respite in the form of controlled discharge or choreographed display. The differentiations and divisions which render human pleasures visible in civilization are codified in a labyrinthine structure of laws and moral interdictions. But they serve to make that which is forbidden even more attractive.

Secondly, his (1970, 1972, 1980, 1988) studies on power and epistemological categories highlight the constructed nature of human law and human being. This theme becomes more prominent in Foucault's writing so that by the end of his life the fallibility and partiality of the normative institutions of power are almost obsessively stated. With the assertion of fallibility and partiality came the recognition that things could be different. Foucault's concept of limit experience does not help very much in pointing to what lies beyond the limit. But it does suggest that in 'a world which no longer recognizes any positive meaning in the sacred' (Foucault 1980: 30), all limits must be critically interrogated and challenged. The lack of universal religious belief confirms the mortal and contextualized character of all laws and interdictions. Testing limits becomes a post-Enlightenment strategy for reuniting experience which Enlightenment epistemology has fragmented and divided.

It does not require much imagination to acknowledge the truly radical character of this position. Foucault's criticisim of the law is universal so it recognizes no restraints on the quest for limit-experience. We know from Miller's (1993: 26–9) biography, that Foucault used his own sexuality to test limits through consensual S/M experience and multiple partners. Miller (1993: 29) himself acknowledges that when Foucault visited the bath-houses in San Francisco on his last trip to California in 1983, he may have been aware that he carried the HIV virus. 'If he already had the virus,' notes Miller (1993: 29) pointedly, 'as he perhaps suspected, then he might be endangering one of his partners. And if any of his partners, as was likely, had the virus, then he might be wagering his own life.' Foucault, it seems, was ready to forgo restraints in his own quest for limit experience which literally invited his self-destruction and the destruction of others.

I think that this appeal to go beyond the limits, even to the point of death, was not singular to Foucault. Because we confront life as a series of limits, the desire to escape the density of restrictions is more or less continuous and familiar to everyone. Especially as many of the restrictions evidently follow from flawed laws built on values which some of us do not happen to share. The popularity of drug abuse and pornography in leisure practice is evident throughout the Western world. In my view, it only makes sense in the context of a quest for limit experience. Certain types of violence against each other, between men and women and between humans and animals also recurs repetitively in Western experience. People are always attracted to the forbidden and the out-of-reach. A cliché in the social control literature is that banning activities has the unintended consequence of increasing their attraction. No ban can be successfully enforced upon human potential. And as Freud's psychology demonstrated, human potential is 'polymorphously perverse'.

Perhaps controversially, I suggest that the forms of violence, which take as their object the accumulation of forbidden pleasure, should also be examined as part of the search for limit experience. And further that it is the legitimate business of students of leisure to study them. These propositions may be controversial in some circles because decades of scientific endeavour have inured us to seeing these forms of violence as 'pathological'. My objection to this is that by pathologizing violent behaviour we treat it as a category which is foreign to leisure and popular culture and which belongs instead to those interested in the study of human morbidity. Against this I wish to insist on the normal character of violence in leisure practice and popular culture. To make these proposals involves bringing together categories of human experience which are normally held apart. I submit that leisure studies is dominated by a meliorist, progressive tradition which holds that leisure is unequivocally a social good. So there is inherent resistance against examining the use of violence in the pursuit of pleasure as a type of leisure activity. Even those critical traditions like Marxism and feminism within the field of study, which acknowledge that power corrupts the human experience of fulfilment and pleasure in leisure practice, pursue the goal of social transformation in order to achieve a qualitative improvement in the current state of affairs. I do not doubt that improvement is desirable, nor do I oppose those who struggle to bring it about. My purpose is simply to propose that limit experience is a condition of every known form of human existence. I cannot foresee any social transformation in which the subject will not be reinstated in some form or another. Our polymorphous perversity will always seek new ways of expression. Further, so long as this is the case, violence will naturally be used to break down perceived barriers or restrictions to the expression of human capacities of pleasure. It is not a question of whether one approves or disapproves of this state of affairs. Rather, I maintain that it is the state of affairs in which we reside and in which leisure practice is situated. Presently, I will come to examine some forms of limit experience in leisure which involve the use of violence against others. Before doing so, I wish to come back to Lyng's concept of edgework and to go on to examine Bataille's concept of surplus energy in more detail.

Pace my discussion of limit experience, it should be stated plainly that edgework as a type of liminal leisure activity does not typically involve law-breaking activity. Bending the rules is something that we are all familiar with; and it need hardly be added that it does not necessarily lead to the internalization of a deviant identity. The capacity for challenging the rule of law is inherent in edgework because it involves individuals in objectifying and attacking moral and routine physical constraints on behaviour. However, because of this, there is elective affinity between edgework in liminal leisure and criminal activity. In the words of O'Malley and Mugford (1991):

> What 'evildoers' have in common with morally and legally legitimate edgeworkers is that they sweep aside the rational constraints of modern western culture in order to achieve emotional transcendence via the effects of strong (moral, emotional and sensual) sensations. Escape from (or transcendence of) an intolerable mundane order connected with modern, rational consciousness, social space and time-space order is key to the experience of these people, criminal or not.

Edgework and moral transcendence would not be so generally distributed in modern society without the dominant presence of strong tendencies designed to elicit routine and predictable behaviour. The rationalization and disenchantment of the world are strong themes in Weberian sociology. Wilhem Reich (1980, 1992), working in the Freudian tradition, argued that the indices of control are registered in the 'character armour' of the human body. He believed that rigid bodily posture, inflexible movement, and mannered bodily deportment, are tangible signs of the cultural organization of physical and emotional drives. Elias's (1978, 1982) study of the civilizing process also draws a parallel between the organization of the individual personality and body with the organization of culture.[2] Indeed, it is Elias and Dunning (1986) who introduced the concept of 'unexciting societies' in the study of leisure. They argue that the control structure in modern society mitigates opportunities for uncontrolled outbursts of strong communal excitement. Sudden eruptions of strong feelings are secluded in the realm of the private world. Only on rare occasions do they find expression in public life. As Elias and Dunning (1986: 65) wrote in a revised version of their 1967 paper:

> To see grown-up men and women shaken by tears and abandon themselves to their bitter sorrow in public, or panic in wild fear,

or beat each other savagely under the impact of their violent excitement has ceased to be regarded as normal. It is usually a matter of embarrassment for the unlooker and often a matter of shame and regret for those who have allowed themselves to be carried away by their excitement. To be rated as normal, adults bought up in societies such as ours are expected to check the rising upsurge of their excitement in good time.

As Elias and Dunning go on to note, the controls on strong emotions are in part, automatic. We learn them through the socialization process.

The ordinary discipline of self-control and emotional restraint with others is one reason why events like the death and funeral of Princess Diana in the summer of 1997 have such a surreal quality in people's memories. This was one occasion in which public grief was visibly expressed. In Britain at least, especially on the day of the funeral, the sight of men and women driven to tears and abandoning ordinary emotional controls was quite common. Interestingly, the emotional release acted as a catalyst for much wider claims for overthrowing restraint. The public reaction to the death of the Princess was presented as a lever for unbuttoning British reserve in relation to obedience to class hierarchy, the Monarchy and ultimately, to the very concept of the 'nation'. If Elias and Dunning are right, the relaxation of reserve and the abandonment of restraint is bound to be temporary. The network of controls which support the civilizing process will reassert themselves because they are built into the personality structure.

A possible criticism of Elias and Dunning's position is that it does not pay enough attention to the chronic distribution of edgework in modern society. By concentrating on *communal* forms of leisure in which excess energy and emotion is discharged, they obscure the manifold ways in which excess energy and bending the rules occur in the highly differentiated, individualized settings of modern, industrial society. Merely because an activity is secluded one should not disregard its importance in discharging surplus energy. Excessive drinking alone, taking drugs in private and consensual sexual pain may be interpreted as ways of discharging strong feelings in relatively safe ways. Cumulatively, these practices may weaken the fabric of the body and constitute threats to life. But in the management of strong emotions they function as viable solutions.

Although Elias and Dunning's work raises the problem of privatized existence, it does not deal in a satisfactory way with the qualities of the phenomenon. Concepts like 'chains of interdependence' and 'functional democratization' are employed to explain changes in the personality structure. But they do not adequately confront the egoism inherent in highly differentiated, specialized societies. Indeed, there is an equalizing character in both concepts, for they stress our interconnectedness with one another. What is missing is the sense of standing apart from others and living in one's own world in a culture built around reservation. Egoistic tendencies are the corollary of the differentiation and social distanciation that characterize post-emotionalism and reservation culture. By emphasizing our unique, solitary characteristics we provide a moral basis for separating ourselves from others. For example, egoism explains deviant behaviour by invoking the judgement that deviants are not people 'like us'. Lasch's (1979, 1984) work on the cult of narcissism and the minimal self argues that the rise of mass society involves emotional disengagement, the growth of a general sense of victimization and the rise of a fascination with extreme situations in everyday life. The narcissistic personality is preoccupied with developing and protecting personal characteristics which repudiate standardization. It emphasizes personal difference above communal solidarity and autonomy above commitment. Foucault's (1981, 1988) work on the ethic of 'care for the self' reinforces many of these themes. Like Lasch, Foucault paints a picture of the modern self beset by a sea of troubles and dangers. Knowledge of the variety and intensity of threats to bodily health, the encroaching awareness of an expanding, invasive machinery of surveillance designed to monitor and regulate the activities of the self, the medicalization of private life, all contribute to a general sense of powerlessness and 'ontological insecurity' (Laing 1960; Giddens 1992).

It is easy to see that in these conditions reflexivity is heightened in personal consciousness and cultural relations (Beck, Giddens and Lash 1994). We are oppressively aware of the risks that lie in the paths of our life-course and our inability to make ourselves invulnerable. Reflexivity helps us to see more clearly the pathos of egoism. For however much we may insist on our individual separateness and difference we are conscious of the collective risks that confront us and the limitations of devising personal solutions to handle them. Reflexivity also helps to clarify the attractions of edgework. The reflexive self is acutely aware of the limits on interpersonal behaviour and the gap between private and public life.

Edgework in leisure is a way of taking controlled risks. By bending the rules of everyday life we express our own sense of individuality and also reveal the fragile, arbitrary character of the constraints that bind us. This behaviour is intrinsically exciting because it opposes the dominant tendencies in society which operate to maintain and reinforce self-control. Edgework in leisure might be thought of as expressing surplus desire and surplus energy. This brings me to the third theoretical strand that I wish to consider in this section of the book.

Surplus Energy

I touched upon the question of surplus energy in the last chapter in discussing the contributions of Mumford and Bataille. Classical political economy teaches us to conceptualize economic and social problems in terms of scarcity. It is the lack of wealth and opportunities in some strata that produces unrest and conflict in the whole society. The utilitarian principle in classical political economy attempts to solve the problem by making the greatest good of the greatest number the allocative principle of resource distribution in moral regulation and economic planning. The work ethic, the philosophy of self-denial and the disapproval of wasteful consumption, all follow from the principle of scarcity. Mumford and Bataille attempt to stand classical political economy on its head by proposing that resource allocation is actually determined by the principle of surplus not scarcity. They start with the problem of abundance. Society, particularly industrial society, produces too much, not too little. A corollary of this is that the moral economy of scarcity is inappropriate for existing material conditions. Thus, the moral censure directed against idleness and conspicuous consumption is incongruous because it does not recognize the true character of social and economic life. Bataille (1991a/b) even proposes that idleness and conspicuous consumption are functional requirements for the stability of the society of abundance. He (1991a: 119) maintains:

> Society (cannot) consume all its products. Hence it must somehow destroy the surplus resources it has at its disposal. Idleness is the simplest means for this purpose. The man of leisure destroys the products necessary for his subsistence no less fully than does fire ... We obtain the same result if we ingest a substance, such as alcohol, whose consumption does not enable us to work more – or even deprives us, for a time, of our strength to produce.

Idleness . . . or alcohol have the advantage of consuming without return – without a profit – the resources that they use. They simply *satisfy* us; they correspond to the *unnecessary choice* that we make of them.

The sheer abundance and profligacy of industrial society makes the question of scarcity particularly acute. However, Bataille (1991b) insists that the problem of what to do with surplus energy and products is a deeply rooted feature of human society. He (1988: 129–47) analyzes the Roman Saturnalia and the Witches Sabbath as spontaneous solutions to the allocation of surplus. He regards both as attempts to transcend the prohibitions of society by inverting moral interdictions and cultural limits. Of course, he recognizes that excess is doomed to alternate with prohibition and limits.

Weber's (1922: 157–8) discussion of the orgy confirms many aspects of Bataille's position and further supports Turner's concept of liminal leisure and Lyng's concept of edgework. Weber argues that the orgy is an attempt to find greater intensity to life by treating prohibitions as alienable moral and physical restrictions. The loosening of organic inhibitions is a prerequisite in this process. Weber (1922: 157) notes that it is typically achieved through acute intoxicated states produced by alcohol, tobacco or other drugs; music and dance; and nudity and sexuality. All of these practices result in a chemical reaction in the body which intensifies our sense of the elasticity of the world and our propinquity to liberation. However, he (1922: 158) is careful to add that the states of ecstasy induced through the orgy must be evanescent. The implication is that society cannot survive by allowing leisure, let alone extreme forms of leisure, to dominate. The social order requires moral limits and the pacification of physical desires. Freud (1939) was later to make broadly the same point in his thesis that civilization is built upon the renunciation of physical instincts.

Bataille (1991b: 404–10) agrees that society is unworkable without moral restraints on our aggressive and sexual drives. He proposes that Calvinism and Lutheranism were puritan responses to the problems of surplus and excess. They controlled instinctual drives by sublimating them into work and the religious quest for salvation. Yet as Weber also recognized, in his (1948, 1976) analysis of rationalization and the Protestant ethic, strict adherence to the Puritan code results in this-worldly routines of experience which are so stark that they become scarcely endurable. The Puritan abjures excess in favour of the promise of eternal life, but the price of voluntary restraint is anxiety and a gnawing sense of permanent dissatisfaction.

Calvinism and Lutheranism are extreme forms of denial which create the demand for transcendence by supplying a closed universe of moral axioms. The problem with all moral prohibitions, as Bataille (1991b) correctly intimates, is that they carry within them the seeds of their own destruction. However, the quest for transcendence can never be pursued without introducing unanticipated limits and prohibitons. As he (1991b: 407) puts it:

> We are faced with a dilemma: we are adults, we actually overthrow the established order, but we cannot intend to put freedom in the place of constraint, we have to impose some new constraint, less burdensome perhaps, but a constraint such that society as a whole does not cease to acknowledge the primacy of useful activity.

Bataille concludes that the subliminal desire behind the quest for transcendence is the rediscovery of order. He (1991b: 408–9) writes:

> The question is always whether we are exceeding the limit *despite* the awareness we have of exceeding it dangerously, and *despite* our respect for the weakness of a world predicated on the limit. If we are aware of the danger of the destruction of *things*, we acknowledge in some way (in the feeling of sin, but also in the vexation that intended to pay no heed to anything) the respect that is deserved by the prohibitions we violate.

According to this view, liminal forms of leisure are ways of discharging surplus energies. By testing the limits of moral restraint and physical pacification leisure activity has the capacity to change the moral and physical order of everyday relations. Foucault (1980) acknowledged his debt to Bataille's work on transgression. Without Bataille, Foucault would have found it more difficult to formulate his concept of limit-experience.

The permissive culture of the 1960s was perhaps the last major example of the generalized testing of limit experience. At this time, social experimentation on the limits of received role models, sexual experience, drugs, dropping out of society, were all rife. Bataille did not live to see the full effects of 1960s permissive culture. His thinking was more directly influenced by the culture of the 1920s which flaunted conspicuous consumption and turned the body to dance rather than the uses of war that it had endured between 1914 and 1919. In any case, liminal discharge into the wider body politic is eventually reconstituted in the form of new moral and physical limits. Thus, the roaring twenties came to an abrupt end with the Wall Street crash, and were succeeded by the austerity of the 1930s. Similarly, the permissive culture of the 1960s which celebrated expressiveness, experimentation and anti-materialism was truncated by the OPEC oil crisis in 1974 and the new economic realities which followed. Rationalization and delayering in the labour market removed the economic security that prevailed in the late 1950s and throughout the 60s. The emergence of AIDS overshadowed the 80s and 90s and was interpreted by moralists as a judgement on permissiveness. This blockage of permissive energy created space for the recrudescence of what Wagner (1997) calls 'the new temperance'. This defined the Thatcher/Major, Reagan/Bush years and it remains a major characteristic, albeit muted, of the Clinton and Blair administrations. Blair in particular, is emerging as a Christian Puritan who believes in family values and a 'third way' in politics. However, a significant aspect of Bataille's account is that the surplus can never be entirely repressed by the agencies of moral and physical repression. Liminal leisure may be driven underground, or it may sublimate surplus energy into politicized campaigns for freedom, but in a society based on asceticism and the work ethic it will not disappear.

This is perhaps a good point in which to summarize the import of the various strands of the discussion for studying and understanding abnormal leisure. Traditional society supported 'antistructures' of time and space in which individuals could stand outside the axioms and conventions of the day. In these liminal zones, collective ritual and symbolic behaviour enabled emotional discharge from the ordinary restraints of everyday life. The effect of liminal activity was not to transform society, but to reinforce it by providing a safety valve for the release of excess emotions and energies. The effect was cathartic inasmuch as excess energies were discharged and the readiness to capitulate to collective order was ultimately reaffirmed.

In highly specialized, secularized and differentiated societies organized around performative, reservation cultures, liminal leisure ceases to be concentrated in time and space which has uniform, binding power over individuals. For example, although the spirit of the carnivalesque palpably remains in Western modern industrial society, the provision for a period of carnival in which the rules of everyday life are collectively overturned for an extended period of time is not common. Instead, the highly individualized character of modern life supports liminal leisure in a variety of diversified settings. Edgework and the discharging of excess emotions and energy are chronically distributed. For example, they may occur in settings as banal as deliberately breaking the speed limit, jay walking, engaging in acts of trespass, bending or sending up the axioms and mores of collective life through conversation, comedy and dramatic entertainment. At the other extreme, they may involve acts of physical violence, either conducted against the self or against others, theft, pornography and subversion. It is important to insist that acts as mundane as speeding through a red light, and engaging in self-abuse through the ingestion of excess alcohol or illegal mind-expanding or behaviour-changing drugs, belong to the same category of liminal leisure. That is, a vital component in the culture of leisure in Western society is limit experience. This may be broadly defined as the desire to achieve moral transcendence from the collective restraints which chain behaviour to standardized, routine practices. It is not helpful to think of edgework or moral transcendence in terms of a leisure 'career'. Only in extreme cases can one identify careers of risk-taking, rule-bending or law-breaking in leisure forms. Rather edgework and moral transcendence are expressions of flow (Deleuze and Guattari 1988; Castells 1998; Shields 1997). That is, they involve variations in intensity; they are not consciously committed to idealist, conscious goals or objects; they are motored both by rational-purposive and emotional drives; and individuals do not have to embrace a deviant leisure career to pursue them, rather, in the highly differentiated, specialized societies of the present day it is more accurate to say that most individuals drift in and out of edgework experience.

A VOLUNTARISTIC APPROACH TO LEISURE?

Durkheim did more than raise the question of the abnormal division of labour, he devised a classification of its forms. I propose that something similar is possible in the analysis of abnormal forms of leisure. But before attempting it, we must return to some of the problems with Durkheim's method. Durkheim (1895: 55) argued

that normal forms of human behaviour can be identified by applying the quantitative criterion of that which is 'generally distributed'.
As we have seen, there are significant difficulties in his application
of this criterion to the division of labour. Specifically, and briefly,
his distinction between the inevitability of 'normal' forms and the
aberrant character of 'abnormal' forms rests finally upon his private value judgements concerning what he desired and believed to
be functionally necessary for the health of modern, industrial society.
He also misjudged the capacities of modern industrial technologies
and systems of economic organization to produce surplus and the
centrality of the work ethic in conditions where expectations of
and opportunities for leisure were exploding.

In addition, Durkheim's methodology is vulnerable to the criticism that what appears to be 'generally distributed' is not necessarily
what is *actually* generally distributed. For example, in Britain during the 1980s, the 'Keep Sunday Special' campaign sought to curtail
trading and entertainment on Sundays on the grounds that it prevented people from being with their families. Sunday was identified
as a day for spending leisure with one's children and reaffirming
community values. Campaigners even held that rising rates of crime
in society were attributable to the commercialization of Sunday and
the seduction of the 'Lord's time' by work values. The biggest problem
with the campaign was that it ignored the realities of British family
and household life. The government's own statistics show that the
number of divorces has risen dramatically in the postwar period,
and that less than 50 per cent of households conform to the
classification of 'married couple with dependent children' (*Social
Trends* 1989: 43). Similarly, religious attendance at Church which
is central to separating Sunday from the rest of the week, has suffered
a dramatic decline in the postwar years (Wilson 1982). The
enlargement of weekend work patterns, the increase in geographical mobility, the growing popularity of secularism and the rise of
multiculturalism have combined to reduce the rule of Sunday
observance. The 'Keep Sunday Special' campaign drew on a fund
of assumptions and images about traditional family life which were
incommensurate with real social conditions.

The lag between common, ultimately ideological, beliefs concerning
the organization of everyday life and the actual organization of
everyday life is a perennnial theme in sociology. But it does not
present the only methodological difficulty in applying Durkheim's
principle of 'general distribution' in the analysis of 'normal' everyday

life. As criminologists know only too well, official statistics disguise a hidden quantity or 'dark number' of activities which take place beneath the observable surface of daily life. The point is made in relation to criminal activity where there are obvious reasons why people disguise behaviour which breaks the law. In leisure the same caveat applies. Because so much leisure occurs in private it is difficult to acquire a clear picture of what people actually do in their free time. For example, male respondents may be quite willing to give information on the programmes they watch on television, the books they read or the CDs they buy; one might expect them to be less forthcoming about their use of pornography or their involvement with prostitutes. Similarly, there are good reasons why respondents may want to disguise illegal drug use or excessive alcohol abuse. Of course, it is not my intention to suggest that pornography, prostitution, illegal drug use, excessive alcohol abuse and analogous activities dominate leisure. My argument is twofold: first, it is difficult to get accurate information about the extent of these activities in Western leisure activity; and secondly, that the persistence of these forms of behaviour suggest that they are a significant component of leisure practice.

Another general problem in investigating abnormal leisure forms is that they challenge categoric definitions about what constitutes leisure. There are two aspects to this point. First, a doctrinal issue within leisure studies relating to what leisure means; and secondly, a wider issue concerning the concept of leisure in relation to the medicalization and legalization of everyday life. To begin with the doctrinal issue: within leisure studies there is vast disagreement about the meaning of leisure. Some authors argue that it only has meaning in relation to work (Wilensky 1960, Parker 1983); others maintain that it is a construct of capitalist ideology or patriarchy (Adorno and Horkheimer 1944; Van Moorst 1982; Wimbush and Talbot 1988; Baudrillard 1998). The view taken here is that leisure consists of time and space in which the compunctions inhibiting voluntary action are relaxed. Compunction here is used as an aspect of the concept of flow which was discussed in Chapter 1. I want to avoid the suggestion that some compunction is present in some behaviours and absent in others. The force of compunction in influencing personal behaviour is a question of balance involving issues of relativity and intensity. The flow of behaviour is subject to stronger or weaker constraints but it never occurs independently of constraints. All behaviour is *situated* and personal choice is a matter of how individuals define and operate the situations in which they are situated. This assumes that in certain social settings, notably work and family life, powerful types of compunction exist to ensure that individuals remain in role. Examples include managerial monitoring devices, self-monitoring devices, worksheets, meal times, school times and so on.

In leisure, individuals believe that they have more voluntary freedom to act as they please. Of course, this belief may be illusory. In addition, voluntary freedom is always relative since even the 'freest' leisure behaviour involves a degree of role-playing. The crucial principle is the belief of social actors that their leisure consists of uses of time and space which are voluntarily chosen by themselves. One difficulty with this argument is that voluntarism is a notoriously problematic category. This brings me to the second issue that needs to be commented on here.

In highly medicalized societies many forms of abnormal behaviour are categorized as addictions. Excessive drug and alcohol use, pornography, flagrant risk-taking and violence have all been analyzed in these terms (Wagner 1997). In placing such strong emphasis upon the belief in voluntarism as the determinant of leisure, the researcher is constantly faced with the question of deciding when behaviour is a choice or an addiction? Typically, violent behaviour against others, fantasies about murdering, acts of murder, drug addiction and alcohol abuse are labelled as illnesses. There are good reasons why this should be the case. The aetiology of violent and self-destructive behaviour in individuals is related to influences which cause helplessness, aggression against others and self-destructive tendencies. Criminologists have related this to a variety of conditions including dysfunctional family experience, material deprivation and genetic predispositions (Taylor, Walton and Young 1973). I have no quarrel with approaching deviant behaviour in this way. My point is simply that to comply with models of deviance which pathologize deviant behaviour by interpreting it in medical terms, ignores the influence of leisure cultures in promoting transgression through limit experience, edgework and the search for moral transcendence. My argument is that leisure cultures release inhibitions and encourage individuals to expel pent-up emotions. This is not an extreme event in leisure, it occurs as part of ordinary leisure practices. Lasch's (1979) account of the cult of narcissism draws attention to the fascination with extreme situations in contemporary society. Kidnapping, murder, stalking and drug abuse are staple themes of popular television. Cinema and literature has developed *genres* like the *film noir*, the crime thriller and the horror story to cater for demand. These *genres* are significant for understanding leisure because they are concentrated overwhelmingly in leisure space and leisure time. At the level of popular fantasy one can justifiably speak of the presence of fantasy edgework in ordinary leisure practice in which, through reveries and daydreams, we situate ourselves in extreme, life-threatening situations.

Of course, feminist literature has highlighted the role of patriarchal culture in propagating these fantasies. It has also drawn attention to the real risks that we, and especially women, face in cultures dominated by patriarchal values (Brackenridge, Summer and Woodward 1995, Burton-Nelson 1994). But, as these authors would no doubt recognize, it is unsatisfactory to lay all of the causes for aggressive and self-destructive behaviour and fantasy edgework at the door of patriarchal culture. Why is this? To begin with, fantasies of aggression and self-destruction are not exclusive to either sex. Interest in extreme responses to inequality, injustice, humiliation is a shared response. It is shared, because excessive emotions of imaginary transcendence are entirely typical, ordinary responses to the frustrations of the reservation culture of modern life (Katz 1988). Whatever sex, race or class we are, we are drawn to limit experience which takes us beyond familiar social forms or practices.

Secondly, only in comparatively rare cases does one find that emotions of transcendence become chronic, unmanageable aspects of personal experience and lifestyle. While most of us yearn for moral transcendence as a consequence of facing the constraints and changing conditions of everyday life, we discharge our yearning through the ordinary mediations of flow. That is, we drift into yearnings for transcendence and, from time to time, may relate to these yearnings as crucial features of our leisure experience. But through the gyrations of flow we turn back into the controlled contours of acceptable selfhood. The solidification of personality types based in the hatred of the opposite sex, or in the pursuit of self-destruction, is comparatively rare. If contemporary society is highly medicalized it is also highly legalized. We think of forms of human behaviour in terms of disconnected boxes and a large phalanx of influential professionals make it their business to legitimate these rational-legal divisions. But over-legalization leads to unimaginative, tunnel vision.

This is particularly a problem in leisure studies because, in our culture, the concept of leisure is so heavily imbued with general associations of 'pleasure', 'satisfaction', 'health' and 'well-being', that to argue that some forms of leisure involve people in gaining pleasure from hurting themselves or others invites a critical backlash. Thus, Aitchison (1996: 10) proposes that

> When we start naming violence, abuse and violation of human rights as activities within the realm of 'leisure', then it will be time for the feminists, philosophers in ethics and sociologists interested in citizenship to move back to our disciplines or on to other subject fields. Violence, abuse and violations of human rights may well play a part in exploitative leisure relations but these acts themselves are not acts of leisure – they are acts of violence and should be named and researched as such.

There are a number of difficulties with this proposition. In the first place it is historically insupportable, since we know that from the Roman games to the freakshows of the nineteenth and twentieth centuries, violence and abuse were prominent themes in leisure (Bogdan 1988). Abuse and violence continue to be elements of many spectator sports. As Elias and Dunning (1986) argue, it is possible to regard many contest sports as providing mimetic outlets in which our aggressive emotions can be discharged.

Secondly, Aitchison mistakes the character of contemporary society. We live in violent societies. Violence is glorified in film, songs and verse. Our culture eulogizes 'heroic killers'. As Yablonsky (1997: 25–6) notes, Al Capone was venerated in the 1920s; John Dillinger and Bonnie and Clyde were folk heroes in the 1930s; Sam Giancana, John Gotti and other Mafioso leaders have been venerated in recent years. In Britain, the Kray twins continue to be a source of fascination in popular culture. As Yablonsky (1997: 26) rightly maintains:

> In contemporary society, a large segment of the population both black and white seem to adore murderous sociopathic film heroes. Stallone, Willis, Norris, Schwarzenegger, and others reflect this public worship of the heroic, sociopathic killer who, against impossible odds, wins by indiscriminately murdering dozens if not hundreds of their enemies in a two-hour movie. The validation of this mad macho-syndrome is affirmed by the billion dollar box office receipts at movie theatres, not only in America but around the world.

Violence and abuse, I suggest, are perfectly ordinary, routine features of our leisure experience. Although the evidence concerning
the effects of these representational forms of violence upon real
behaviour is equivocal (Barker and Petley 1997), there is no doubt
that millions of people enjoy these leisure forms either vicariously
or through direct participation. Further, we know from studies of
gang and hooligan cultures and serial killers, that violence plays
an enormous part in the leisure conduct of real strata in society
(Dunning, Murphy and Williams 1988; Katz 1988). Moreover, how
can one examine the statistics on drug and alcohol abuse and the
cancer rates associated with cigarettes, without reaching the conclusion that self-destructive edgework is omnipresent in our society?
In our leisure many of us are routinely and unapologetically violent to ourselves. The fact that abuse exists in one box and violence
in another may satisfy Aitchison's naive and politically partisan view
of contemporary culture, but it is no basis for a mature and detached approach to leisure studies.

I want to insist on the ordinary character of fantasy edgework
and limit experience in everyday life. Leisure in popular culture is,
I suggest, a crucial outlet for the release of repressed aggressive
and sexual emotions. Through film, television and *genre* literatures
we vicariously expel tensions and play with social forms that are
denied in our staple life. As I have already noted, Elias and Dunning
(1986) argue that sport performs a release function in contemporary society. It permits the discharge of pent-up strong emotions
in relatively safe ways. My position is similar, except I want to insist that in advanced consumer culture there are powerful stimulations
which make fantasy edgework a continuous aspect of behavioural
flows. It is no longer a question of discharging our repressed emotions at a soccer game or rugby match. In post-emotional society
we are continuously bombarded with escape messages which fanta-
size about the prospect of transcending the edges of everyday life.
Advertising, television, film, pop music, magazines and the other
branches of the mass media, provide countless outlets for the arousal
and discharge of strong emotions around the prospect of going over
the edge. Our incentives to offload aggression vicariously are so
inexorable that we have trouble recognizing real forms of aggression when they occur.

Following Mestrovic (1997), the media saturation of personality
structure has introduced the law of diminishing returns into our
emotional discharge. The post-emotional state is a consequence of

media-overload which prevents us from having strong feelings about anything except that which impacts upon the buoyancy of what Lasch (1984) calls 'the minimal self'. This is why Mestrovic (1997) was justifiably able to condemn the cool responses in the West to the excesses of Serbian aggression in the war in former Yugoslavia in the early 1990s. We knew about the horror and the genocide. We chose to get on with our own lives and turned a deaf ear to those who called for Western military involvement on the grounds that we didn't want another Vietnam.

If all of this is correct, it suggests that it is essential to revise the balance of Stebbins's (1992) distinction between 'serious and casual leisure'. In particular, casual leisure emerges as a much more significant component of contemporary leisure experience than Stebbins seems to allow. We may develop a sense of career and self-discipline by following serious leisure pursuits, but our personalities are formed by the flow of representations of escape, release and transcendence which form a continuous part of commodity culture.

A further problem with voluntaristic approaches to leisure remains. That is, they have a tendency to overstate individual freedom. This is a routine criticism of the early functionalist and conservative approaches to leisure (Roberts 1978, 1981; Parker 1983: Dower *et al.* 1981). Yet unless one grants reflexivity and choice to social actors one falls into the same trap as structuralists who exaggerate determinism in leisure behaviour. Individuals are not atomized, autonomous actors. Everyone is situated in a cultural and material network of relations which influences personal behaviour flow. Structuralist approaches overstate the situated character of behaviour. In the most egregious cases, personal choice disappears and the individual is reduced to a cypher blindly fulfilling social forces. On the other hand, agency approaches to leisure seriously exaggerate personal freedom. In the most concentrated examples the individual is analyzed as exercising choice and self-determination autonomously, so that the situated character of personal choice is neglected.

The reality lies in between structure and agency. In analytical terms it has probably been captured to best effect in approaches like Giddens's (1984) structuration theory which seeks to convey the recursive character of human interactions and, more recently, those philosophical and geographical approaches to human behaviour which have developed the concept of flow (Deleuze and Guattari 1988; Castells 1998; Shields 1997). A final problem with voluntarism is cultural and historical relativism. If it is allowed that behaviour is situated, and that compunction applies in behavioural flow, it follows that the cultural and historical conditions of situated behaviour and behavioural flow is a crucial requirement of analysis. In enquiring into what is generally distributed in one culture one must not make the mistake of attributing universal characteristics to the behaviour in question.

These problems and difficulties have been discussed at some length in order to combat some of the more simplistic assumptions made with regard to voluntaristic approaches to leisure. For all of the troublesome caveats that one must make in advocating and applying voluntaristic models of behavioural flow they have the crowning advantage of placing the intentions, beliefs and values of social actors at the centre of analysis.

TRUST AND ONTOLOGICAL INSECURITY IN LEISURE

As I will argue at greater length in the next chapter, the foundation of meaningful human relationships is respect and trust. Where these qualities are breeched or denied, relationships may cease to be viable. In our society, most people, most of the time, experience sufficient trust and respect in leisure relationships to remain attached to them and to reciprocate with others. But on some occasions people are caught up in leisure relationships which are pregnant with inauthenticity and which engender bad faith. Laingian psychology partly examined these relationships in the context of family life. Laing (1960), Laing and Esterson (1964) argued that where men and women feel trapped in relationships which are built around layers of inauthenticity and bad faith they experience anxiety, invalidation and distress. In the worst cases they laspe into a state of chronic non-identity. Laing (1960) identified three clinical conditions associated with this state:

1) *Engulfment.* The fear of being overwhelmed by strong emotions so that personal safety is sought in isolation.
2) *Implosion.* The fear that relationships are continuously on the brink of disintegrating, so that the individual must build defences to avoid extinction.
3) *Petrification.* The fear that others have the power to turn one to stone, so treating others as 'things' becomes the safest way to protect oneself.

In abnormal leisure relationships feelings of fears of engulfment, implosion and petrification are, to a lesser or greater degree, usually present. Individuals feel that their true self is buried and the external face which they present to the world is embroiled in false and meaningless relationships. Unable to confirm what they see as their true identity with others, they may feel the anguish of seeing themselves as essentially lost or destroyed. In such circumstances, they may decide that self-destruction is the safest place to be. For other individuals the despair of being locked into false and meaningless relationships leads to the feeling that one has become stripped of individuality. One perceives oneself as a thing among other things. In these circumstances the temptation to strike out at others or to find ways of eliminating them may prove irresistible. For if something is experienced as an obstacle without the capacity for trust or respect, the natural tendency is to eliminate it.

Laing's clinical psychology was extremely persuasive. Where he went wrong in his later work was to extend these clinical observations to the whole of society (see Laing 1967; 1970). In his most egregious passages, he presents madness as a 'voyage' of regression into more authentic states of being and he argues that modern bureaucratic, capitalist, big city culture is making us all mad. This exaggerates, and ultimately renders implausible, the extremely useful concept of 'ontological insecurity' which, Laing (1960, 1967) argues, is a common condition among men and women in contemporary culture.

Laing's discussion parallels Simmel's (1971; 1978) discussion of the psychology of modern life. Simmel argued that one of the chief characteristics of modern life is the increasing velocity and density of relations. The acceleration of daily life is evident in the rapid oscillation of information flows and the transport and communication revolutions which compresses time and space. For Simmel, two personality types have emerged from this condition. Neurasthenic personalities are characterized by a high state of anxiety and restlessness. They are information and fashion junkies who constantly react to the latest trends. In Riesman's (1950) terms, they are 'other-directed', in that they follow the stimulations of the culture industry as role and status models. Neurasthenic personalities live for the moment. But their desire to consume the latest commodities and experiences of consumer culture is overshadowed by a sense of pathos. Neurasthenic people know that nothing lasts. So they are wary of making commitments to others or dedicating themselves to long-term goals. Their leisure is marked by restlessness and a sense of homelessness. It is oriented to the outside world and is driven by a search for fresh stimulation.

The blasé personality is distinguished by a state of indifference to the external world. Everything seems flat, repetitive and monotonous. In Riesman's (1950) terms, blasé people are 'inner directed'. They act as if they and their immediate family are the only reality in society. The culture of the external world is beyond their capacity to influence. Their leisure is privatized and repetitive. Distrustful of new sensations, they rely on familiar and safe patterns of behaviour.

Simmel treats these personality types as reactions to the accelerated velocity of everyday life. They are ways of coping with the instability and insecurity of constant change. They help to explain why a sense of place and the element of fantasy have become prominent features of leisure in this century. In circumstances where everything is changing people seek symbolic continuity in fixed horizons and stable spaces. The desire to preserve places of outstanding natural beauty from industrial or commercial development and the growth of interest in cultural heritage, can be interpreted as expressions of the modern desire for stability. Yet simply because modern life requires you to change or perish, there are few remaining spaces in which solidarity and belonging can be expressed and reaffirmed (Lowenthal 1985).

Fantasy has emerged as a symbolic space in which these feelings can be exchanged. We feel closer to each other when we watch a sentimental film, than when we are implored by the state or voluntary organizations to band together to tackle poverty or homelessness. Infantilism is a very strong component here. The desire to return to safety and security is palpable in many modern leisure forms.

We hunger after security for good reasons. An elementary fact about our world is that it is undependable. As Beck (1992) implies in risk society, modern life is living without a safety net. There are few guarantees, and no guardian angels. Ontological insecurity is certainly an appropriate response to our situation. It is very evident in popular leisure forms. Much of our most popular film, television drama, literature and music is concerned with the themes of inauthenticity, annihilation and extinction. Beckett, Albee and Pinter return to the theme of chronic non-identity again and again in their plays. In movies like *Natural Born Killers* (1994), *Pulp Fiction* (1994), *Seven* (1995), *LA Confidential* (1997), the characters radiate a profound lack of trust in others and a sense that others are obstacles which must be eliminated through acts of violence. Many of the dramatic play forms in popular leisure deal with extreme situations in which individuals face the risk of personal extinction. Exley, the good cop in *LA Confidential*, can only eliminate the inauthenticity and bad faith around him by shooting his corrupt police commander in the back. For this act Exley is not punished, but receives an award for bravery, and promotion. The elimination of rivals and inauthentic characters is also a prominent theme in popular music from 60s soul and protest music through to rap and hip hop. As Clarke (1995: 553), quoting a popular rap artist, puts it:

> NWA's Easy-E sings:
>
> Do I look like a motherfucking role model?
> To a kid looking up to me
> Life ain't nothing but bitches and money

> The rest of us may appear to behave ourselves, but there is little evidence that we care about anything more than Easy-E does. All the rapper knows is what he sees, and he does not see a society which is interested in any kind of justice.

Rap portrays the ordinary world as enmeshed in inauthenticity and self-delusion so that violence which refuses to play the game acquires an incandescent purity. Feelings of engulfment, implosion and petrifaction are dramatized in the music. The limitations experienced in everyday life are subject to violent parody. The music capitalizes the sense of righteousness which derives from exposing the hypocrisy of dominant cultural values. Rap flings a gauntlet in the face of performative and reservation culture and comments on the atavism of the real world.

To claim this much is to make a covert plea for the reassessment of the concept of alienation in popular culture. Alienation is a difficult term and its over-use in the 60s and 70s leads to unfortunate assertions. I have already mentioned Laing's phenomenology and its appeal to madness as a voyage out of the alienation of everyday life. In this period the term alienation became a catch-all for every kind of disappointment and dissatisfaction, thus draining the concept of its analytic power. I submit that it is time to reassess the concept. Briefly, the term alienation is most closely associated with the writings of Marx, especially the *Economic and Philosophic Manuscripts* (1964) originally published in 1844. Marx argues that alienation is an inevitable consequence of the capitalist mode of production. Workers are alienated in three ways:

1. *Necessity to sell their labour power for the means of subsistence.* Marx held that the historical tendency of capitalism is to re-place common rights and property with individual rights and property. By depriving workers of the means to guarantee their own subsistence, capitalism forces workers to turn to the mar-ket and sell their labour power to capitalists. Essential to Marx's argument is the proposition that workers have no choice in this matter. By handing over their energy and time to the capitalist, workers feel estranged from the work process.
2. *No property rights in the fruits of production.* Capitalism forces workers to work for the owners of the means of production. But it does not allow them to retain control or ownership of what they produce. Instead, the fruits of production belong to the capitalist and are sold on the market as commodities. Workers are conscious of living in a world which they have created but which just as obviously, cannot be influenced by them, and does not belong to them. The world is experienced as a theatre in which the props and script are controlled by others. Feelings of powerlessness and meaninglessness follow from this situation (see also Blauner 1964).
3. *Sense of invalidation.* Because work in capitalist society does not satisfy basic needs or desires, workers feel inauthentic and invalidated. Their work occupies most of their conscious life, but it provides no element of self-affirmation, beyond monetary reward. Workers do not feel at home in their work, nor do they feel at home in their leisure.

Marx collapsed each argument into the general proposition that work under capitalism, is the source of an overarching universe of alienation. Workers are not fulfilled in their work experience and they deaden their dissatisfaction in leisure by intoxicating and un-demanding pursuits.

Although few writers today take alienation as their chief theme, it is part of the background assumptions in many critical approaches to society and culture. For example, Lowe (1995: 166–70), writing on the body in late-capitalist society, proposes that commodity culture is 'sociopathic'. The constant shopping around for different life-styles, the concern with physical appearance, the fear of ageing, the desire to escape the limitations imposed by consumer culture, produce psychological depression and physical illness. They are symptoms of neurasthenia which, in Simmel's sociology, features as a general condition of Modernity. The body in Modern society has lost its connection with the relations of traditional society. It has become the nexus of exchange value in which impersonal and remote relations dominate. McLaren (1997) writes from a contrasting perspective, but reaches similar conclusions. He argues that commodity culture connects with racism to produce an inhuman system of oppression which can only be transcended through revolutionary action.

There is then, a wide body of literature which maintains that the conditions of everyday life in contemporary society are dehumanizing and alienating. Sociopathic conditions are conducive to psychopathology. Cultures which generate alienation create dehumanized people who have low trust in or respect for others and a poor self-image. Most of us, most of the time, handle these feelings through denial, parody or irony. We distance ourselves from the pain of feeling invalidated. As Mestrovic (1997) argues, post-emotionalism is part of the common currency in which everyday life is now conducted. Our sense of social reality has shrunk to ourselves and our immediate family so that the rest of humanity is operationally neutralized as 'strangers' or 'others' about whom we can be relatively indifferent. But the retreat into distance, reservation and denial is sometimes difficult. They reinforce the general sense of invalidation and inauthenticity. For some people these stock responses become untenable. They use their free time to unleash the unsatisfied emotions bottled up inside. This is when people notice that some forms of free-time activity become abnormal.

THE ABNORMAL FORMS OF LEISURE

If life seems like a series of material and cultural limitations, the attractions of escape are heightened. As I have already intimated, this is one reason why our modern leisure pursuits have an historically high level of fantasy content. We play at being in different circumstances by consuming film, television, music, theatre and popular music. For some people, playing out practices changes the life course. They begin to treat their bodies in leisure as objects to be pushed beyond the limits of ordinary experience (Katz 1988). This may end up in pathological practice. Individuals who use their bodies to escape from mundane reality through drug or alcohol abuse may kill themselves. But it is important to my general argument that limit experience is an ordinary part of leisure. In particular, I want to avoid the tendency to medicalize limit experience as a condition to be corrected through a regime of medical intervention. Abnormal leisure may be defined as pushing limit experience so that it threatens the self or others. This is a deliberately broad definition. I wish to treat some types of behaviour which have hitherto been described as 'crime' or 'illness' as part of the spectrum of leisure. I do not mean to be understood as claiming that criminologists and medical sociologists should abandon their careers in the study of deviance and the aetiology of pathology in order to switch to leisure studies! My point is rather, that leisure studies must break with the habit of regarding deviance and illness as segregated from leisure practice. I accept that this is a difficult and agonizing break to make. Ideologically speaking, the concept of leisure is bound up with capitalist ideology which presents free time as the reward for work. Leisure is overwhelmingly associated with positive characteristics, most commonly, freedom, choice and self-determination. This is one reason why it is so difficult to discuss leisure time and space as the root of negative personal experience or social alienation. To break with the ideologically dominant equation between leisure and positive experience is to run against the grain of how leisure is conceptualized both by specialists and at the level of common sense. However, I propose that unless the break is made the potential of leisure studies will always be restricted. There are two reasons for this. Firstly, the common and ordinary occurrence of deviance in leisure behaviour will be ignored; and secondly, the ambivalent character of many leisure situations in which ordinary practice can swing into deviance and law-breaking will be mistaken.

Abnormal leisure occurs when the individual refuses to bestow respect or trust on the other. The density of contemporary life often pitches us into this kind of relationship with others. The number and velocity of daily contacts and collisions that we have with others neutralizes our feelings for them. For most of us, most of the time, we cope with the impersonality and anonymity of daily life by intensifying our attachments to our family and delving deeper into our fantasy lives. But we are aware of a surplus residue in our relationships which is much greater than the spheres of intimacy and mutual understanding in which we ordinarily operate. This residue is generally referred to as 'society'. When we encounter conflict with 'society' we have coping mechanisms to reconcile the problem. Most of us hold the general belief that the court of civility will convene to correct damaging behaviour. If appeals to civility – the inherent decency of one's fellows – fail, the individual always has recourse to rational-legal judgements embodied in the law and judiciary. So while society may seem anonymous and impersonal for most of us, there is a mechanism for translating our desire for redress and fairness in relations with others into a tangible outcome. But for some people, some of the time, faith in civil or rational-legal standards is dislocated or entirely absent. For these people, the other is often experienced, albeit tacitly, as threatening and oppositional. Their emotions become petrified.

Another response is to label the other as an object of personal gratification. The other may be defined in a generalized, abstract form such as the state, the police, the gang, the company or the stranger. Or it may apply to a concrete individual with whom one has a relationship.

Although the forms and practices show a great variety, abnormal leisure typically involves treating the other as immune to valid feelings. It is easy to imagine how this might apply to strangers. The examples of rioting at leisure events discussed by Cunnen *et al.* (1989), joy-riding by Presedee (1994) and computer hacking Stanley (1997) all involve individuals moving into aggressive and abusive relations with generalized, abstract others in which the rights of others are neutralized. Similarly, feminist research has shown how free time in domestic space can tip over into violent behaviour, usually involving men attacking women (Green *et al.* 1987). In my frame of reference computer hacking and crowd disturbances fall into the category of leisure activity. They derive some of their energy from the relaxation of inhibitions that is typically associated with leisure time and leisure space.

However, I want to extend the meaning of invalidation in leisure experience to apply to one's self. I propose that acts of, for example, alcohol and drug abuse are directed by the individual against those aspects of the self which are regarded or experienced as invalid. For some of us, leisure is the category of human experience in which we seek to annihilate or punish those aspects of the self which we relate to as invalid. Of course, not all leisure conforms to this category of experience. Many forms of leisure are oriented to enriching the self through participation with others. However, I am electing to concentrate on the category of leisure experience which revolves around invalidity experience because I think it is the basis for understanding abnormal leisure forms.

I suggest that there are three types of abnormal leisure forms:

Invasive

The individual engages in leisure practices that involve a lack of respect for or trust in an element of one's own self. The individual is unable to build enriching or viable relationships with others in leisure practice. Leisure becomes a place in the life-course in which the individual retreats and practices ways of burying the elements of the self which are experienced as invalid. The feelings of invalidity may arise from the wider experience of alienation in society. But they are concentrated on the self and not others. Invasive leisure experience may therefore involve the outward display of *bonhomie* and companionship with others; but in the inner world, the individual feels split, both from others who require him or her to go through the motions of companionable leisure, and from elements in his or her own personality which are experienced as irretrievably invalid. In such a condition individuals use leisure to drown out their sorrows or blank out their inability to be like others.

An important strand in writing about drugs emphasizes the relationship between drugs and liberation (Leary 1970, 1990; Lee and Shlain 1985; Melechi 1997). I have no reason to repudiate the relationship, although I submit that it is overstated. I propose that the liberation that people feel through the recreational use of stimulants must also take account of the widespread feelings of invalidity or deadness that people experience in other aspects of their ordinary lives. The sense of oppressive limits creates an adjoining desire for escape or liberation. In excessive cases invalidation involves the individual in pushing limit experience beyond the barrier of physical and mental tolerance. Repeated, gross stimulant abuse involves punishing the invalid element of the personality. Individuals often legitimate it to themselves as an heroic attempt to go beyond life and death. The prominence of the element of the personality which experiences everyday life as a series of invalid encounters supports this heroic delusion, often with catastrophic consequences. Recreational use of stimulants can impair physical and mental health and it may lead to death.

Conrad's (1997) fascinating study of absinthe demonstrates how the drink was associated with 'respectable suicide'. Poets like Alfred de Musset, Charles Baudelaire, Paul Verlaine and Arthur Rimbaud and painters like Claude Manet, Edgar Degas, Toulouse-Lautrec, Paul Gaugin and Vincent Van Gogh, all used absinthe to expand consciousness. An earlier generation of artists, headed by Coleridge and De Quincey, used opium for the same purpose. Yet so far from enlivening and expanding visionary life, the excessive and prolonged use of absinthe and opium, stupefied the imagination, destroyed artistic energy and ruined the physical well-being of the drinker. In the cases of de Musset, Baudelaire, Van Gogh, Coleridge and De Quincey, continued use was palpably a method of neutralizing the sense of invalidity or incapacity in themselves. The leisure of these individuals ceased to be about creation and became a matter of obliteration. What started as a way of opening up and heightening consciousness, turned into a way of dulling an inner sense of failure.

The respondents in Pearson's (1987) study of heroin use in Britain gave a variety of reasons for turning to the drug. Some took heroin to avoid the stress and degradation associated with unemployment; others became addicted through peer-group pressure; others use the drug to cope with family pressures. What emerges most unequivocally from Pearson's study is the addict's sense of being distinct and separate from the rest of society. His respondents speak of not being able to find the right job, failing in personal relationships or finding the entertainments and amusements in straight society inadequate and insufficient. Although few admit to being in a state of dependence, nearly all reveal major incapacities in being able to control the use of the drug. Feeding the habit often puts the user at additional risk through burglary, shop-lifting and prostitution. The question arises of whether heroin use can in any meaningful sense be called leisure activity. Two points must be made. First, Pearson's study clearly shows that occasional users take the drug as an adjunct of recreational culture. Secondly, addicts take the choice to use heroin in preference to other forms of stimulation. That is, they choose not to make the recreational choices of non-users. The stereotype of the helpless addict unable to break out of the cycle of need and dependency ignores the active choices that addicts make in favour of the drug.

Invasive leisure often involves slowly retreating from a society which is seen as unfulfilling, performative (hence, inauthentic) and over-reserved or gradually abandoning a part of the self which is no longer regarded as having a capacity for ordinary life. A spirit of listlessness accompanies the individual's participation in leisure and recreation. This leads to a general shrinking away from engaging with others and the cultivation of retiring, solitary recreational habits. In many cases invasive leisure patterns may be shared with a partner or a family, so that the reserved, solitary leisure forms characterize the entire social unit. But as with the case of heroin use with peers, the experience is ultimately a solitary one which serves to emphasize one's difference from the rest of society. There is some historical evidence to suggest that patterns of invasive leisure may have been more widespread in the early years of industrialization. For example, Berridge and Edwards (1987: 262) show that between 1830 and 1869 average home consumption of opium per thousand population was between 2 and 3lb of opium per head. There is nothing new about the desire to use drugs to turn one's back on reality.

Mephitic

The individual directs a lack of respect or trust onto others. The term mephitic comes from *mephitis* which means a noxious emanation or foul-smelling or poisonous stench. I use the term figuratively, although I also want to convey the view that mephitic forms of leisure offend the moral order. This is also true of invasive leisure patterns. But whereas invasive leisure typically involves a self-contained destiny, mephitic forms spill out to damage others.

Mephitic leisure patterns occur when the individual transfers feelings of invalidity onto others; equally, it may involve regarding the self as truly authentic and real and others as inauthentic or unreal. In both cases, others are deprived of genuine feelings and are objectified as sources of physical gratification or mental pleasure. The objectification of others in leisure is closely related to commodification. Several studies of sex tourism demonstrate how organized prostitution operates as a source of attraction for male tourists. Crush and Wellings (1987) argue that prostitution is one of the pillars of tourist promotion in Lesotho and Swaziland. Similarly, Thanh-Dam (1983) has commented on the importance of sex tourism to the leisure economies of Thailand, the Philippines, South Korea and Taiwan. As Craik (1991: 104) observes, sex tourism is often resented by residents, but a combination of a lack of alternative employment prospects, low wages and harassment by the tour operators makes it hard to combat.

Many forms of sexuality and sexual practice are situated on the borderlines of straight society. As such, they are attractive for edgeworkers seeking to exploit limit-experience. People who use other bodies for physical gratification do so for a variety of reasons. The desire to go beyond conventional limits is certainly one of them. Given the nature of sexual inequality, this desire is more developed and practised by men. The use of prostitutes in male leisure experience undoubtedly involves high levels of male-dominated fantasy content. The same is true of go-go bars, strip clubs, massage parlours, S&M dungeons, porn videos and phone sex. But as Plachy and Ridgeway (1996) argue, it is ingenuous to regard relationships between men and women in the sex industry as universally revolving around sexual stereotypes and clichés. The gratification of male power is often attributed to male clients who use the sex industry. Although this is certainly confirmed by many relationships it should not be allowed to obscure the variety of relationships between men and women in the sex industry. Men are often drawn to prostitutes and massage parlours by feelings of personal invalidation. They feel unworthy of having a relationship, so turn to serial sexual encounters which bring a quick-fix of sexual release. Dependence not power is the key in this kind of relationship. Studies of sex workers also clearly show that some workers build up nurturing ties with clients which are closer to friendships than business relationships.

Nevertheless, underlying sex work is the philosophy that the sex worker is finally an object to be used as one pleases for monetary payment. Sex workers are treated as individuals who operate solely on the edges of limit-experience. They are defined as 'hot' or 'horny' rather than workers who are selling themselves as a commodity, rather than mothers, daughters or sisters. In this sense sex work is an example of mephitic leisure because it involves treating the other as finally, an object in which trust and respect are not a precondition of interaction.

For writers like Laing (1960) and Lowe (1995), invalidation is a consequence of alienation. In critical psychoanalysis the phenomenon of invalidation is studied in acts of self-abuse and self-destruction, but also in acts of abuse and destruction which are directed against others. These abusive acts are not typically encountered in the sphere of work because the monitoring system which supports civil behaviour is well articulated. The same articulation does not apply to leisure. Sex work is unusual in this respect, because abuse and harassment are often implicit in the work relationship. But mephitic leisure practice is more usually conducted outside the work sphere, in the home and in areas of 'free' time. Statistically, most acts of violence are concentrated in non-work space and time such as the home, public streets, clubs, bars, parks, beaches and woodlands.

In some cases the feelings that others do not deserve respect or trust are so strong that the individual fantasizes and takes steps to eliminate others. Studies of serial killers have shown that fantasies about eliminating others bulk large in the killer's leisure time (Norris 1988; Jenkins 1994; Pron 1995). Most acts of homicide are spontaneous and occur in a fit, frenzy or temper. Also, the majority of homicides occur between an assailant and victim who know each other (Archer and Gartner 1984; Mitchell 1990). In contrast, serial killings involve high levels of fantasy work and mental preparation in eliminating strangers. This fantasy work is situated overwhelmingly in the leisure time of the killer. Speculatively, one might add that leisure is also the time in which people feel most solitary and in which the atmosphere of invalidation is likely to be most concentrated.

The direction of the argument is leading me to make propositions which I am conscious will disturb many proponents of leisure studies. The idea that some people 'kill for leisure' is abhorrent to many people. It is particularly difficult for teachers and researchers involved in leisure to entertain the possibility, since most of them are emotionally involved with the belief that leisure is unquestionably a social and personal benefit. For such people, the proposition that some individuals devote their free time to fantasizing about killing others and, in some cases, plan and commit murders is too ghastly to contemplate. All that one can say in response to this type of position is that the evidence reveals a different picture. Studies of serial killers by Leyton (1986), Norris (1988) and Pron (1995) show a close correlation between serial killing and recreation. Their case studies of serial killers show, beyond reasonable doubt, that the recreation of the killer is dominated with fantasies and plans to murder others. Recent cases reported in the press and current events literature support the argument. For example, the Home Office psychologist called in to analyze the multiple killings committed by Fred and Rosemary West, concluded that the murders at 25, Cromwell Street were, in part, a search for 'peak experience' (Britton 1995). That is, a quality of emotional experience not available in everyday life. The Moors murderer, Ian Brady (1997) has written in similar terms in describing his relationship in serial killing with Myra Hindley:

She regarded periodic homicide as rituals of reciprocal innerva-
tion, marriage ceremonies theoretically binding us ever closer . . .
we experimented with the concept of total possibility.

Brady's allusion to ritual and the marriage ceremony is interesting.
It suggests that he thought of serial killing as a path to deeper
emotional reality. Again, a consideration of the countless books
and newspaper reports on Brady and Hindley leave the dispassion-
ate observer in no doubt that the prospect of killing others
overshadowed the leisure fantasies and behaviour of the two pro-
tagonists. Analysis of the Canadian couple, Paul Bernardo and Karla
Homolka, who were tried and found guilty of multiple murders in
the early 1990s, shows a broadly similar picture. Pron (1995) reports
that fantasies about multiple murder dominated Bernardo's leisure.
Homolka even videotaped the rapes of women victims for her hus-
band's 'enjoyment'. Here, one might also note that Brady and Hindley
in the 1960s tape-recorded the pleas for mercy made by their child
victims which they later played back for their 'pleasure'.

There is no doubt that these serial murderers recognized something invalid in themselves which needed to be dramatically
countermanded. They chose serial murder as the means to achieve
this end. In doing so, they treated others as invalid and destroyed
them. These are deep waters. Perhaps it is beyond the capacity of
social science to find answers as to why some people decide to kill
others. All that I wish to submit here is three propositions. First,
that some forms of murder and leisure often have a close, largely
unexplored, correlation. Secondly, that the choices to kill others
are currently made in the context of a society in which fantasy
content about violent acts against others is a staple feature of leisure and recreation cultures. Thirdly, some forms of serial killing
are an example of mephitic leisure because they involve the use of
leisure time and space in the construction of fantasies and acts of
violence against others who are defined as invalid beings.

Given what I have said about the relationship between fantasy,
post-emotionalism and invalidization processes, it should be clear
that I hold the view that the climate of leisure and recreational
cultures predisposes some individuals to engage in illicit forms of
edgework that involve killing others. To be absolutely clear, I am
proposing that the culture of leisure and recreation is not inciden-
tal or peripheral in accounting for some forms of serial killing.
Rather it is of central significance. Of course, serial killing is an

extreme case. Statistically speaking, both serial killing and homicide are not major problems in urban-industrial civil society. In England and Wales the homicide rate is among the lowest in the world. To put this in perspective, in 1993 the rate in New York was 25 times the English rate. There are obvious problems with the reliability of statistics. Many serial killers are never discovered. Leyton (1995a: 22) quotes unofficial US Justice Department estimates which suggest that currently, there may be as many as 100 serial killers active in the USA. Only a relatively small proportion are caught and the deaths are 'lost' to official statistics by being defined as accidental or natural.

Serial killing was not very frequent in pre-industrial society. Bataille's (1991) account of the crimes and trial of the fifteenth-century child murderer, Gilles de Rais, is notable precisely because serial murder was such an unusual crime in the Middle Ages. True, the general level of violence was much higher. In England homicide rates in the thirteenth century were twice as high as those of the sixteenth and seventeenth centuries and five times the current US average (Leyton 1995b: 114–16). But rates of serial killing were low.

It is only when social and geographical mobility becomes generalized that the number of serial killers grows. This uprooting of fixed relations was well understood by Marx and Engels (1848). They argued that the cause lay in the acceleration of the industrialization process. But it is only in the twentieth century that writers such as Freud, Simmel and Laing began to speculate on the psychological and social consequences of ontological insecurity. In late twentieth-century society the pace of acceleration has increased dramatically with new technologies dissolving whole industries and communities, rendering old patterns of social life obsolete. Etzioni's (1993) highly public attempts to reintroduce new binding ethics of community is one reaction to this state of affairs. But it is bedevilled by the widespread belief that few foundational principles underpinning everyday life remain (Gitlin 1995).

In performative, reservation cultures the majority of people are active citizens in the restricted sense of acting on behalf of themselves and their immediate families. Wider notions of community and nation have been permeated with the doctrine of individual rights and, in particular, the doctrine of the freedom of the individual. In advanced capitalist societies freedom is disconnected from responsibility. Wagner's (1997: 140–44) study of the 'New Temperance' movement shows that the 'personal politics' developed in the

1980s and 90s drew on a complex mix of resources. Crucially it relied on the mobilization of evangelical and fundamentalist factions and it fused this with widespread worries about social change and economic uncertainty. The result was to elevate individual responsibility for one's own life into the new credo of sexual and welfare policies. Where the content of everyday life depends so much on the supply of fantasy images via the culture industry, the descent into indifference about others is the least line of resistance. Delusional fantasies also accompany this situation. Feelings of omnipotence and self-righteousness are most easily nurtured in conditions of reservation culture, in which we do not have to directly relate with others. Where we don't have to bargain and negotiate about our true feelings, and where we are encouraged to regard the pursuit of individualism as the ultimate moral responsibility, we are apt to assign pre-eminence to our own feelings, so that the feelings and interests of others cease to matter.

Mephitic leisure patterns are prominent in commodity cultures. In circumstances where experience is commodified there is a natural inclination to relate to providers and recipients of commodities in commodified codes. The gratification of pleasures of the individual is organized around techniques of socially excluding others. For example, the consumption of cheap leisure goods in the advanced Western world is in many cases only possible by sweatshop labour in economically underdeveloped areas. Mephitic leisure forms do not recognize sweatshop labour as an issue let alone a problem. Personal gratification is the name of the game, so that the condition of others is irrelevant. MacCannell (1992: 172–80) gives a chilling example of this in his analysis of the Locke case. This involved the sale of an entire human community based in Locke, California to the Asian City Development Inc. Locke was home to the descendants of Chinese farm labourers who were among the earliest non-Europeans to labour in California. The Asian City Development Inc. planned to turn the community into a tourist attraction. Plans were announced to build a giant Buddha, a temple and pavilions representing six Asian countries, a country club, a yacht basin, a restaurant and top-rate condominiums. The irony of purchasing an entire community in a country which abolished slavery after the Civil War is not lost on MacCannell. But what is also good about his discussion is that it exposes how ordinary consumers collude in mephitic leisure patterns simply by treating some forms of human life as alienable property. This extends to the natural world. For example, the hunting of animals for pleasure refuses to acknowledge the relevance of animal rights. In general, mephitic forms aggrandize individual desire and submerge the rights of others.

Wild

The individual exploits and develops the ambiguities in edgework to push limit-experience momentarily over the edge for the purposes of personal gratification and pleasure. Invasive and Mephitic patterns of leisure imply continuity in personality formation and repetitive behaviour In contrast, wild leisure patterns tend to be opportunity-based and sporadic. They involve contingent transgressions over the question of the 'limit' rather than the formations of 'identities' (Presedee 1994: 180–81).

I associate the term 'wild' in the context of transgressive behaviour with the work of Presedee (1994) and Stanley (1997). In the context of a discussion of youth culture, Stanley (1997: 37) defines 'the wild zone' as

> that space nominated as deregulated. It is 'fenced off' as the neglected space of industrial erosion... These spaces are not without law, but rather are the spaces of the without-laws... The contemporary wild zone reflects both the impossibility of control within the global city and also alternative patterns of consumption... The wild zone as a disordered and deregulated area enables competing configurations in the manifestation of solidarity and desire in a strategic subversion of the rationalized space of the tame zone.

Presedee (1994: 181) contends that resistance, challenge and excitement are integral to limit-experience. The creation of a limit to human potential produces its own antithetical time and space in which the limit is unravelled and inverted. The paradox of policing is therefore that the world of order inevitably creates an underworld of values and behavioural forms. This is unavoidable in every attempt to impose laws of behaviour upon others.

Because the legal and juridical system of Western industrial societies staunchly favours rational behaviour and values, excitement and release are typically centred upon forms of conduct which celebrate the body. Wild leisure patterns typically celebrate excesses of bodily behaviour, the surplus energies and capacities that are repressed in the modern social order. They arise from the realization that what we experience in the 'civilized' order based around 'mind' and 'rationality', isolates us from the 'delight' and 'desire' of 'pre-rational' society (Stanley 1997: 49). The argument is as old as Freud's (1939) postulate, that the price of civilization is the repression of our aggressive and sexual instincts. Freud understood only too well that, since these instincts are life-affirming, there is a sense in which civilization requires us to constantly torment ourselves so as to endorse our compact with 'normality'.

Wild leisure patterns are frequently associated with crowd behaviour. Freud argued that crowds release repressed infantile emotions. As he (quoted in Gatrell 1996: 72–3) put it:

> In the togetherness of mass individuals, all individual inhibitions fall away and all the cruel, brutal, destructive instincts which lie dormant in each person as relics of the primitive era, are awakened for free-drive gratification.

We are group animals. In general, we feel higher levels of excitement and emotional release in large groups rather than small ones. In large groups we can be carried away by the tide of human emotion and lose ourselves in collective identity. We feel less compulsion to control our feelings of anger, disapproval or pleasure. Not so long ago, public executions offered crowds opportunities of licit mass excitement and emotional arousal. Gatrell (1996: 56) notes that the public hangings of famous murderers, traitors, thieves or rich men attracted crowds of several thousand. Over 100 000 were said to have attended the executions and decapitations of the Cato Street conspirators in 1820 and the hangings of the forgers Fauntleroy in 1824 and Hunton in 1828. These numbers are larger than the crowds which today attend international sporting fixtures at Wembley stadium. Contemporary accounts refer to the 'jocularity' and 'frivolity' of the crowd. Public hangings often incited a 'festive' mood, which was fuelled by gin, beer and other intoxicants. Contemporary commentators often described the execution crowd as composed of the lowest and roughest members of society. In some accounts the use of the term 'mob' is interchangeable with 'crowd'. Gatrell's (1996: 62–4) discussion shows a different picture. It makes it clear that the execution crowd consisted of elements from all walks of society. Only the rich could afford the window boxes adjoining the gallows which offered the best view, while tradesmen and professionals joined the common people in the crowd. Gatrell (1996: 71–2) also reveals the specialist culture industry that formed around executions. Woodcuts and pamphlets often depicted semi-porno-graphic drawings of murders and executions. These lurid documents clearly aimed to appeal to sexual instincts quite as much as aggressive ones. Execution crowds in Hanoverian and Victorian England often exhibited the boisterous and disorderly behaviour that is typical of wild leisure. The drunkenness and debauchery of the crowd were among the main reasons why middle-class reformers campaigned to ban public executions. These emotions were offensive to 'civilized' values. They were also dangerous, since the crowd was clearly able to sympathize with those prisoners who had been unfairly or unjustly condemned to die.

To some extent, a margin for wildness is still built into the modern social order. For example, celebrations like New Year's Eve, visibly involve the general relaxation of public codes of behaviour. On New Year's Eve in most capital cities it is possible to blow whistles and horns, throw streamers, shout and hoot at strangers and go skinny-dipping in public fountains, lakes and rivers. Most police even turn a blind eye to drunkenness, casual nudity and soft drug use. A general loosening of civil culture occurs.

However, in most cases wild leisure patterns are not part of licit behaviour. Gatherings of strangers at sporting or leisure events induce a spirit of collective effervescence which is intrinsically exciting and pleasurable. On some occasions collective effervescence flares up into violent clashes with the authorities. Cunnen *et al.* (1989) give a good example in their discussion of the dynamics of the riots at Bathurst. In the 1980s, the Australian Motorcycling Grand Prix held on Easter Saturday in Bathurst gained notoriety for being an occasion for regular crowd trouble. Cunnen *et al.* (1989: 171–2) show how the riots grew out of the spirit of relaxation and effervescence that accompanied the sporting-leisure event. The riots were not a reaction to external force, nor were they animated by the politics of class. Rather they grew out of the relaxation of inhibitions that accompanied the events. As Cunnen *et al.* (1989: 171) put it, 'the play events did not disappear but were "carried over" into the conflict' (op. cit.). Cunnen *et al.*'s (1989: 171–2) account draws on the work of Geertz (1973) in emphasizing the *reflexive* character of the riots. The crowd engaged in mock gestures and applied the rituals of street carnival in order to achieve a momentary sense of identity as a social body pitted against the authorities who define limit-experience. As with other examples of wild leisure, the use of carnivalesque *patois* and theatrical styles of defiance was opportunistic and sporadic. The riots seized the atmosphere of collective effervescence and momentarily pushed it over the edge.

The same pattern of opportunistic and sporadic collective effervescence was evident in the riots in Brixton and Toxteth which occurred in the early 1980s, and in parts of Los Angeles following the acquittal of white policemen in the Rodney King trial. In covering these incidents the media stressed the significance of racial motivation in breaking down law and order. But it is over-simplistic to regard the looting and vandalism in these incidents in terms of disadvantaged strata in the black population waging war against white dominance. For one thing, non-black elements were also agents in the disturbances. More significantly, in terms of the preoccupations of the present study, the disorder did not constitute a break with ordinary codes of containment and resistance, and in an *ad hoc*, opportunistic, sporadic fashion, translated them into a different key of intensity. The rioters and looters drew on codes of street behaviour developed in ordinary practices of hanging out and killing time, and pushed them over the edge of the usual acceptable limits. The ordinary values entailed in urban culture and leisure were pumped up to a new level of intensity. When the flashes of aggression and violence were spent, behaviour reverted to the usual codes of containment and resistance.

In emphasizing the connection between rioting, looting and ordinary cultures of leisure, as opposed to presenting them in terms of class, gender or race, I do not mean to suggest that wild leisure patterns have no relation to social stratification. On the contrary, Dunning *et al.*'s (1988) analysis of soccer humanism strongly suggests that the propensity to engage in wild leisure is stratified along class and gender lines. They maintain that 'aggressive masculinity' is a characteristic of working-class cultures. These cultures tolerate relatively high levels of aggression in social relations. This is a product of ordinary leisure and play patterns which, in early life, are focused on the streets, where the 'ability to handle oneself' is a transparent mark of status. Working-class parents tolerate higher levels of spontaneity in the behaviour of their children. Pressures to practise self-control over aggressive instincts are less extensively developed than in middle and upper-class homes. In addition, the greater use of physical punishment leads working-class children to internalize violence and aggression as standard features of adult role models. The result is lower inhibitions against aggression and the development of an association between the capacity to use violence 'to look after yourself' and manliness. This is reinforced by the paucity of chances that working-class children have to gain status, meaning and gratification in the professional and managerial world. Unable to acquire the status rewards available to the middle class, they have a greater propensity to locate status in terms of fighting, physical intimidation, heavy drinking and exploitative sexual relations. However, one should note that not all working-class children turn to violence. Working-class life is composed of a complex network of taste cultures which are influenced primarily by kinship patterns and geographical locality. Individuals are located in these taste cultures, often as a matter of birth. They operate to increase and decrease the propensity to violence. It is not therefore enough to explain violence in class terms. The cultural dimension must also be addressed.

Dunning *et al.*'s (1988) work argues that there is a connection between patterns of what I term, 'wild leisure' behaviour and class and gender. However, what needs to be stressed here is that wild leisure patterns are the unavoidable adjunct of rational-legal systems of authority. They are the result of what Weber (1968: 217) called the rational-bureaucratic system in which a person's 'dispositions and actions' are subject to an 'impersonal order'. While there may be differences in the tendencies of strata to engage in wild leisure behaviour, the propensity is a universal feature of rational-bureaucractic cultures. The desire to go beyond limits is connected with the mere presence and imposition of limits. In this sense, the specific character of the limits is irrelevant. The surplus of energy in repressed human capacities will always find a means of expression.

So far, I have discussed wild leisure behaviour in relation to crowd conduct. But it should be obvious from my twinning of rational-bureaucratic authority with the propensity for going beyond limits, that wildness is an intrinsic element in personal leisure relationships. Indeed, the rise of the information society has produced a quantum leap in the opportunities to go 'beyond limits' (Poster 1990; Castells 1996; 1997). As I write, it is possible for someone in an English provincial city like Nottingham, to download pictures of paedophile events in Denver, footage of public executions in Saudi Arabia and what purport to be *paparazzi* mug-shots of the injured and dying Princess Diana, all in the comfort of one's living room. Foucault's model of the panopticon culture has been inverted. Now it is the net-browser who possesses the all-seeing eye, monitoring world events that governments and private individuals would prefer to keep hidden from view. Computer hacking also involves breaking the walls of secrecy. Browsing the net and hacking test limit-experience in relatively low-risk ways. The global character of the communications system militates against effective policing. Network society permits us to gain access to illict information and hidden knowledge in the grey area in which the law is deliberately broken without serious fear of detection and conviction. It allows us to play at being deviant and engage in what Katz (1988) describes as 'the delight of being deviant'. The expansion of network society lays the foundation for the enlargement of wild leisure patterns. For, it renders rational-legal limits permeable and simultaneously neutralizes the identity of the viewer. The opportunities for voyeuristic and vicarious experience are significantly enlarged.

Wild leisure is not the antithesis of rational-legal forms of leisure behaviour. Rather it is more accurate to analyze it in terms of continuities in ordinary leisure behaviour. Wild leisure exploits and develops capacities which are unfulfilled in everyday relations governed by rational-legal codes of practice. It takes behaviour over the edge. In most cases, the encoding of rational-legal values snaps behaviour back into the mode of everyday familiarity. But in cases where encoding has been weakened, the wild leisure pattern may become chronic.

CONCLUSION: THE ELASTICITY OF EVERYDAY LIFE

One of the first things that every undergraduate who studies leisure learns is the etymological root of the term. As the *Collins Dictionary of Sociology* notes:

> Leisure, derived from the Latin *licere* 'to be allowed', shares a common root with 'licence'. It thus contains within itself the dualism of freedom and control, individual agency and constraint (Jary and Jary 1995: 365).

What is and is not 'allowed' in everyday life varies historically and contextually. For example, bear-baiting, cock-fighting and public executions used to be legally permitted in Britain. People used to flock to them as part of the normal calendar of leisure events. The practices were gradually outlawed by public pressure, largely middle class in origin and often attached to the rational recreation movement.

Most of us now feel repelled by these activities and condemn those countries in which they still occur.

Yet everyday life still retains a high level of elasticity in standards of public behaviour. Thus, we are taught that violence against others is wrong; but violence against a mugger or a terrorist is assigned heroic status by many people. 'Have-a-go-heroes' are lionized by the tabloid press. Similarly, we are taught that the use of drugs is wrong; but by banning drugs we deprive users of the means of receiving public education about the worst effects of the drug before casual use turns to addiction. Moreover, we know that society condemns drug-use, but we also know that people from 'good' backgrounds who use illegal stimulants have a higher chance of avoiding prosecution than others. Many of the prohibitions against our behaviour in 'free' time and space are compromised by double-standards and shifty moral precepts.

Imagine how a child sees the prohibitions that obtain in our 'free' time behaviour. Boys are taught to be resilient and self-sufficient. Yet when some men feel that part of themselves is invalidated through this process of masculine socialization, and turn to alcoholism, drug addiction or violence to attempt to deal with the problem, we condemn them as failures. Girls are taught to be appealing to the opposite sex, but if they cultivate feminine allure too frankly, through dress or body codes, they are accused of being sluts. The magazines and adverts which form the backdrop of our leisure urge us to use clothes, hairstyles, perfumes and other cosmetics to feel good about ourselves and to be attractive to others. Yet when we use these products and fail to feel good about ourselves, or to attract others, we are dismissed for being unrealistic about our life-expectations and urged to make the best of what we've got. Every child realizes the gross hypocrisy that underpins ordinary adult life. Most surrender and join the game. Leisure becomes a way of sublimating unfulfilled energy. Through it we act out fantasies and vicariously enjoy pleasures which are denied or at least rationed in everyday life.

But not everyone joins the game. From the standpoint of someone caught up in invasive, mephitic or wild leisure patterns of leisure, the behaviour of ordinary people seems transparently inauthentic and life-destroying. Those who voluntarily submit to the 9–5 routine are the *abnormal* ones. The invasive, mephitic and wild types, reassure themselves that they are separated from the herd. They either regard themselves as petrified beings somehow left over in time, or believe themselves to be superior versions of the docile, obeisant human machines that they see walking around them.

But no sooner do we make the distinction between them and us, than we are forced to abandon it. There is only 'us'. If we can understand the life-stuff of petrification or violent tendencies towards others, it is because we are composed of the same life-stuff. Throughout this study it has been necessary to insist on the common matrix that links extraordinary, 'inhuman' behaviour with the ordinary, day-to-day routines that everyone follows. Bauman's (1989) clear-eyed attempt to make sense of the holocaust, showed how ordinary men and women in Nazi Germany were able to participate in the unjust, enforced incarceration of Jews, the illegal seizing of Jewish property and the transportation of Jewish men, women and children to death camps. These same men and women drew their pay every month, shopped in the local bakery, drank beer in the neighbourhood pubs, played with their children, took exercise, watched sports, enjoyed musical concerts, read their Goethe – in short maintained all of the essentials of normal family life and leisure – without being immobilized by the ghastly incongruity of their actions. Nor is it satisfactory to write this off in a smug, xenophobic way, as a 'German thing'. Rudé's (1975) study of revolutionary France shows ordinary French men and women doing the same thing during the Great Terror in the summer of 1794. *'Peuple, je meurs innocent'* ('My people, I die an innocent man') cried Louis XVI from the scaffold. *'Vive la nation!'* chanted the crowd in response (Keane 1995: 369). One shudders to think how many others proclaimed their innocence before indifferent ordinary men and women sheltering beneath the logic of abstract necessity, in St Petersburg, Mylai, Phnompenh, Amritsar in this, the bloodiest of all centuries. In our own time, genocide in Rwanda and Bosnia, sectarian killing in Northern Ireland and the indiscriminate mainland bombing campaigns of the IRA in England, show the human animal pursuing its lust for the excitement of violence and the lure of blood. I use the word 'animal' deliberately. Too many arm-chair philosophers draw laboured distinctions between 'mass murder', serial killing and homicide, without recognizing the animal instincts that underly all of these activities.

The case of Paul Bernardo, the Canadian serial killer, illustrates the thin, elastic line between the mundane rules that we are taught to live by, and behaviour which goes over the edge. Bernardo was a student in commerce at the Scarborough campus of the University of Toronto. His bedroom was decorated with two poster images that represent the standard icons of wealth and pleasure for a certain kind of male youth today (Pron 1995: 72). It was dominated by one poster showing a Caribbean beach, the embodiment of the Western ideal of 'no worries' and the easy life, and a second poster of a red Porsche, the ultimate success symbol for many. Bernardo had bought in to the ethic of success in a big way. He decorated a third wall with popular sayings that most Puritans would have enthusiastically condoned: 'Time is money'; 'Money never sleeps'; 'There are winners, and there are whiners'; 'Self-denial leads to self mastery'. Even the popular sayings which Puritans would probably disapprove of, are the conventions of the business trading floor or the managerial away day: 'Think big. Be big'; 'You'll never make the grade by playing it safe'; 'The game is won in the final quarter'; 'Poverty sucks'; 'Give me liberty, or give me death'. It is not for me to claim that these sayings reveal the soul of the serial killer. I merely wish to record how snugly they dovetail with most 'common-sense wisdom' about the rules of everyday life and, in particular, how to get ahead. Business success is often reliant on thinking big and taking risks that others flinch from. The rewards that follow from success are overpowering in the sense of mastery conveyed to others. Country mansions, city town houses, fast cars, the best clothes, all fall into the lap of the successful business risk-taker. In 1997 over £1 billion was distributed to City of London stock exchange traders in the form of bonuses. One wonders what rules were bent, what liberties were taken in order to secure these business 'killings'. A successful businessman is nothing but an effective edgeworker. They function on the basis that limits are there to be broken and conventions exist to be overturned when conditions allow. The biggest successes come to those who are prepared to take the biggest risks. Innovation under capitalism would be impossible without this business mentality. Yet the numerous scandals in the 80s and 90s about insider-trading and share-rigging underline that business practices in testing limits and conventions often involve illegality. 'Greed is good' said the corrupt trader, Gordon Gekko in Oliver Stone's film *Wall Street* (1987). For some, the huge rewards that lie tantalizingly on the other side of the limit, justify adopting whatever means necessary to acquire them.

The horrid court-room descriptions of Bernardo's arousal and excitement in the act of killing his victims (Pron 1995), and the newspaper reports of the frenzy and bloodlust during the genocide in Bosnia and Rwanda, highlight the pleasure that the human animal gains from torturing and killing others. Press reports of the public execution of 22 prisoners in Rwanda in April 1998 were full of Bakhtinian overtones. The crowd included many dressed 'in their Sunday best', 'desperate in their attempt to get a better view', 'wild', 'festive' (Rojos 1998). These are people vying with each other to watch other humans, in their misery, being executed by a close-range firing squad. The executed were associated with the Hutu extremist Democratic Republican Movement. They had themselves authorized or participated in the mass killings of Tutsis.

The jubilation of the crowd can in part be understood as a way of purging feelings of outrage and injustice. But if it is only understood in these terms, it will not be understood very accurately. Transgression has its own, self-defining appeal. Human beings are attracted to behaviour which goes beyond limits, because the limits that govern everyday life often seem arbitrary. Unless students of leisure wean themselves from the comforting view that leisure is, *sui generis*, positive and enriching, they will never grasp the dynamics of transgression in free time behaviour. Invasive, mephitic and wild personality types will be dismissed as 'morbid' and left to medical practice to research and theorize. The connections with the culture of leisure will never be made and leisure studies will be left telling only half the story.

5 Conclusion: Engaged Freedom

It is a feature of modernization to raise utopian hopes while delivering a dystopian lifeworld. The precept should be kept in mind in evaluating current claims that we are moving into a 'post-work' society (Aronowitz and Di Fazio 1994; Aronowitz and Cutler 1998; Hochschild 1997). Similar claims have been uttered in every century since the Renaissance. Thus, in the seventeenth century the English Ranters articulated a fully developed anti-work philosophy; in the eighteenth century, Enlightenment *savants* like Adam Smith, Turgot and St. Simon estimated that if National Income were more fairly distributed, nobody would be poor and nobody need work more than a few hours a day; in the nineteenth century, utopian socialists like Fourier and Proudhon, predicted that socialist transformation would minimize work obligations and result in 'the realm of freedom'; and as we saw earlier in this study, twentieth-century commentators like Mumford and Bataille argued that technology and productivity have outpaced the work ethic and that human beings need to devise a new social and moral discipline to live happily in the new technological and economic conditions.

Yet the work ethic endures. So much so that Western workers today are widely held to be trapped between chronic overwork and periodic or long-term unemployment (Schor 1992; Hoschschild 1997). What makes the post-work society argument today different? Three points must be made.

First, the cybernation of work is no longer the stuff of science fiction writers. It has become part of the condition of everyday life. A single domestic computer can now do the work that required an office of full-time staff twenty years ago. The labour market reflects this state of affairs. Two-thirds of the jobs created in the UK between 1993 and 1998 have not been permanent. In the last twenty years the notions of a job for life and full employment have themselves been pensioned off by new management strategists and political ideologues. The hallmark of the new economic reality is the casualization of paid labour and the erosion of the concept of 'work career' (Bayliss 1998). In addition the new work space emerging

196

in society is increasingly 'virtual'. The use of domestic personal computers, lap-tops and mobile phones contribute to the disappearance of old-style dedicated work space as separate from the rest of life.

Throughout the Industrial Revolution workers have become used to the idea of travelling to work. Indeed, the establishment of the factory and the office is regarded by some writers as the prerequisite for the time and discipline regimes which underpinned the Industrial Revolution (Thompson 1967; Foucault 1975). Bayliss (1998) argues that the daily commute for most service workers in the twenty-first century will typically be no further than from the kitchen to the study. A customized orientation to work and leisure which fits work and leisure time around work and leisure needs is emerging. This goes hand in hand with the replacement of Fordism with flexible accumulation as the spearhead of capitalist growth (Harvey 1989; Castells 1996, 1997, 1998).

Secondly, the expansion of the cultural sphere via new technologies of communication and entertainment has vastly increased the appeal of non-work activity. Fordism stimulated interest in relations of consumption. Adorno and Horkheimer (1944) and Marcuse (1964) equated the turn to consumption with the standardization and mechanization of leisure. Ritzer (1992) adduces evidence of this in his 'McDonaldization thesis' which claims to unearth the standardization of relations of production and consumption through the application of uniform criteria of efficiency, calculability, predictability and control. There is much to learn from the analysis of culture presented by the Frankfurt School and Ritzer. Yet it is a striking fact that workers often use more skill and ingenuity in their leisure than in their work. For most of the postwar period, commentators have taken it as read that the intrinsic value of work has declined for most workers. Typically, the main attraction of work is the extrinsic reward that it brings in the form of financial reward and social status (Goldthorpe *et al.* 1968). Gorz (1982, 1983) argues that the purpose of work today for most workers is to finance leisure interests and activities. The point which emerges most powerfully from this literature is the immense seduction offered by relations of leisure and consumption as areas of human fulfilment and enrichment. The expansion of the cultural sphere has reduced the importance of work as the central life interest in contemporary society. As a result, the notion of post-work society no longer carries with it the spectre of mass idleness that horrified the rational recreation movement at the turn of the century. Post-work frees up the individual for more leisure.

Thirdly, the percentage of the population passing through tertiary education has grown dramatically. Most Western societies now send between 35 per cent and 60 per cent of all 18-year-olds through the university system. This has transformed the character of the body politic. A greater, and growing number, now earn their living through employment in the service sector. As I have already noted, in the UK today more people are employed in making films and television than assembling automobiles. It is now commonplace in the sociology of industrial society to maintain that greater reflexivity is an attribute of late modernity (Beck, Giddens and Lash 1994). The universities have played a major role in increasing reflexivity. Academic sociology, cultural studies, communication studies and media studies have been so successful in drawing attention to the constructed character of media relations and everyday life that people now 'naturally' read ordinary relations with others in this way. Specialized academic terms like 'charisma', 'bureaucracy', 'deferred gratification', 'reference group', 'alienation' and 'instrumentality' are now used in everyday speech. The IQ of the body politic may not have increased during the postwar years. But their ability to interpret events in terms of social power perspectives and their abstract background knowledge of how the lifeworld is structured has certainly grown. An unintended effect of this is that they are probably harder to govern. Greater reflexivity engenders a more questioning attitude to government and fragments the body politic into stratified lifestyle and interest groups. The organization of everyday life around questions of intimacy and the concomitant emergence of 'identity politics' mirrors the expansion of reflexivity in ordinary life-course relations (Giddens 1990, 1991).

TIME AND POST-WORK SOCIETY

The subject of government is central to thinking through the composition of post-work society. Following Schor (1992) and Aronowitz and Cutler (1998), the work ethic no longer provides satisfactory allocative principles to distribute time. Its persistence results in a skewed division of labour. This is already a social and economic problem and it is likely to grow in significance. The skewed division of labour has four variants:

Overwork

The overworked worker remains committed to the work ethic but devotes too much time to paid labour. Overwork partly reflects the worker's attachment to the values of consumer society. For people who do not have a property income, the desire to consume more typically means that they are obliged to work more. The main defect of overwork is that it produces a sense of permanent time-famine. Overworked workers never feel that they have enough time to devote to doing a job properly or to enjoy leisure. This is associated with high general levels of stress and frustration.

Underemployment

The underemployed worker is usually committed to the work ethic but spends a large portion of the working day engaged in performative labour. The appearance of being busy is the best defence against being classified as surplus to requirements. Paper-pushing and pen-pushing become the benchmark of work activity. In this way, the means of work are detached from the ends of work. Underemployed workers typically suffer from strong feelings that their work is not intrinsically rewarding and that their working lives are meaningless. This is associated with high levels of anxiety and purposelessness.

Alienation

Alienated workers regard work as non-satisfying and the source of misery. They feel disinvolved in the work process and divorced from the products and services which they produce. They are conscious of a mismatch between their aptitudes and work responsibilities. Blauner (1964), in a classic contribution to the sociology of alienation, argued that alienated workers suffer from a sense of powerlessness, meaninglessness, normlessness, isolation and self-estrangement. Alienated workers may retain a strong attachment to the work ethic, yet experience work as a chain of repression.

Unemployment

Unemployed workers are typically socialized into the work ethic. The absence of work in their lives is therefore psychologically experienced as a cause for self-reproach and guilt. Unemployed workers often feel useless and depressed. The failure to meet the requirements of the work ethic intensifies a sense of social isolation and reinforces a feeling of retreating from the rest of society.

These four variants are exhaustively discussed in the literature on the sociology of work (Esland and Salaman 1975; Hill 1981; Thompson 1983). Indeed, if critics of work and analysts of leisure agree on one thing it is that a revision of the allocative principles determining the distribution of time would increase the happiness and well-being of most people in society.[1] The proposition is often connected with a critique of consumer culture and materialism as the proper social value for the conduct of life. But if there is broad consensus that the old-fashioned work ethic has had its day, what should replace it?

I have already considered the proposals on the allocation of time in post-work society devised by Schor (1992) and Aronowitz and Di Fazio (1994). But a good way of reviewing the theme again is to examine the thought of Andre Gorz (1982, 1983, 1989). Gorz is useful because his work both anticipates some of the proposals made by Schor and Aronowitz and Di Fazio, and presents them more boldly and at greater length.

Gorz is a maverick figure. Like others of his generation, his earliest mentor and intellectual role model was Sartre. The existentialist axiom that freedom is the basis of the human condition never deserted him. However, the Sartrean notion of freedom was soon mitigated in his work by the influence of Marxism. Gorz's Marxism is dedicated to the goal of advancing human liberation. This is at the heart of his denunciation of capitalism and his attacks on Old Left strategy. Gorz's Marxism recognizes deep divisions within the working class, the necessity of building a platform of economic reform around an ecologically sound policy and the importance of leisure and consumption as opposed to traditional Old Left concepts of 'work' and 'community' in the organization and practice of identity. These themes coalesce with maximum force in his politics of time. Gorz (1982: 134) contends that productivity (output per hour of work) has jumped twelvefold this century. There is no end in sight to this productivity gain. Indeed the cybernation of labour, which is still underway, is bound to accelerate the process. Technology has solved the philosopher's riddle and promises, exponentially, to produce more with less. As we have seen, the application of the work ethic in these circumstances generates a skewed division of labour which contributes to human unhappiness. For Gorz the solution is to make the reduction of work time the object of productivity gains. This is justified by the old Marxist belief that free and full development occurs in voluntary chosen activity. That is, in activity situated in the realm of freedom and not the realm of necessity (Marx 1867).

How is this to be financed? Gorz (1994: 108–12; 1989: 199–202) advocates extending indirect taxation. In effect, he proposes that legislation should be enacted to levy a luxury tax on goods. I use the term 'luxury tax' because Gorz envisages a rate of taxation proportionate to the exchange-value of the goods. The luxury tax is not intended to keep people in subsistence. To take that course would be foreign to Gorz's insistence that the goal of socialism is human liberation. Instead, Gorz proposes that the luxury tax functions to provide a guaranteed income flow which will free labour to perform socially useful work. Gorz therefore reiterates the classical Marxist view that the need to work is a 'species need' of human beings. It can no more be jettisoned than the human need for love or hope. The basis that Gorz uses for recognizing the desire to perform socially useful work is actually rather conservative. He (1989: 211) writes:

> The essential aspect of an obligation to work in exchange for a guaranteed full income is that this obligation provides the basis for a corresponding right: by obliging individuals to produce by working the income which is guaranteed to them, society obliges itself to guarantee them the opportunity to work and gives them the right to demand this. The obligation it imposes on them is the basis for the right they have over it, the right to be full citizens.

Gorz's understanding of citizenship under the politics of time implies full participation of group members in policy, strategy, work and management.

Gorz's proposals suggest a fundamental transformation in the social and economic system. It calls upon all of us to recognize time, not money, as the most important resource at our command. Human liberation is maximized through the free use of time which, in itself, is an argument for the reduction of working hours. Gorz (1989: 190, 219–42) identifies the trade unions as an important lever for change. It is essential for the unions to restrict sectarianism in wage bargaining in favour of a positive politics of time. Gorz's proposals assume the full democratization of the work place and economic strategy. For the first time in industrialization, the direct producers will be in control of working time and the production process. Once this control is established the essential political and economic requirements for human liberation are in place.

CRITIQUE OF GORZ

Gorz has been ill served by minor hagiographers who follow his liberationist desires but minimize the flaws in his political economy (see especially Lodziak and Tatman 1997, but also Bowring 1995). His politics of time is wonderfully seductive, but so, it might be said, are most utopian systems. The real issue is the practicality of his proposals. Here three points, dealing respectively with the historical, psychological and epistemological character of his analysis, must be made.

First, historically speaking, there is no sound precedent in industrialization for the Gorzian politics of time. In Europe, the most developed system of workers' self-management occurred under Tito's non-aligned path to communism in former Yugoslavia. Here, between the 1950s and 70s, an ambitious attempt was made to erase work hierarchies and create genuine workers' control. Self-management was devised as a solution to the nation's need for rapid industrialization and the seemingly intractable history of ethnic tension in the region between the Serbs, Croats, Bosnians and Montenegrins. The urgent requirements of postwar reconstruction initially produced a high level of harmony and economic growth. This was helped by Tito's decision to pursue a strategy of non-alignment with the Soviet bloc which ensured preferential loan arrangements and foreign aid from the West. By the late 1960s, workers' self-management in Yugoslavia was foundering. Uneven development in the region meant that the more industrialized North was forced to subsidize the less efficient South. This fuelled latent ethnic tensions and became a cause for protest and unrest in the 1970s and 80s. In addition, sectarian patterns of wage-bargaining, long familiar to the postwar economies of Western Europe and the USA, quickly took root on Yugoslav soil. There is some evidence that quality of life and welfare issues had a higher profile

throughout Yugoslav industrial relations in the period under consideration. But these issues appear to have been more pronounced
in the relatively underdeveloped South (Rus 1978; Jovanov 1979;
Sacks 1983; Rojek and Wilson 1987). In the North, issues of higher
wages and competitive efficiency quickly became the focus of industrial relations strategy. In the 1980s, declining economic
competitiveness and rising indebtedness contributed to the meltdown
of the system. This, in turn, directly led to the ethnic wars and
programmes of 'ethnic cleansing' which became an object of world
horror and condemnation in the 1990s. The Yugoslav system was
unable to prevent sectarian wage bargaining and the demand for
more work from destroying the self-management system.

Hunnicutt's (1988) work on the history of the American labour
movement tells a similar story. Until the late 1920s the movement
was generally committed to reducing hours and increasing the general quality of life of the workers. After 1945 issues of pay moved
to the centre-stage of American collective bargaining. This reinforced the tendency in commodity culture to make relations of
consumption the central life interest. It also fuelled the trend towards
sectarianism since some unions were more successful in gaining
higher pay for their members than others. Faced with the choice
of working longer hours or limiting their propensity to consume,
American workers chose to work longer hours. Schor's (1992) argument that making this choice actually deprived workers of quality
time to enjoy the fruits of their labour may be true, but it has not
stopped workers choosing again and again to put more hours in
for more take-home pay.

Secondly, there are difficulties with the Gorzian model of the
psychology of the workforce. Gorz argues that the objective interest
of workers is in the direction of human liberation. Further, the
contradictions of capitalism ensure that they are, in ever greater
numbers, becoming subjectively aware of where their objective interest
lies. He maintains that the severity of the problems of time-famine,
environmental attrition and skewed patterns of employment will
culminate in a campaign for the democratization of economic
decision-making. This will restore quality of life issues and questions of leisure-use to the top of the radical agenda and, eventually,
ease in the new politics of time. But this underestimates the
stabilization of capitalist systems of control.

Although it is flawed in many respects,[2] the Frankfurt School
thesis that capitalist consumer culture has profoundly *transformed*

the psychology of the masses remains relevant (Adorno and Horkheimer 1944; Adorno 1991; Marcuse 1955, 1964). According to the Frankfurt School there is no reason to hold that the subjective recognition of objective interests will translate into the mobiliza-tion of the masses. On the contrary, they argue that subjective recognition of objective common interests is habitually diverted into fatalism, distraction, nationalism and other psychological reactions as an *ordinary* part of capitalist control. Utopian socialism has always held a romantic notion that, once the contradictions of capitalism reach a certain point of development, workers will spontaneously recognize the fetters that bind them and take the necessary steps to dismantle the system. Gorz's proposals belong to this tradition. They underestimate the extent to which workers are internally divided by relations of consumption, ethnicity, sexuality, gender, regionalism and nationalism. Further, they minimize the rootedness of these divisions in the workers' psyche and the ordinary structures and practices of everyday life.

The point becomes especially relevant when one considers the question of how the politics of time will be practically applied. Gorz's proposals are predicated upon the democratization of economic decision-making on a society-wide basis. In an earlier work, Gorz (1975) identifies the party as the catalyst of democratization. He argues that the party must always be the servant of the interests of the people, and never aspire to be the master. As he (1975: 35) puts it:

> The party is to be the means of the working class's own con-quest of power and not a new machine for exercising power on *behalf* of the working class. Without a revolutionary party that stimulates effective self-expression from below and offers a unifying political perspective to autonomous and 'spontaneous' struggles, there can be no lasting revolutionary movement (emphasis in original).

Later in the same work, Gorz (1975: 36, 63–4) admonishes against any tendency for the party to become authoritarian, repressive or domineering. By the time he developed his (1982) politics of time, Gorz had retreated somewhat from his advocacy of the party. None-theless, it is unrealistic to envisage the democratization of decision-making throughout society without some kind of central co-ordination. Without it there would be an uneven development of services and standards. A central force is necessary to adjudicate between the regions and localities. With adjudication come powers of enforcement. If this is accepted, what will the Gorzian party do to guarantee that it will not make the same mistakes of other parties in this century, operating out of Moscow, Peking or Warsaw? The answer of course, is that the Gorzian party will remain true to the ideal of advancing human liberation. This belief is ultimately founded upon a rational principle which Gorz himself formulated in 1967:

> Once a certain level of culture has been reached, the need for autonomy, the need to develop one's abilities freely and to give a purpose to one's life is experienced with the same intensity as an unsatisfied physiological necessity.

While one can accept that humans harbour a need for autonomy, there is nothing to suggest that this need will be expressed in the same way. The practice of autonomy is likely to be a source of conflict rather than harmony, precisely because we don't all think in the same ways or find the same things attractive or compelling. As soon as autonomy is constrained by external rules or moral precepts, it ceases to be autonomy. Gorz's libertarian arguments should have made him an anarchist since anarchy is the only political system truly compatible with the pursuit of autonomy. But Gorz is a socialist and his socialism takes the form of exaggerating the utopian side of human collectivity and minimizing the dark side of individual and group life. This brings me to my third and final criticism.

Gorz's concept of autonomy is based upon a category error. He argues that under capitalism leisure provides time and space for autonomy. However, the logic of capitalist accumulation, especially as it is iterated through consumer culture, perverts autonomy by commodifying experience. Once capitalism is uprooted, he suggests, the perversions in individual and group life will disappear. So Gorz uses the Marxist belief in the essential and universal goodness of humans to underwrite the quality of life under the politics of time. But in this respect the Freudian view of human beings is superior. Freudianism presents human beings as *innately*, polymorphously perverse. Group attempts to contain human life by social contract, are always subject to transgressive urges which attempt to transcend the integument of the current rules governing human desires. We are born with an *as if* capacity that requires us to compare life as it is, with life as it might be. Human energy cannot be contained by boundaries. There is always a movement in life with others to go beyond the boundaries.

In Huizinga's (1947) work this capacity is identified as the source of creativity in the development of the human species. *Homo ludens*, argues Huizinga, is the model for innovative behaviour in the arts, humanities and sciences. His discussion tends to emphasize the positive qualities of the *as if* quality in human life. It was left to Bataille (1988, 1991a, 1991b) to theorize the specifically social aspects of the dark side of the surplus. Following from Bataille, the invasive, mephitic and wild forms of leisure described in the last chapter are essential to the organization of free time in all forms of human life. However, bountiful and generous the material conditions of life become, there will always be individuals and groups who splinter into retreatism, rebellion and – by the prevailing standards of the day – deviance.

To be fair, Gorz would hardly dissent from this common-sense point of view. On the other hand, he does not deal with the question of deviance under the new politics of time. His discussion is therefore unbalanced in favour of accentuating the positive. In particular there is no appreciation of the polymorphously perverse character of human beings. On the contrary, Gorz's proposals for the politics of time imply that deviance and negative forms of human behaviour are simply the consequence of the faulty organization of society. The import of the analysis of leisure presented in this book is that human boundaries will always be challenged. The emergence of liminal space and antistructures of behaviour are not aberrations in human behaviour. Rather, they are essential to the human condition.

LEISURE CHOICES AND LEISURE POLICY

What then, should we – polymorphously perverse humans – strive to achieve in our leisure? And what should we present as the requirements of leisure policy? These questions are usually wrapped up in issues concerning class, race and gender inequality (Henry 1993). The discussion in Chapter 2 of this book suggests that there is a good reason for this. Inequality is part of every known society. As such, issues of inequality are central to leisure. The bankruptcy of the functionalist approach to leisure lies precisely in its failure to deal with questions of inequality in a convincing way (Parker

1983, Roberts 1978, 1981). But the critical analysis of Marxist writers on leisure (Clarke and Critcher 1985) or feminist commentators (Bialeschki and Henderson 1986; Scraton and Talbot 1989), hardly suggests more tenable responses. Each emphasizes the looming presence of respectively, class and gender in leisure relations, so that the genuine autonomy achieved in leisure practice is obscured. In dealing with leisure we are dealing with human relations in which people believe themselves to be more free than in other parts of their lives. Regardless of how deeply tainted this belief is by the ideology of capitalism and patriarchy, the nub of our enquiry must be the individual quest for freedom. In leisure, people exercise the capacity of going 'beyond the bounds'. This is one reason why leisure has always exerted such strong attraction throughout the ages (Applebaum 1992).

The first requirement of a durable and relevant leisure policy is that it must recognize people's innate desire to go beyond the bounds. This will always be a controversial issue in leisure because people's leisure choices and values are multidimensional. One person's freedom of expression, will be another person's cause for complaint. Pornography is a good example of this. In the USA during the 1970s and early 80s the anti-pornography laws were progressively liberalized. Films like *Deep Throat* and *The Devil in Miss Jones* became openly available in video stores. Most of the EC states, apart from Britain and Ireland, followed suit. But the tendency was criticized by the far right, Christian and moral authoritarian movement and an energetic lobby of the women's movement. This unlikely alliance combined and agitated to stem the tide of liberalization. For example, the Minneapolis Ordinances of 1993 were drafted to place a feminist definition of pornography on the statute books. Written by the radical feminist activists, Catherine MacKinnon and Andrea Dworkin, the Ordinances require the police and public to regard pornography as a thing and not an interpretation. Its primary characteristic is that it uses words and images to present women as 'dehumanized sexual objects' and is therefore discriminatory on the basis of sex. But is this the right way of conceptualizing pornography? Feminist authors like Lynne Segal (1992), Camille Paglia (1992), Wendy McElroy (1995), Drucilla Cornell (1995), have pointed to the dangers of censorship and queried the legitimacy of the feminist anti-porn lobby's attribution of false consciousness to women who work in the sex industry and female consumers of pornography. The anti-porn case ultimately depends upon proving that pornographic material has a tendency to corrupt. O'Toole's (1998: 39–45) review of the scientific findings suggests that there is no tenable evidence to prove this case. Indeed, he maintains that the evidence suggests that liberalization is associated with lower levels of attacks against women. Be that as it may, the attempt to treat pornography as a thing and not an interpretation, ignores our multidimensional response to phenomena. It is not just that different people will interpret the same cultural object in different ways. In addition, we interpret the same object in various ways at different stages in the life-cycle. The attempt to deny multidimensionality and variance by an act of political fiat is dehumanizing because it seeks to neutralize our human capacity to be different.

It is hard to extract any objective principles or precepts from the debate or the history of anti-pornography. If pornography is a thing and not an interpretation it is immensely difficult to decide what thing it is and what effects it has. What is censored in one decade often becomes required study in another. Think of the banning of James Joyce's *Ulysses* in the 1920s and later D.H. Lawrence's, *Lady Chatterley's Lover*. We now think of these works as part of the literary canon and we look back at the attempts to suppress them as evidence of less sophisticated moral cultures.

Pornography, like drugs, is used daily by millions of people in Britain and Ireland. While males are the main consumers, the evidence suggests that 30 per cent of consumption involves women, either as sole consumers or consumers who consume with their partners (O'Toole 1998: 55). In Britain and Ireland these people are subject to criminal prosecution if found in possession. These commodities cannot be disinvented. Nor in the age of the internet, can the distribution of pornographic images be effectively controlled, which raises the auxiliary question of whether a law that cannot be properly enforced makes much sense. Moreover, the scientific evidence that pornography and drugs are inherently and universally addictive, and possess a tendency to deprave is simply not credible. If leisure policy respects freedom of expression, it follows that the laws on pornography and drug-use in Britain and Ireland should be relaxed. More generally, as British and Irish society move towards multiculturalism and as they become further integrated into the European Community, current policies on pornography and drugs are bound to seem more anomalous. Leisure policy must recognize, as Pieper (1952) acknowledged over forty years ago, that leisure is the basis of culture and that culture is not a thing but a field of interpretation. Different views and disagreements are basic to any field of interpretation. The desire to go beyond the bounds is not an aberration, but a characteristic of the surplus energy inherent in all human cultures and all human beings.

The second requirement of a durable leisure policy is that it must be founded upon, and seek to propagate, care and respect for the other. In the ferment of literature and debate around postmodernism and poststructuralism we have become inured to seeing difference and fragmentation everywhere and unity and solidarity nowhere. Bryan Turner's (1984, 1993) sociology provides a helpful contrasting viewpoint. Turner argues that two universals in human society are the frailty of the body and the precariousness of the environment. All of us have bodies which are subject to illness and which age and eventually die; and all of us inhabit a natural and physical environment which can be damaged and lose its capacity to sustain life. Frailty and precariousness are the universal basis upon which a moral and civil order ultimately rests. Of course they are patterned in different ways in different societies. But insofar as there is anything common to life with others everywhere in the world, it is the need to cope with frailty and precariousness.

A moral injunction of leisure practice should be to respect the actual or potential frailty of others and to care for the actual or potential threat to the precariousness of the environment posed by a given form of practice. Given the velocity, density and innovativeness of contemporary life, *ex post facto* agreements on these matters are probably the best we can hope for. Nonetheless, the principles of frailty and precariousness should underly all leisure policy. Because they are held in common by human beings, they should override any particular personal or group interest.

A third feature of leisure policy should be to acknowledge that leisure activity is ethically constituted. Moral boundaries shaping activity may shift, but leisure choices and practices are irremediably part of a moral universe. This is important because leisure is not a sphere of activity in which anything goes. Not all behaviour is equivalent. Actions which run counter to frailty and precariousness must be hindered. Some forms of leisure practice are better than others. For example, it is better to watch dramatized violence in the cinema than to engage in violence in real life. Similarly, it is better to inhibit forms of free expression which destroy the environment than to assist them. The emphasis on the ethical content of leisure practice is stressed here because so much writing in leisure policy is concerned with technical issues which are divorced from ethical considerations. For example, the politics of time debate is essentially technocratic. It revolves around determining new parameters for the distribution of free time. How this time is used is either treated in an abstract quasi-utopian way – that is, 'for the good of mankind' or in the cause of human progress, or it is reduced to the mere will of individuals. In contrast I contend that the fundamental issues in leisure are ethical. They have to do with who we are and who we want to be. These issues cannot be confined to the discourse of abstract philosophy or the sphere of individual choice. They must be practically worked through in our life with others. We have to start with the ethical content of life with others now, how this compares with conditions in other times and different cultures and what we want to achieve in our ethical composition through leisure policy.

Fourthly, the religious, civil and legal foundations of the work ethic need to be revised. We can no longer, in good conscience, socialize and train our populations to expect to experience lifelong adult paid labour between the ages of 18 and 65. The economy no longer requires it (Schor 1992; Aronowitz and Di Fazio 1994; Aronowitz and Cutler 1998). In addition, the quality of life in the body polity would certainly be improved if surplus labour were diverted into social issues. Housing, health, old age care, environmental protection and wildlife preservation would all benefit from more people being involved in participating in these causes. To some extent, people have already voted with their feet. The enormous growth of the voluntary sector – the so-called 'third sector' of the economy – during the cuts in welfare state expenditure during the 1980s and 1990s is testament to the enormous reservoir of goodwill in people with regard to questions of frailty, precariousness and need. But this labour is discharged as a social credit, usually after paid-work time duties are completed. Voluntaristic activity in the third sector is therefore usually committed after the hours of paid labour and does not carry recognition from the employer. It is 'added on' to the working day, rather than being recognized as an integral part of work. This voluntary labour is arguably akin to the gift of blood (Titmuss 1970) in being one of the noblest things that humans can do for one another. If leisure policy should be concerned with enlarging the ethical content of life with others, voluntary labour in caring for others in need should be a high priority.

But all of these policies belong to the kingdom of good intentions unless we recognize the scale of the challenges facing us. We live in global, essentially capitalist societies. The key actor in these societies is not the individual, classes or the state, but corporations intent on maximizing profits and minimizing costs. The hoary old problems in the critical sociology of leisure relating to commodification, alienation and oppression will never be expressed correctly unless we get to grips with the immense power of the business corporation in ordinary leisure practice. In addition, it is no longer enough to consider the activities of the corporation as confined to national boundaries. One of the greatest errors of the Left in the 1960s and 70s was to underestimate the global nature of corporate capitalism. This led to an exaggerated view of the importance of national traditions. It also produced the myth that it is possible to find national solutions to global problems. As Bauman (1998) argues, corporate capitalists think globally. The boundaries of the nation-state are irrelevant to most of their business decisions.

So must they be in any thinking about how to restructure leisure. Of course, this is not to make the local disappear by a theoretical trick of some vanishing mirror. No-one can take charge of their own lives if they wait to address the global level. Responsibility must be executed at the most immediate phenomenal level: life with others. In the areas of life which mean most to us, in our workplaces, our schools, our universities, our places of consumption and in our communities, we must *engage*.

The barriers to engagement are formidable. Performative cultures carry strong tendencies to encourage people to limit themselves to their own narrow interests. The inequality of power between individuals and state organizations and multinational corporations is stacked against individuals. Practically speaking, the condition boils down to getting on with your own life while leaving the wider questions of the conduct of life with others to others. But if the experience of the interventionist and free-market policies of the postwar period teaches us anything, it is that if we confine ourselves merely to getting on with our own lives, society and culture pass us by. We become enmeshed in precepts and habits of behaviour determined by others which we experience as a train of blockages. Environmental risks, moral prohibitions, policies on heritage preservation and traffic control, grow up around us without our involvement or consent. Of course, advanced urban-industrial societies are complex and they depend upon systems of representative democracy to take decisions. We cannot be involved in everything.

In addition, because leisure is ideologically presented as free time, most of us relate to it as an area in social life which enables us to get away from the cares of the day.

But freedom is not a gift donated to us by others. Freedom depends upon personal engagement. It carries responsibilities of care for the self and the guarantee of freedom for others. The debate on the ethical content of leisure practice has been obscured by consumer culture. Commodity capitalism presents commodities as alienated items, separate from the network of human relations that produced them. It also pursues the dynamic of continuous commodity replacement so that consumer life is apt to seem like an endless parade of new commodities. The questions of who we are in our free, private time and what we should aspire to be are all too easily lost in the rituals of commodified leisure practice. But just as freedom ultimately depends upon personal engagement, private life has a public dimension. If this book has a dominant message it is that leisure studies has reached a stage of maturity in which the question of the cultural dimensions of private life must occupy the centre stage. The fate of Nietzsche's (1986: 360) 'pleasure tourists' is to succumb to the mechancial rituals of performative culture. We have a different option open to us: escape.

Notes

1 FROM RITUAL TO PERFORMATIVE CULTURE

1. Looking back, 'the good society' was an amazingly imprecise construct. It included freedom, equality, justice and affluence. But it was never really convincingly explained how exploitation and aggression were to be overcome. Kerr *et al.* (1973) predicted the emergence of what they called 'the new bohemianism'. In some ways this anticipated later postmodern theories by proposing that the future will be marked by increasing diversity, tolerance and multiculturalism. But questions of social exclusion and new forms of exploitation are simply shrugged off. The whole post-industrial society moment is a curious amalgam of pre-scient insights about the rise of new information technologies and associated technocultures of change and naive hopes that technology will allow Enlightenment humanism to flourish undimmed in the late twentieth and twenty-first centuries.
2. The black, or informal economy, refers to undeclared wage earnings. It is immensely difficult to gain an accurate impression of the size of this component of the national economy. But it is clearly a significant feature of the labour market in advanced industrial society.
3. It is sociologically implausible to propose that competition will die out overnight. Even if the status of pecuniary reward is diminished, the sociologically plausible outcome will be that new reward distinctions will emerge leading to new, unanticipated systems of stratification.

2 'THE LEISURE CLASS' TODAY

1. Post-colonialism has two aspects to it. First, it refers to the subjectivities that arise in reaction to colonial occupation. The second meaning refers to the discursive practices involving resistance to colonialism. For an informative and reliable discussion of post-colonialism see Child and Williams (1997).
2. EPCOT refers to the Experimental Prototypical Community of Tomorrow devised by Walt Disney for the Disneyworld park. Disney intended it to consist of inhabitants living and working with the most advanced technologies. From the standpoint of the tourist the effect would be a futuristic encounter with new lifestyles and conditions of life. Gates seems to see his house in the same light.

3 THE CULTURAL CONTEXT OF LEISURE PRACTICE

1. Hall's view of theoretical work drew heavily on Gramsci's concept of

213

'the organic intellectual'. Hall interpreted this as consisting of two components. On one side, it was the duty of the organic intellectual to develop better, more accurate forms of knowledge than traditional intellectuals. This view gave an important sense of moral superiority to Cultural Studies work since it implied that the work of traditional intellectuals was intrinsically flawed. The second dimension of the organic intellectual was to disseminate knowledge and theories to meaningful social forces. In Hall's early work this was more or less synonymous with the working class. Later gender and race relations became more significant.

2. At the time of writing Celia Brackenridge and Sheila Scraton are on the editorial board; Karla Henderson and Betsy Wearing are members of the editorial advisory board.

3. The failure to engage with poststructuralist and postmodern thought is particularly striking. Working in the field of leisure theory often feels like being becalmed in the theoretical debates of the 1970s.

4   THE ABNORMAL FORMS OF LEISURE

1. These spaces can be thought of as prototypical liminal zones in industrial society – that is, cultural spaces in which boundaries on narratives, especially critical narratives, are semi-suspended.

2. Figurational sociology refutes the notion of the isolated individual. Essential to Elias's method is that we are bound by relations of interdependence to the generations that preceded us and also to others in the world today. Functional democratization refers to the tendency for power to be distributed along functional lines as processes of social development advance. The effect of this is to make each individual more reliant upon functionally specialized labour and hence to reinforce the chains of interdependence linking each to all.

5   CONCLUSION: ENGAGED FREEDOM

1. Although of course, there is widespread disagreement about the nature and form of reorganization.

2. The Frankfurt School is regarded to ultimately reinforce an elitist view of leisure and popular culture and to be over-pessimistic about the prospects of social transformation

Bibliography

Adorno, T. (1991), 'Resignation' pp. 171–5 (in) *The Culture Industry*, ed. with an Introduction by J.M. Bernstein, London, Routledge.

Adorno, T. and Horkheimer, M. (1944), *Dialectic of Enlightenment*, London, Verso.

Aitchison, K. (1996), 'A Critical Response to Rojek's "Killing for Leisure"', *Leisure Studies Association Newsletter*, 45, pp. 10–11.

Ang, I. (1985), *Watching Dallas*, London, Methuen.

Ang, T. (1996), *Living Room Wars*, London, Routledge.

Applebaum, H. (1992), *The Concept of Work*, Albany, State University of New York Press.

Archer, D. and Gartner, R. (1984), *Violence and Crime in Cross-National Perspective*, New Haven, Yale University Press.

Arendt, H. (1958), *The Human Condition*, Chicago, Chicago University Press.

Arnold, M. (1869), *Culture and Anarchy*, London, Nelson.

Aronowitz, S. and DiFazio, W. (1994), *The Jobless Future*, Minneapolis, University of Minnesota Press.

Aronowitz, S. and Cutler, J. (eds) (1998), *Post-Work*, New York, Routledge.

Bachelard, G. (1968), *The Psychoanalysis of Fire*, Boston, Beacon Press.

Bailey, P. (1987), *Leisure and Class in Victorian England*, London, Methuen.

Bakhtin, M. (1968), *Rabelais and His World*, Cambridge, MIT Press.

Barker, M. and Petley, J. (eds) (1997), *Ill Effects*, London, Routledge.

Bataille, G. (1986), *Eroticism*, London, Marion Boyars.

Bataille, G. (1988), *The Accursed Share*, Vols 1–3, New York, Zone Books.

Bataille, G. (1991a), *The Accursed Share: An Essay on General Economy: Consumption*, New York, Zone Books.

Bataille, G. (1991b), *The Accursed Share: An Essay on General Economy: Eroticism; Sovereignty*, New York, Zone Books.

Bataille, G. (1991), *The Trial of Gilles de Rais*, Monroe, Amok.

Baudrillard, J. (1975), *The Mirror of Production*, St Louis, Telos.

Baudrillard, J. (1983), *Simulations*, New York, Semiotext.

Baudrillard, J. (1998), *The Consumer Society*, London, Sage.

Bauman, Z. (1989), *Modernity and the Holocaust*, Cambridge, Polity.

Bauman, Z. (1992), *Intimations of Postmodernity*, London, Routledge.

Bauman, Z. (1998), *Postmodernity and its Discontents*, Cambridge, Polity.

Bayliss, V. (1998), *Redefining Work*, London, Royal Society for the Encouragement of Arts, Manufacture & Commerce.

Beck, S., Giddens, A. and Lash, S. (1994), *Reflexive Modernization*, Cambridge, Polity.

Beck, U. (1992), *Risk Society*, London, Sage.

Bell, D. (1973), *The Coming of Post-Industrial Society*, Harmondsworth, Penguin.

Bell, D. (1976), *The Cultural Contradictions of Capitalism*, London, Heinemann.

Benjamin, W. (1970), *Charles Baudelaire*, London, Verso.
Bennett, T. (1986), 'A Thousand and One Troubles: Blackpool Pleasure Beach', pp. 138–55, in *Formations of Pleasure*, London, Routledge.
Beresford, P. (1997), 'Introduction', *Sunday Times Rich List, Sunday Times*, April.
Bernstein, B. (1971), *Class, Codes and Control*, Vol 1, London, RKP.
Berridge, V. and Edwards, G. (1987), *Opium and the People*, New York, Yale University Press.
Bhabba, H. (1994), *The Location of Culture*, London, Routledge.
Bialeschki, D. and Henderson, K. (1986), 'Leisure in the Common World of Women', *Leisure Studies*, 5(1): 299–308.
Billig, M. (1992), *Talking about the Royal Family*, Routledge, London.
Blackburn, R. (1997), 'The Rich and the Poor', Cambridge, Occasional Paper, Dept of Economic and Political Science, Cambridge University.
Blauner, R. (1964), *Alienation and Freedom*, Chicago, Chicago University Press.
Bogdan, R. (1988), *Freak Show: Presenting Human Oddities, for Amusement and Profit*, Chicago, Chicago University Press.
Bourdieu, P. (1984), *Distinction*, Routledge.
Bourdieu, P. and Passeron, J.C. (1990), *Reproduction in Education, Society and Culture*, London, Sage.
Bowring, F. (1995), 'Gorz: Ecology, System and Lifeworld', *Capitalism, Nature and Socialism*, 6:4.
Brackenridge, C., Summer, D. and Woodward, D. (1995), 'Educating for Child Protection in Sport', in Lawrence, L., Murdoch, E. and Parker, S. (eds) *Professional and Development Issues in Leisure, Sport and Education*, LSA Publication 56, Eastbourne, Leisure Studies Association.
Brady, I. (1997), 'Letter to Home Office', extracts printed in *The Guardian*, 9 December.
Braverman, H. (1974), *Labour and Monopoly Capital*, New York, Monthly Review Press.
Britton, P. (1995), 'They Grew into Monsters: Why?' *Sunday Times*, 26 November 1995.
Brundson, C. (1996), 'A Thief in the Night: stories of feminism in the 1970s at CCCS', pp. 276–86 in Morley, D. and Chen, K.H. (eds) *Stuart Hall: Critical Dialogues in Cultural Studies*, London, Routledge.
Buck, N. *et al.* (1994), *Changing Households: The British Household Panel Study 1990–1992*, ESRC Centre on Micro Social Change, Essex University.
Burton-Nelson, M. (1994), *The Stronger Women Get, the More Men Love Football*, New York, Avon.
Butler, J. (1993), *Bodies That Matter*, London, Routledge.
Carmichael, S. (1968), 'Black Power', pp. 150–74 in Cooper, D. (ed.) *The Dialectics of Liberation*, Harmondsworth, Penguin.
Castells, M. (1996), *The Rise of Network Society*, Oxford, Blackwell.
Castells, M. (1997), *The Power of Identity*, Oxford, Blackwell.
Castells, M. (1998), *The End of the Millennium*, Oxford, Blackwell.
Chaney, D. (1996), *Lifestyles*, London, Routledge.
Cheney, C.R. (1961), 'Rule for the Observance of Feast Days in Medieval England', *Bulletin of the Institute of Historical Research* 34 (November): 117–21.

Child, P. and Williams, P. (1997), *An Introduction to Post-Colonial Theory*, Hemel Hempstead, Prentice Hall-Harvester Wheatsheaf.

Clarke, D. (1995), *The Rise and Fall of Popular Music*, Harmondsworth, Penguin.

Clarke, J. and Critcher, C. (1985), *The Devil Makes Work*, London, Macmillan.

Cohen, S. and Taylor, L. (1993), *Escape Attempts*, London, Routledge.

Conrad, B. (1997), *Absinthe: History in a Bottle*, New York, Chronice Books.

Cooper, D. (1974), *The Grammar of Living*, Harmondsworth, Penguin.

Cornell, D. (1995), *The Imaginary Domain*, New York, Routledge.

Corrigan, P. and Sayer, D. (1985), *The Great Arch*, Oxford, Blackwell.

Craik, J. (1991), *Resorting to Tourism*, Sydney, Allen & Unwin.

Cross, G. (1988), *Time and Money*, London, Routledge.

Crotts, J. (1996), 'Theoretical Perspectives on Tourist Criminal Victimisation', *Journal of Tourism Studies*, 7:1, 1–9.

Crush, J. and Wellings, P. (1987), 'Forbidden Fruit and the Export Vice', (in) Britton, S. and Clarke, W. (eds), *Ambiguous Alternative: Tourism in Small Developing Countries*, Suva, Fiji: University of South Pacific Press.

Csikszentmihalyi, M. (1975), *Beyond Boredom and Anxiety*, San Francisco, Josey-Bass.

Cunnen, C., Findlay, M., Lynch, R. and Tupper, V. (1989), *Dynamics of Collective Conflict: Riots and the Bathurst Bike Races*, North Ryde, The Law Book Company.

Cunningham, H. (1980) *Leisure in the Industrial Revolution*, Beckenham, Croom-Helm.

Davidoff, L. (1973), *The Best Circles*, Beckenham, Croom Helm.

Davis, M. (1990), *City of Quartz*, London, Verso.

Debord, G. (1967), *The Society of the Spectacle*, London, Rebel Press.

De Grazia, S. (1962), *Of Time, Work and Leisure*, Garden City, Doubleday.

Deem, R. (1986), *All Work and No Play*, Milton Keynes, Open University Press.

Deleuze, G. and Guattari, F. (1988), *A Thousand Plateaus*, Minneapolis, University of Minnesota Press.

Di Fazio, W. (1985), *Longshoremen: Community and Resistance on the Brooklyn Waterfront*, South Hadley, MA, Bergin and Garvey.

Domhoff, G. (1967), *Who Rules America?*, New Jersey, Prentice Hall.

Dower, M., Rapaport, R., Strelitz, Z. and Kew, S. (1981), *Leisure Provision and People's Needs*, London, HMSO.

Du Gay, P. (1996), *Consumption and Identity at Work*, London, Sage.

Dunning, E., Murphy, and P. Williams, J. (1988), *The Roots of Football Hooliganism*, London, Routledge.

Durkheim, E. (1895), *The Rules of Sociological Method*, New York, Free Press.

Durkheim, E. (1897), *Suicide*, London, RKP.

Durkheim, E. (1902), *The Division of Labour in Society*, New York, Free Press.

Durkheim, E. (1915), *The Elementary Forms of Religious Life*, New York, Free Press.

Dyer, R. (1997), *White*, London, Routledge.

Eco, U. (1990), *The Limits of Interpretation*, Bloomington, Indiana University Press.

Eco, U. (1994), *Apocalypse Postponed*, Bloomington, Indiana University Press.

Edgell, S. (1993), *Class*, London, Routledge.

Ehrenreich, B. (1989), *Fear of Failing: the Inner Life of the Middle Class*, New York, Pantheon.

Eliade, M. (1957), *The Sacred and the Profane*, New York, Harcourt, Brace and Ward.

Elias, N. (1978a), *What Is Sociology?*, London, Hutchinson.

Elias, N. (1978b), *The Civilizing Process*, Vol 1: The History of Manners, Oxford, Blackwell.

Elias, N. (1982), *The Civilizing Process*, Vol 2: State Formation and Civilization, Oxford, Blackwell.

Elias, N. and Dunning, E.G. (1969), 'The Quest for Excitement in Leisure', *Society and Leisure*, 2: 388–402.

Elias, N. and Dunning, E.G. (1986) *Quest for Excitement*, Oxford, Blackwell.

Eliot, T.S. (1948), *Notes Towards the Definition of Culture*, London, Faber.

Esland, G. and Salaman, G. (eds) (1975) 'Towards a Sociology of Work (in) G. Esland, G. Salaman and M. Speakman (eds), *People and Work*, Edinburgh, Holmes-MacDougall/Open University.

Etzioni, A. (1993), *The Spirit of Community: Rights, Responsibilities and the Communitarian Agenda*, New York, Crown.

Evans-Pritchard, E. (1976), *Witchcraft, Magic and the Oracles, Among the Azande*, Oxford, Clarendon Press.

Ewen, S. (1976), *The Captains of Consciousness*, New York, McGraw Hill.

Ewen, S. (1988), *All Consuming Images*, New York, Basic Books.

Featherstone, M. (1990), *Consumer Culture and Postmodernism*, London, Sage.

Featherstone, M. and Burrows, R. (1995), *Cyberspace, Cyberbodies, Cyberpunk*, London, Sage.

Finch, J. and Mason, J. (1993), *Negotiating Family Responsibilities*, London, Tavistock/Routledge.

Fiske, J. (1987), *Television Culture*, London, Methuen.

Fiske, J. (1989), *Reading Popular Culture*, London, Unwin Hyman.

'For Leisure', Leisure Studies Association Newsletter, 45: 10–11.

Foster, H. (ed.) (1985), *Postmodern Culture*, London, Pluto.

Foucault, M. (1961), *Madness and Civilization*, London, Tavistock.

Foucault, M. (1970), *The Order of Things*, London, Tavistock.

Foucault, M. (1972), *The Archaeology of Knowledge*, London, Tavistock.

Foucault, M. (1975), *Discipline and Punish*, Harmondsworth, Penguin.

Foucault, M. (1979), *Power, Truth and Strategy* (eds) M. Morris and P. Patton, Sydney, Feral Publications.

Foucault, M. (1980), *Power/Knowledge: Selected Interviews and Other Essays 1972–77*, (ed.) C. Gordon, Brighton, Harvester.

Foucault, M. (1981), *The History of Sexuality*, Vol. 1, Harmondsworth, Penguin.

Foucault, M. (1988), *Politics, Philosophy, Culture* (ed.) L. Kirtzman, London, Routledge.

Frank, R. and Cook, P. (1995), *The Winner-Takes-All Society*, New York, Penguin.
Fraser, N. (1989), *Unruly Practices*, Cambridge, Polity.
Freud, S. (1939), *Civilization and its Discontents*, London, Hogarth Press.
Galbraith, J.K. (1974), *The New Industrial State*, Harmondsworth, Penguin.
Game, A. (1991), *Undoing the Social*, Milton Keynes, Open University Press.
Gates, B. (1995), *The Road Ahead*, New York, Viking.
Gatrell, V. (1996), *The Hanging Tree: Execution and the English People 1770–1868*, Oxford, Oxford University Press.
Gay, P. (1994), *The Cultivation of Hatred*, London, Harper Collins.
Geertz, C. (1973), *The Interpretation of Cultures*, New York, Basic Books.
Gershuny, J. (1993), *Social Innovation and the Division of Labour*, Oxford, Oxford University Press.
Giddens, A. (1984), *The Constitution of Society*, Cambridge, Polity.
Giddens, A. (1990), *The Consequences of Modernity*, Cambridge, Polity.
Giddens, A. (1991), *Modernity and Self Identity*, Cambridge, Polity.
Giddens, A. (1992), *The Transformation of Intimacy*, Cambridge, Polity.
Gilbert, D. and Kahl, J. (1987), *The American Class Structure*, Belmont, Wadsworth.
Gillies, E. (1976), 'Introduction', (in) Evans-Pritchard, E.E., *Witchcraft Oracles and Magic Among the Azande*, Oxford, Oxford University Press, pp vii–xxix.
Gitlin, T. (1984), *Inside Prime Time*, New York, Pantheon.
Gitlin, T. (1995), *The Twilight of Common Dreams*, New York, Owl Books.
Glotz, G. (1927), *Ancient Greece at Work*, New York, Knopf.
Goffman, E. (1959), *Asylums*, Harmondsworth, Penguin.
Goffman, E. (1963), *Stigma*, Harmondsworth, Penguin.
Goffman, E. (1967), *Interaction Ritual*, New York, Pantheon.
Goffman, E. (1971), *Relations in Public*, Harmondsworth, Penguin.
Goffman, E. (1974), *Frame Analysis*, New York, Harper & Rowe.
Goldthorpe, J.H., Lockwood, D., Bechhofer, F. and Platt, J. (1968), *The Affluent Worker*, Cambridge, Cambridge University Press.
Gorz, A. (1967), *A Strategy for Labour*, Boston, Beacon Press.
Gorz, A. (1975), *Ecology as Politics*, London, Pluto.
Gorz, A. (1982), *Farewell to the Working Class*, London, Pluto.
Gorz, A. (1983), *Paths to Paradise: on the Liberation from Work*, London, Pluto.
Gorz, A. (1989), *Critique of Economic Reason*, London, Verso.
Gorz, A. (1994), *Capitalism, Socialism, Ecology*, London, Verso.
Goudsblom, J. (1992), *Fire and Civilization*, Harmondsworth, Penguin.
Gray, R. (1981), *The Aristocracy of Labour*, London, Macmillan.
Green, E., Hebron, S. and Woodward, D. 'Women's Leisure in Sheffield', mimeo (1987), Dept. of Applied Social Studies, Sheffield Hallam University.
Grossberg, L. (1983), 'Cultural Studies Revisited and Revised, in M.S. Mander (ed.) *Communications in Transition*, New York, Praeger, pp. 392–421.
Grossberg, L. (1984), 'I'd rather feel bad than not feel anything at all', *Enclitic*, 8: 94–111.

Grossberg, L. (1986), 'History, Politics and Postmodernism: Stuart Hall and Cultural Studies', *Journal of Communication Inquiry*, 10(2): 61–77.
Grosz, E. and Probyn, E. (eds) (1995), *Sexy Bodies*, London, Routledge.
Gurevich, A. (1985), *Categories of Medieval Culture*, London, RKP.
Habermas, J. (1962), *The Structural Transformation of the Public Sphere*, Cambridge, Polity.
Hall, S. and Jacques, M. (eds) (1989), *New Times*, London, Lawrence & Wishart.
Hall, S. and Jefferson, T. (1975) (eds), *Resistance through Rituals*, London, Hutchinson.
Hall, S., Critcher, C., Jefferson, T., Clarke, J. and Roberts, R. (1978), *Policing the Crisis*, London, Macmillan.
Hall, S., Hobson, D., Lowe, A. and Willis, P. (eds) (1980), *Culture, Media, Language: Working Papers in Cultural Studies, 1972–79*, Hutchinson/CCCS, London.
Haraway, D. (1991), *Simians, Cyborgs and Women*, London, Free Association Books.
Hargreaves, J. (1986), *Sport, Power and Culture*, Cambridge, Polity.
Harriman, A. (1982), *The Work/Leisure Trade Off*, New York, Praeger.
Harris, D. (1992), *From Class Struggle to the Politics of Pleasure*, London, Routledge.
Hartley, J. (1996), *Popular Reality*, London, Edward Arnold.
Harvey, D. (1989), *The Condition of Postmodernity*, Oxford, Blackwell.
Hebdige, D. (1979), *Subculture*, London, Routledge.
Hebdige, D. (1987), *Cut 'n' Mix*, London, Comedia.
Henderson, K., Bialeschki, M., Shaw, S. and Freysinger, V. (1989), *A Leisure of One's Own: A Feminist Perspective on Women's Leisure*, State College, PA, Venture.
Henderson, K., Bialeschki, M., Shaw, S. and Freysinger, V. (1996), *Both Gains and Gaps: Feminist Perspectives on Women's Leisure*, State College, PA, Venture.
Henry, I. (1993), *The Politics of Leisure Policy*, London, Macmillan.
Hill, S. (1981), *Competition and Control at Work*, London, Heinemann.
Hindess, B. (1986), *Freedom, Equality and the Market*, London, Tavistock.
HMSO (1997), *Social Trends*, London, HMSO.
HMSO (1998), *Social Trends*, London, HMSO.
Hochschild, A.R. (1997), *The Time Bind*, New York, Metropolitan Books.
Huizinga, J. (1947), *Homo Ludens*, London, RKP.
Hunnicutt, B.K. (1988), *Work without End*, Philadelphia, Temple University Press.
Hutton, W. (1996), *The State We're In*, London, Vintage.
Huyssen, A. (1986), *After the Great Divide*, Bloomington, Indiana University Press.
Jackson, T. (1995), *Virgin King*, London, Harper Collins.
Jary, D. and Jary, J. (1995), *Dictionary of Sociology*, London, Harper Collins.
Jenkins, P. (1994), *Using Murder: the Social Construction of Serial Homicide*, New York, Aldine de Gruyter.
Jenkins, R. (1983), *Lads, Citizens and Ordinary Kids*, London, Routledge.
Jenks, C. (1993), *Culture*, London, Routledge.

Jhally, S. (1990), *The Codes of Advertising*, London, Routledge.

Jovanov, N. (1979), *Radnicki strajokvi u socijalistickoj federativnojrepublici Jugoslaviji od 1958 do 1969*, Belgrade: Zapis.

Katz, J. (1988), Seductions of Crime, New York, Basic Books.

Keane, J. (1995), *Tom Paine: A Political Life*, London, Bloomsbury.

Kellner, D. (1994), *Media Culture*, London, Routledge.

Kelly, J. (1987), *Freedom to Be?*, New York, Macmillan.

Kerr, C., Dunlop, J.T., Harbison, F.H. and Meyers, C. (1973), *Industrialism and Industrial Man*, Harmondsworth, Penguin.

Kracauer, S. (1995), *The Mass Ornament*, Harvard University Press, Cambridge, MA.

Laing, R.D. (1960), *The Divided Self*, London, Tavistock.

Laing, R.D. (1967), *The Politics of Experience and the Bird of Paradise*, London, Penguin.

Laing, R.D. (1968), 'The Obvious', pp. 13–33 (in) Cooper, D. (ed.) *The Dialectics of Liberation*, Harmondsworth, Penguin.

Laing, R.D. (1970), *Knots*, London, Tavistock.

Laing, R.D. and Esterson, A. (1964), *Sanity, Madness and the Family*, London, Tavistock.

Lasch, C. (1979), *The Culture of Narcissism*, London, Abacus.

Lasch, C. (1984), *The Minimal Self*, London, Paladin.

Lash, S. and Urry, J. (1987), *The End of Organized Capitalism*, Cambridge, Polity.

Lash, S. and Urry, J. (1994), *Economies of Signs and Space*, London, Sage.

Leary, T. (1970), *The Politics of Ecstasy*, London, Paladin.

Leary, T. (1990), *Flashbacks*, New York, Tarcher/Putnam.

Lee, M. and Shlain, B. (1985), *Acid Dreams: The Complete Social History of LSD*, New York, Grove Press.

Lefebvre, H. (1991), *Critique of Everyday Life*, Oxford, Blackwell.

Lenzener, R. (1993), 'Warren Buffett's Idea of Heaven: "I Don't Have to Work with People I Don't Like"', *Forbes*, 18 October.

Leyton, E. (1986), *Hunting Humans*, Toronto, McLelland & Stewart.

Leyton, E. (1995a), *Men of Blood*, London, Constable.

Leyton, E. (1995b), 'Preface to the new Canadian edition', pp. ix–xv, *Hunting Humans*, London, Constable.

Lhamon, W.T. (1993), *Deliberate Speed*, Washington, Smithsonian Institute.

Linder, S. (1970), *The Harried Leisure Class*, New York, Norton.

Lodziak, C. and Tatman, J. (1997), *Andre Gorz*, London, Pluto.

Lowe, D. (1995), *The Body in Late Capitalist USA*, Durham, Duke University Press.

Lowenstein, R. (1995), *Buffett: The Making of an American Capitalist*, London, Orion.

Lowenthal, D. (1985), *The Past is a Foreign Country*, Cambridge, Cambridge University Press.

Lowenthal, L. (1944), 'Biographies in Popular Magazines', in Lazarsfeld, P. and Stanton, F. (eds), *Radio Research 1942–43*, New York, Duell, Sloan and Pearce.

Lyng, S. (1990), 'Edgework: a social psychological analysis of voluntary risk taking', *American Journal of Sociology*, 95: 887–921.

Lyng, S. (1991), 'Edgework revisited: reply to Miller', *American Journal of Sociology*, 96: 1534–9.

Lyotard, J.-F. (1984), *The Postmodern Condition*, Manchester, Manchester University Press.

MacCannell, D. (1992), *Empty Meeting Grounds*, London, Routledge.

MacQuarrie, F. and Jackson, E. (1996), 'Connections between negotiation of leisure constraints and serious leisure', *Loisir et Société*, 19:1, 459–83.

Marcus, G. (1989), *Lipstick Traces*, London, Secker & Warburg.

Marcuse, H. (1955), *Eros and Civilization*, London, Abacus.

Marcuse, H. (1964), *One Dimensional Man*, London, Abacus.

Marshall, G. (1997), *Repositioning Class*, London, Sage.

Martin, P. (1994), 'The consumer market for interactive services: observing past trends and current demographics', *Telephony* 226(18): 126–30.

Marx, K. (1844), *Economic and Philosophic Manuscripts*, New York, International Press.

Marx, K. (1867), *Capital Vol. 1*, London, Lawrence & Wishart.

Marx, K. (1888), *Capital Vol. 3*, London, Lawrence & Wishart.

Marx, K. (1965), *The German Ideology*, Moscow, Progress Publishers.

Marx, K. and Engels, F. (1968), *Selected Works*, London, Lawrence & Wishart.

Mauss, M. (1925), *The Gift*, London, Routledge.

McElroy, W. (1995), *XXX: A Woman's Right to Pornography*, New York, St Martin's Press.

McGuigan, J. (1992), *Cultural Populism*, London, Routledge.

McGuigan, J. (1996), *Culture and the Public Sphere*, London, Routledge.

McLaren, P. (1997), *Revolutionary Multiculturalism*, Boulder, Westview.

McLintock, A. (1995), *Imperial Leather*, New York, Routledge.

McLuhan, M. (1997), *Essential McLuhan* (eds), McLuhan, E. and Zingrone, F., London, Routledge.

McRobbie, A. (1978) 'Working class girls and the culture of femininity', in Women's Studies Group, Centre for Contemporary Cultural Studies, *Women Take Issue*, London, Hutchinson.

McRobbie, A. (1994), *Postmodernism and Popular Culture*, London, Routledge.

Melechi, A. (ed.) (1997), *Psychedelic Britannica: Hallucinogenic Drugs in Britain*, London, Turnaround.

Merton, R. (1968), *Social Theory and Social Structure*, New York, Free Press.

Mestrovic, S. (1997), *Post-Emotional Society*, London, Sage.

Miller, J. (1993), *The Passion of Michel Foucault*, London, Harper Collins.

Mills, C.W. (1956), *The Power Elite*, New York, Oxford University Press.

Mitchell, B. (1990), *Murder and Penal Policy*, London, Macmillan.

Mugford, S. and O'Malley, P. (1991), 'Crime, Excitement and Modernity', mimeo, paper presented at The American Society of Criminology Conference, San Francisco.

Mumford, L. (1967), *The Myth of the Machine*, London, Secker & Warburg.

Mumford, L. (1970), *The Pentagon of Power*, New York, Harcourt, Brace & Jovanovich.

Nietzsche, F. (1986), *Human All Too Human*, Cambridge, Cambridge University Press.

Norris, J. (1988), *Serial Killers*, New York, Doubleday.
O'Connor, D. (1997), 'Lines of (F)light: The Visual Apparatus in Foucault and Deleuze', *Space and Culture*, 1:1, 49–66.
O'Malley, P. and Mugford, S. (1991), 'Crime, Excitement and Modernity', Mimeo Paper, presented at The American Society of Criminology Conference, San Francisco.
O'Toole, L. (1998), *Pornocopia*, London, Serpent's Tale.
Offe, C. (1984), *Contradictions of the Welfare State*, London, Hutchinson.
Paglia, C. (1992), *Sex, Art and Politics*, Harmondsworth, Penguin.
Pahl, R. (1984), *Divisions of Labour*, Oxford, Blackwell.
Pahl, R. (1995), *After Success*, Cambridge, Polity.
Pakulski, J. and Waters, M. (1996), *The Death of Class*, London, Sage.
Parker, S. (1983), *Leisure and Work*, London, Macmillan.
Pearson, G. (1987), *Hooligan: a History of Respectable Fears*, London, Macmillan.
Pieper, J. (1952), *Leisure: the Basis of Culture*, New York, Mentor.
Plachy, S. and Ridgeway, J. (1996), *Red Light: Inside the Sex Industry*, New York, Powerhouse Books.
Plant, S. (1992), *Most Radical Gesture*, London, Routledge.
Poster, M. (1990), *The Mode of Information*, Cambridge, Polity.
Presedee, M. (1994), 'Young People, Culture and the Construction of Crime: Doing Wrong versus Doing Crime', pp. 179–87 in Barak, G. (ed.) *Varieties of Criminology*, Westport, Praeger.
Probyn, E. (1991), *Sexing the Self*, London, Routledge.
Pron, N. (1995), *Lethal Marriage: the Unspeakable Crimes of Paul Bernardo and Karla Homolka*, Toronto, McLelland-Bantam.
Reich, W. (1980), *Character Analysis*, New York, Farrar Strauss.
Reich, W. (1992), *The Mass Psychology of Fascism*, London, Souvenir Books.
Reuth, R.G. (1993), *Goebbels*, London, Constable.
Rheingold, H. (1994), *The Virtual Community*, London, Secker and Warburg.
Riesman, D. (1950), *The Lonely Crowd*, New York, Doubleday.
Riesman, D. (1964), *Abundance for What?*, London, Chatto & Windus.
Ritchie, B. and Goldsmith, W. (1987) (eds), *The New Elite: the Secrets of Britain's Top Chief Executives' Success*, Harmondsworth, Penguin.
Ritzer, G. (1992), *The McDonaldization of Society*, Thousand Oaks, Pine Forge.
Ritzer, G. (1995), *Expressing America*, Thousand Oaks, Pine Forge.
Roberts, K. (1978), *Contemporary Society and the Growth of Leisure*, London, Longman.
Roberts, K. (1981), *Leisure*, London, Longman.
Roberts, K. (1998), 'Why Old Questions are the Right Response to New Challenges: the Sociology of Leisure in the 1990s', *Loisir et Société*, 20:2, 369–83.
Robertson, R. (1992), *Globalization*, London, Sage.
Robinson, D. (1973), *World Cinema 1895–1980*, London, Eyre Methuen.
Rodgers, E. (1940), *Discussions of Holidays in the Later Middle Ages*, New York, Columbia University Press.
Rojek, C. (1993), *Ways of Escape*, London, Macmillan.
Rojek, C. (1995), *Decentring Leisure*, London, Sage.

Rojek, C. (1998), 'Stuart Hall and the Antinomian Tradition', *International Journal of Cultural Studies*, 1:1, 45–65.

Rojek, C. and Wilson, D. (1987), 'Workers' self management in the world system: the Yugoslav case', *Organization Studies*, 8:4, 297–308.

Rojos, A. (1998), 'Justice is revenge in Kigali's bloody arena', *The Guardian*, 25 April, p. 3.

Routh, G. (1987), *Occupations of the People of Great Britain 1801–1981*, London, Macmillan.

Rudé, G. (1975), *Revolutionary Europe: 1793–1815*, London, Fontana.

Rus, V. (1978), 'External and internal influences in enterprises', in J. Obradovic and W. Dunn (eds), *Workers's Self Management and Organizational Power in Yugoslavia*, Pittsburgh: Center for International Studies, pp. 25–43.

Ruskin, J. (1903–12), *Works* (39 Vols), (eds) E.T. Cook and A. Wedderbrun, George Allen, London.

Ryan, C. (1991), *Recreational Tourism*, London, Routledge.

Sacks, S. (1983), *Self Management and Efficiency: Large Corporations in Yugoslavia*, London: Allen & Unwin.

Sahlins, M. (1985), *Islands of History*, Chicago, Chicago University Press.

Said, E. (1978), *Orientalism*, London, Routledge.

Savage, M., Barlow, J., Dickens, P. and Fielding, J. (1992), *Property, Bureaucracy and Culture*, London, Routledge.

Sayers, S. (1987), 'The Need To Work', *Radical Philosophy*, 46: 17–26.

Schor, J. (1992), *The Over-Worked American*, New York, Basic Books.

Schwagger, J.D. (1992), *The New Market Wizards: Conversations with America's Top Traders*, London, Harper Collins.

Scott, J. (1982), *The Upper Class*, London, Macmillan.

Scott, J. (1985), *Corporations, Classes and Capitalism*, London, Hutchinson.

Scott, J. (1991), *Who Rules Britain?*, Cambridge, Polity.

Scraton, S. (1993), 'Feminism, "Post-feminism" and Leisure Mimeo', International Leisure Studies Association.

Scraton, S. and Talbot, M. (1989), 'A Response to "Leisure, Lifestyle and Status"', *Leisure Studies*, 8(2): 155–8.

Segal, L. (1992), *Straight Sex: the Politics of Pleasure*, London, Virago.

Sennett, R. (1973), *The Uses of Disorder*, Harmondsworth, Penguin.

Sennett, R. (1977), *The Fall of Public Man*, Cambridge, Cambridge University Press.

Shaw, S.M. (1985), 'Gender and leisure: an examination of women's and men's everyday experience and perceptions of family time', *Journal of Leisure Research*, 17(4): 266–82.

Shaw, S.M. (1994), 'Gender, leisure and constraint: towards a framework for the analysis of women's leisure', *National Recreation and Park Association*, 26(1): 8–22.

Shields, R. (1997), 'Flow', *Space and Culture*, 1:1, 1–9.

Simmel, G. (1971), *On Individuality and Social Forms*, Chicago, Chicago University Press.

Simmel, G. (1978), *The Philosophy of Money*, London, Routledge.

Slater, P. (1971), *The Pursuit of Loneliness*, Penguin, Harmondsworth.

Stanley, C. (1997), 'Not Drowning but Waving: Urban Narratives of Dissent in the Wild Zone', pp. 36–54, in S. Redhead, D. Wynne and J. O'Connor (eds), *The Club Cultures Reader*, Oxford, Blackwell.

Stebbins, R. (1992), *Amateurs, Professionals and Serious Leisure*, Montreal, McGill University Press.

Stebbins, R. (1997), 'Casual Leisure: A Conceptual Statement', *Leisure Studies*, 16:1, 17–26.

Storey, J. (1995), *Cultural Theory and Popular Culture*, Hemel Hempstead, Harvester Wheatsheaf.

Talbot, M. (1988), '"Their own worst enemy?"', in E. Wimbush and M. Talbot (eds), *Relative Freedoms, Women and Leisure*, Milton Keynes, Open University Press, pp. 161–76.

Taylor, I., Walton, P. and Young, J. (1973), *The New Criminology*, London, RKP.

Thanh-Dam, T. (1983), 'The Dynamics of Sex Tourism', *Development and Change*, 14: 533–53.

Thompson, E.P. (1967), 'Time, Work Discipline and Industrial Capitalism,' *Past and Present*, 38: 56–97.

Thompson, J. (1995), *The Media and Modernity*, Cambridge, Polity.

Thompson, K. (1982), *Emile Durkheim*, London, Tavistock.

Thompson, P. (1983), *The Nature of Work*, London, Macmillan.

Thornton, S. (1995), *Club Cultures*, Cambridge, Polity.

Titmuss, R. (1970), *The Gift Relationship*, London, Allen & Unwin.

Tomlinson, A. (1989), 'Whose Side Are They On?', *Leisure Studies*, 8(2): 97–106.

Tomlinson, A. (1990) (ed.) *Consumption, Identity and Style*, London, Routledge.

Tonnies, F. (1887), *Gemeinschaft and Gesellschaft*, London, RKP.

Touraine, A. (1971), *The Post-Industrial Society*, New York, Random House.

Turner, B.S. (1984), *Body and Society*, Oxford, Blackwell Sage.

Turner, B.S. (ed.) (1993), *Citizenship and Social Theory*, London, Sage.

Turner, V. (1969), *The Ritual Process*, Chicago, Chicago University Press.

Turner, V. (1982), *From Ritual to Theatre: the Human Seriousness of Play*, New York, Cornell.

Turner, V. (1992), *Blazing the Trail*, Tucson, University of Arizona Press.

United Nations (1996), *Human Development Report*, New York, United Nations.

Van Moorst, H. (1982), 'Leisure and Social Theory', *Leisure Studies*, 2: 157–69.

Vattimo, G. (1992), *The Transparent Society*, Cambridge, Polity.

Veblen, T. (1899), *The Theory of the Leisure Class*, London, Allen & Unwin.

Virilio, P. (1986), *Speed and Politics*, New York, Semiotext.

Virilio, P. (1995), *The Vision Machine*, London, British Film Institute.

Wagner, D. (1997), *The New Temperance: The American Obsession with Sin and Vice*, Boulder, Westview.

Walby, S. (1997), *Gender Transformations*, London, Routledge.

Wearing, B. (1998), *Leisure and Feminist Theory*, London, Sage.

Weber, M. (1922), *The Sociology of Religion*, Boston, Beacon Press.

Weber, M. (1948), *From Max Weber*, (eds) H. Gerth and C.W. Mills, London, Routledge.

226 *Bibliography*

Weber, M. (1968), *Economy and Society* (3 vols), New York, Bedminster Press.
Weber, M. (1976), *The Protestant Ethic and the Spirit of Capitalism*, London, Routledge.
Webster, F. (1995), *Theories of the Information Society*, London, Routledge.
Webster, H. (1926), *Rest Days: A Study in Early Law and Morality*, New York, Macmillan.
Wilensky, H. (1960), 'Work, Careers and Social Integration', *International Social Science Journal*, 4: 543–60.
Williams, R. (1958), *Culture and Society*, London, Chatto and Windus.
Williams, R.H. (1982), *Dreamworlds*, Berkeley, University of California Press.
Willis, P. (1977), *Learning to Labour*, London, Saxon House.
Willis, P. (1978), *Profane Culture*, London, Routledge.
Willis, P. (1990), *Common Culture*, Milton Keynes, Open University Press.
Willis, P. (1990b), *Moving Culture – An Enquiry into the Cultural Activities of Young People*, London, Gulbenkian Foundation.
Wilson, B. (1982), *Religion in Sociological Perspective*, Oxford, Oxford University Press.
Wimbush, E. and Talbot, M. (eds) (1988), *Relative Freedoms*, Milton Keynes, Open University Press.
Wolfgang, M. (1958), *Patterns in Criminal Homicide*, Philadelphia, University of Pennsylvania Press.
Yablonsky, L. (1997), *Gangsters*, New York, New York University Press.
Yeo, S. (1976), *Religion and the Voluntary Sector*, Beckenham, Croom Helm.

Index

227